POETRY AND ⸱⸱⸱ OTHERS

For Megan,

With gratitude, admiration, and warm best wishes for your future work. You have been superb w/my MS — eternal thanks for the thrilling occasion in Ann Arbor,

John
10/30/2014

POETRY

AND ITS OTHERS

News, Prayer, Song,
and the Dialogue of Genres

JAHAN RAMAZANI

THE UNIVERSITY OF CHICAGO PRESS
Chicago and London

Jahan Ramazani is the Edgar F. Shannon Professor of English at the University of Virginia. He is the author of four books, most recently of *A Transnational Poetics*, also published by the University of Chicago Press.

The University of Chicago Press, Chicago 60637
The University of Chicago Press, Ltd., London
© 2014 by The University of Chicago
All rights reserved. Published 2014.
Printed in the United States of America

23 22 21 20 19 18 17 16 15 14   1 2 3 4 5

ISBN-13: 978-0-226-08373-5 (cloth)
ISBN-13: 978-0-226-08356-8 (paper)
ISBN-13: 978-0-226-08342-1 (e-book)

DOI: 10.7208/chicago/9780226083421.001.0001

The University of Chicago Press gratefully acknowledges the generous support of the Dean of the College of Arts and Sciences and the Vice President for Research and Graduate Studies at the University of Virginia toward the publication of this book.

Library of Congress Cataloging-in-Publication Data
Ramazani, Jahan, 1960– author.
Poetry and its others : news, prayer, song, and
the dialogue of genres / Jahan Ramazani.
pages cm
Includes bibliographical references and index.
ISBN 978-0-226-08373-5 (cloth : alk. pbk.) —
ISBN 978-0-226-08356-8 (pbk. : alk. pbk.) —
ISBN 978-0-226-08342-1 (e-book)
1. Poetry—History and criticism—20th century.
2. Poetry—History and criticism—21st century. 3. Poetics. I. Title.
PN1072.R36 2014
808.1—dc23
2013028986

For
Helen Vendler
and
Marjorie Perloff

CONTENTS

ACKNOWLEDGMENTS

There are more people to thank than I can enumerate, but I would like to single out a few for special mention. Caroline Rody has been the most incisive and supportive reader I could have hoped for—as well as my beloved companion in parenting our ever-energetic boys, Cyrus and Gabriel. My parents, Nesta and Ruhi, have never failed to rally and sustain, nor my eldest brother and fellow litterateur, Vaheed, to encourage me in my writing. Students and colleagues at the University of Virginia have stimulated, provoked, and challenged ideas that have gone into this book. My astoundingly poetry-attentive colleague Herbert Tucker graciously and scrupulously read the entire manuscript. Cara Lewis has been a resourceful and indefatigable research assistant. Valuable bibliographic and lexical suggestions came from Kevin Hart, Jennifer Peterson, Victor Luftig, Michael Suarez, Bruce Holsinger, Mark Edmundson, Randall Couch, Debra Fried, Frances Dickey, Anthony Cuda, and Stephen Burt. Cynthia Wall has been a wonderfully sustaining department chair, and I acknowledge welcome research funding for book production costs from the dean of the College of Arts and Sciences and the vice president for Research and Social Sciences. Two anonymous readers—later revealed to me as the remarkably acute poetry critics Bonnie Costello and Brian Reed—provided exceptionally thorough and thoughtful reports that helped me push the book toward its final shape. With characteristic shrewdness, my four-time editor at the University of Chicago Press, Alan Thomas, found those readers and offered superb guidance, and Randy Petilos deftly navigated the

ACKNOWLEDGMENTS

publication process. The dedication names two scholars whose luminous readings, if often diverging in emphasis, have been profoundly generative for poetry studies. I owe them debts of gratitude too large ever to be repaid.

I thank my generous hosts for opportunities to give talks that allowed me to try out parts of this book; their and their audiences' questions and comments supplied abundant food for thought: Ato Quayson for the History of Postcolonial Literature Conference at the University of Toronto; Françoise Lionnet, Shu-Mei Shi, Maya Boutaghou, and Greg Cohen for the Cultures in Transnational Perspective Conference at the University of California, Los Angeles; Peter Schmidt, Nathalie Anderson, and Aakash Shuchak at Swarthmore College; Rachel Blau DuPlessis, Sue-Im Lee, and Janet Neigh at Temple University; Christy Burns, Sean Keilen, and Henry Hart for the Cloud Lecture at the College of William and Mary; Moynagh Sullivan and Christopher Morash at the National University of Ireland, Maynooth; Nicholas Allen at the National University of Ireland, Galway; Susannah Gottlieb and Reginald Gibbons for the Poetry and Poetics Workshop at Northwestern University; Brian Richardson for the Modernist Symposium of the University of Maryland, College Park; Esra Santesso at the University of Georgia, Athens; Christopher Gair for the Symbiosis Conference at the University of Glasgow; Justus Nieland at Michigan State University; Jessica Berman and Michele Osherow at the University of Maryland, Baltimore County; Caroline Lusin and Anne Brüske for the Cultural Flows Conference at the University of Heidelberg; Ronald Schuchard at the T. S. Eliot International Summer School; Elizabeth Richmond-Garza, Katie Logan, and Martino Lovato for the Comparative Literature Conference at the University of Texas, Austin; Gautam Kundu for the British Commonwealth and Postcolonial Studies Conference of Georgia Southern University; Emily Wittman at the University of Alabama, Tuscaloosa; and Margaret Harper at the Yeats International Summer School; and Michael Coyle for the T. S. Eliot Memorial Lecture.

I also thank editors and publishers for their invitations to write essays that, conceived with this book in mind, have been published, then disassembled, rewritten, and scattered through the text: Cary Nelson, ed., *The Oxford Handbook of Twentieth-Century American Poetry* (Oxford: Oxford University Press, 2012), 461–86; Ato Quayson, ed., *The Cambridge History of Postcolonial Literature*, 2 vols. (Cambridge: Cambridge University Press, 2012), 2:938–81; Fran Brearton and Alan Gillis, eds., *The Oxford Handbook of Modern Irish Poetry* (Oxford: Oxford University Press, 2012), 548–66; Erik Martiny, ed., *A Companion to Poetic Genre* (Oxford: Blackwell, 2012), 3–16; *Northwest Review* 49, no. 2 (2011): 144–50; and *Contemporary Literature*, special issue ed. Michael Davidson, 52, no. 4 (2011): 716–55 © 2011 by the Board of Regents of the University of Wisconsin System, reproduced courtesy of the University of Wisconsin Press.

1

A DIALOGIC
POETICS

Poetry and the Novel, Theory, and the Law

WHAT IS POETRY? From antiquity to the present, there have been innumerable efforts to grapple with this impossible but unavoidable question—impossible because poetry and its readers redefine it from one time to another, one place to another, perhaps even one work to another; unavoidable because every time we draw up a syllabus, submit a work to a poetry journal or workshop, or choose a poem to read at a wedding or funeral, we act on ideas about what a poem is and isn't. But even if we limit ourselves, as in this book, to English-language works from the twentieth and twenty-first centuries, the difficulty of crafting a precise definition of poetry that could include high-art formalism and creole performance poetry, sonnets and collage poems, W. B. Yeats's line "A terrible beauty is born," Gertrude Stein's "Rose is a rose is a rose is a rose," and Louise Bennett's "Jamaica oman cunny, sah!" should not be underestimated.[1] Like plays, novels, films, and works in other genres and modes, poems are threaded together by family resemblances, but their variousness is hard to fit under one conceptual roof, built out of identifiable formal and thematic characteristics.

If we turn for help to the *Oxford English Dictionary*, we find poetry defined as "[c]omposition in verse or some comparable patterned arrangement of language in which the expression of feelings and ideas is given intensity by the use of distinctive style and rhythm; the art of such a composition. Traditionally associated with explicit formal departure from the patterns of ordinary speech or prose, e.g. in the use of elevated diction, figurative language, and syntactical reordering."[2] Similarly, in an introduction to a poetry anthology, *The Poet's Tongue* (1935), W. H. Auden famously called poetry "memorable speech," explaining that it heightens "audible spoken word and cadence," "power of suggestion and incantation," "alternating periods of effort and rest," and "tension between" personal and inherited rhythms, while emphasizing "[s]imiles, metaphors of image or idea, and auditory metaphors such as rhyme, assonance, and alliteration" and "the aura of suggestion round every word."[3] Though highly useful, these and other distillations are vexed by what they exclude: poems that avoid patterning or intensity, free verse poems without mnemonic structures, poems written not in "elevated diction" but in a vernacular, and so forth. They are also vexed by what they inadvertently include, such as sermons and political speeches, jingles and James Joyce's or Virginia Woolf's novels. Acknowledging the permeability of these boundaries, at the start of an anthology published a year after Auden's, Yeats lineated as poetry a sentence of rhythmic prose by Walter Pater—a reframing that earned Yeats an unlikely spot in a recent anthology of conceptual poetry.[4] Auden, too, was well aware that the qualities he ascribed to poetry—rhythm, figuration, sound patterning, and polysemy—aren't exclusive to it, and so he cited alongside Housman and Shakespeare a popular song and a schoolroom mnemonic for remembering a Latin gender, as well as the "good joke" made by the poetry-phobe who unwittingly "creates poetry."[5] But this laudable theoretical elasticity doesn't resolve all the issues: if it did, and if Auden thought jokes and mnemonics were indeed poems, why didn't he include them alongside the sonnets, ballads, and epigrams indexed in *The Poet's Tongue*?

Some critics believe that poetry's one inarguable distinction is its being written in lines, but even this identifier is imperfect: it would turn menus, shopping lists, and timetables into poems, while excluding oral poetry and prose poems. Poetry draws on and intensifies features of language in other oral and written uses, from which it can never be conclusively separated. As Roman Jakobson noted when grappling with the question "what is poetry?," the fact that the "same alliterations and other types of euphonic devices" appear in other kinds of discourse, including jokes, gossip, and everyday speech, blurs "the line of demarcation between poetry and nonpoetry."[6] As indicated by his example of the echoic, rhyming, assonantal, alliterative campaign slogan "I like Ike," the poetic function, if usually secondary outside poetry, isn't exclusive to poetry; nor is it the only linguistic function operative in poetry (the referential, the emotive, and the conative can also play a role).[7] "The borderline dividing what is a work of poetry from what is not," he wryly observed, "is less stable than the frontiers of the Chinese empire's territories."[8]

One way of trying to get around these difficulties is the adoption of a more circumscribed vocabulary, devolving umbrella terms such as "poetry" and "lyric" into more limited historical and subgeneric groupings, such as "twentieth-century British sonnets" and "modern American elegies." This strategy of disaggregation limits the scope of the problem and avoids flattening historical and cultural differences.[9] But intractable boundary questions remain. What is included and shut out by "British," "American," or "modern"? Does "sonnet" mean any fourteen-line poem, or are specific meters and rhyme patterns and themes also prerequisites, and what about near-sonnets? Does "elegy" include only poems of mourning for individuals or also blues poems and group laments and works of self-mourning? Moreover, can a poetic subgenre be quarantined in a specific time and location? What about poetry's transnational bearings and transhistorical memory? What about the skeins that thread through it from disparate times and places? Whether framed broadly as "poetry" or limited to the sonnets and elegies, villanelles and aubades of a particular era and culture, genres are not easily sequestered.

But to discard "poetry," "sonnet," "elegy," and "epigram" as interpretive frameworks because of their untidiness would be to make unrecognizable the ways in which individual works invoke and resist genre conventions. The "transgression requires a law," writes Tzvetan Todorov, and Jacques Derrida adds that a text "cannot be without or less a genre. Every text participates in one or several genres, there is no genreless text."[10] Genre descriptors such as "poem of mourning for the dead" and "fourteen-line poem"; or "composition in verse," "patterned arrangement," "intensity," "distinctive style and rhythm," and "elevated diction, figurative language, and syntactical reordering"; or "speech" made "memorable" by rhythm, figuration, sound patterning, and polysemy, should be seen not as defining elegies, sonnets, and poems but as pragmatically delineating what cognitive psychologists call "schemas" and what Hans Robert Jauss terms "horizons of expectation," which "can then be varied, extended, corrected, but also transformed, crossed out, or simply reproduced."[11] Like beauty, genre is at least partly in the eye of the beholder. A kitchen note can be reframed as a poem, such as William Carlos Williams's "This Is Just to Say"—an act that in turn reshapes expectations of poetry. Because genres vary across time and space, and because individual works both activate and press against the genre assumptions brought to bear on them, critical use of the term "poetry," as of the terms "elegy," "sonnet," "ballad," "sestina," "epigram," "ghazal," "pantoum," and the like, requires a pragmatic awareness both of the power of genre terms and of their unavoidable overreach and imprecision.

Since its boundaries are porous, its conventions unfixed, poetry is sometimes said to transcend genre altogether—a genreless genre. If genre is restricted to stable, constraining, sharply delimited categories, as in the phrase "genre fiction," surely poetry is no genre. But genre is more fruitfully understood as a web of crisscrossing family resemblances with closer and more distant relatives, which are, writes Alastair Fowler in extending Wittgenstein's metaphor, "related in various ways, without necessar-

inescapable

ily having any single feature shared in common by all."[12] These resemblances may strengthen or dissipate over time, are identifiable at higher ("poetry") and lower levels ("sestina") of abstraction, and are coproduced by hermeneutic acts that build shared horizons of expectation. "Poetry" may be conceptually ragged and historically unstable, but little more so—within period and cultural limits—than other broad areas of cultural production that have richly rewarded genre study, such as film and the novel.

A major reason for poetry's ineluctable messiness as a concept is that genres are not sealed off from one another, transmitted in isolation through the centuries, but responsive, in A. K. Ramanujan's words, "to previous and surrounding traditions; they invert, subvert, and convert their neighbours"; "a whole tradition may invert, negate, rework, and revalue another."[13] Poetry and other genres are "processes," "open systems," in Ralph Cohen's words, and "each genre is related to and defined by others to which it is related."[14] Genres change as they absorb and resist other genres. Hence, all genres are ineluctably intergeneric, and all genres are *genera mixta*. Poets are constantly enlarging (Marianne Moore's welcoming of "'business documents and // school-books'") and narrowing (Stéphane Mallarmé's restrictive "Donner un sens plus pur aux mots de la tribu") the intergeneric scope of what is understood to be "poetry," "lyric," "sonnet," "elegy," "ballad," and so forth.[15] Narrow it too much, and a poetic genre risks choking in self-parody. Enlarge it too much, and it risks vanishing into unrecognizability, unable to activate the genre-based assumptions that propel the hermeneutic circle of literary engagement.

In a dialogic understanding of genre, poetry is infiltrated by and infiltrates its generic others. But not according to the preeminent theorist of the dialogic imagination, Mikhail Bakhtin. He famously conceived of poetry as monologic and exclusionary, "suspended from any mutual interaction with alien discourse, any allusion to alien discourse," "destroying all traces of social heteroglossia and diversity of language." "The language of the poetic genre," he flamboyantly asserted, "is a unitary and singular Ptolemaic world outside of which nothing else exists and nothing else is needed."[16] Although in his influential formulation the novel is the omnigeneric genre par excellence, while poetry is purist and exclusivist, already in Homer epic poetry was an expansive compendium of genres, and while modern epic poems such as the *Cantos, The Waste Land, The Bridge, Trilogy,* and *Paterson* obviously contain generic multitudes, lyric poems also take up, internalize, and refigure other genres. Even if lyric poetry has a stronger centripetal torque than prose fiction, its seemingly monologic tendencies have, at the least, what Bakhtin calls *"dialogic overtones"*:

> However monological the utterance may be (for example, a scientific or philosophical treatise), however much it may concentrate on its own object, it cannot but be, in some measure, a response to what has already been said about the given topic, on the given issue, even though this responsiveness may not have assumed a clear-cut external expression. It will be manifested in the overtones of the style, in the finest nuances of the composition. The utterance is filled with *dialogic overtones*, and they must be taken into account in order to understand fully the style of the utterance. After all, our thought itself—philosophical, scientific, and artistic—is born and shaped in the process of interaction and struggle with others' thought, and this cannot but be reflected in the forms that verbally express our thought as well.[17]

Poetry is deeply influenced by earlier poetry, as writers from T. S. Eliot to Walter Jackson Bate and Harold Bloom have shown, and so a poem is sometimes thought of as being "born and shaped" almost entirely in response to earlier poems. But even though poetry has an especially long and deep memory of earlier works and forms, it is also "born and shaped in the process of interaction and struggle" with other discourses, other genres, other kinds of utterance. Poems come into being partly by echoing, playing on, reshaping, refining, heightening, deforming, inverting, combating, hybridizing, and compressing extrapoetic forms of language.

Recent books on poetry, while usefully extrapolating recurrent and long-lived characteristics, often treat poems as if they were for the most part elements of a self-enclosed system. But a poem faces both inward and outward: it enriches itself in its play on euphonies and dissonances within itself and across an array of earlier poems, and it feasts on, digests, and metabolizes linguistic forms of other kinds. In *The Fourth Dimension of a Poem and Other Essays*, M. H. Abrams distills poetry as utterance that highlights and exploits the "material dimension," "the physical aspect of language."[18] In *Lyric Poetry*, Mutlu Konuk Blasing characterizes poetry as a platform for "the emotionally and historically charged materiality of language," "an excess of 'sense,'" and "a rhythmic beat between sense and nonsense."[19] In *Poetry and the Fate of the Senses*, Susan Stewart sees poetry as "language that retains and projects the force of individual sense experience and yet reaches toward intersubjective meaning," language reliant on "rhythm and musical effects that are known with our entire bodies."[20] The physical, musical, visual, sensual, semantic, sonic, individual, intersubjective, and other dimensions of poetry identified in these and other books also figure prominently in the ensuing analysis. Helping to keep in view "the poetic function," they avoid reductions of poetry to thematic idea, historical document, or cultural or psychological symptom. Already in the 1930s, Jakobson had argued that the poetic function, or "poeticity," "is present when the word is felt as a word and not a mere representation of the object being named or an outburst of emotion, when words and their composition, their meaning, their external and inner form, acquire a weight and value of their own instead of referring indifferently to reality."[21] Poetry turns the material features of language into ends in themselves: "The set (*Einstellung*) toward the message as such, focus on the message for its own sake, is the POETIC function of language."[22]

As valuable as this largely intrinsic conception is, it touches only lightly on poetry's extramural relations. It needs to be supplemented with a more interactive view of poetry's interplay with nonpoetry. The materiality, musicality, and self-reflexivity identified in the immanent structural view need to be set in motion by casting poetry into animated conversation with neighboring discourses. Jakobson should be supplemented by Bakhtin, linguistics by metalinguistics, poetics by dialogics. What I call a dialogic poetics combines "dialogic" in Bakhtin's sense of the term with "poetics" in Jakobson's. It takes seriously both poetry's specificity as poetry and its being shaped by its dialogic interactions with other discourses. Poetry is formed by both its "domestic" and its "foreign" relations. It is constituted both intragenerically and intergenerically.[23] If it is long-memoried and self-referring, it must also be understood, as Cohen states of genre more broadly, "in relation to other genres," because its "aims and purposes at a particular time are defined by its interrelation with and differentiation from others."[24] Its dynamic give-and-take with other genres, its butting up against and assimilation of various codified uses of language, its reversals and co-optations of multiple discursive forms—these engagements aren't secondary but fundamental, and they need to play a part in our thinking about what poetry is and is not, in any given time and place. What we homogenize as poetry is an array of heterogeneous and ever-evolving discursive processes that frequently attach themselves to nonpoetic genres, the incorporation of which stretches and reshapes what is thought to be poetry.

Preoccupied with considering poetry intrinsically, albeit as molded by historical or biographical circumstances, poetry criticism has less frequently explored poetry as an open system, dynamically responsive to other genres. But, to adapt Bakhtin's terms for the novel, poetry dialogizes literary and extraliterary languages, intensifying and hybridizing them, making them collide and rub up against one another.[25] Further, by virtue of its exacting attention to form and language, poetry makes visible the structuring presuppositions behind the genres it assimilates. With its deliberate and irrepressible artifice, it makes "images of languages" it cites.[26] When Williams and Frank O'Hara excerpt newspaper articles (as seen in chapter 2), when T. S. Eliot and Agha Shahid Ali interpolate Christian, Hindu, or Muslim prayers (chapter 3), when Rae Armantrout and Frank Bidart sample popular songs (chapter 4), they decontextualize these discourses as trope and raise to view the assumptions behind them. Even if poetry isn't quoting, it often places as if in quotation marks the languages and genres it absorbs. When Seamus Heaney wrestles with the news's positivism, when Gerard Manley Hopkins adapts prayer's address to the divine, when Patience Agbabi echoes song conventions, their poetry casts these extrageneric characteristics in relief. Despite Bakhtin's antipoetic views, we can say of such poetry, as Bakhtin said of the novel, that it exploits the "ability of a language to represent another language while still retaining the capacity to sound simultaneously both outside it and within it, to talk about it and at the same time to talk in and with it," "simultaneously to serve as an object of representation while continuing to be able to speak to itself."[27] Because poetry can both represent and act within other languages, it provides searching reflections on a range of discursive genres.

The modern and contemporary opening of poetry to its others is in part a return to roots on which poetry has long nourished itself; in Andrew Welsh's account, these include riddle, emblem, chant, charm, and song.[28] Always intertwined with these others, poetry has from time to time deliberately reengaged them, as we will see especially with song. Although poets at various times have echoed classical interdictions against mixing genres, their practice has not always followed their poetics. In the Renaissance, despite protestations to the contrary, poets combined different sorts of poetry not only with one another—sonnet and epigram, satire and eulogy, "tragical-comical-historical-pastoral"—but also with nonpoetic kinds, such as the adage, the law, and the Ignatian spiritual exercise.[29] Notwithstanding commonplaces about neoclassical generic purity and Romantic monologic lyricism, writers in the eighteenth and nineteenth centuries similarly opened poetry to legal, religious, commercial, novelistic, dramatic, and other discourses.[30] In the ensuing chapters, I cite precedents going back to antiquity for modern and contemporary poets' absorption of specific genres.

But the twentieth and twenty-first centuries may be especially fertile ground for a dialogic approach to poetry. Loosening the generic boundaries between literature and other arts, modernism is, in Daniel Albright's view, a movement of intergeneric "collaboration," activating "figures of consonance" among music, literature, and other arts, eroding distinctions among media.[31] Early in the twentieth century, the congress between poetic and other artistic and nonartistic discourses is part of what many landmark poems are about. In the drive for reinvention at a time when generic boundaries and hierarchies were increasingly unstable, when incipient globalization was relativizing aesthetic and spiritual paradigms, when poetry had grown increasingly specialized and its cultural prestige was imperiled, poets drew strength by hybridizing their verse with the formal and linguistic possibilities of the novel, journalism, song, religious discourse, the visual arts, commerce, science, and so forth. An array of genres vividly collide and compete in their intergeneric experiments, including journalistic reportage and love lyric in Claude McKay's *Constab Ballads*; prophecy, popular song, and prayer in Eliot's *Waste Land*; economic policy, hymn, and political theory in Ezra Pound's *Cantos*; forest guide, philosophy, and an overheard remark in Moore's "An Octopus"; newspaper, lyric, and letter in Williams's *Paterson*; and advertising, ode, and prophecy in Hart Crane's *The Bridge*.

Intergeneric dialogue has been an especially pronounced feature of poetry in the late twentieth and early twenty-first centuries, when media spectacle and mass-reproduced or digitally circulated texts, sounds, and images have increasingly permeated the private spaces once thought to be poetry's preserve.[32] Salient examples of the poetics of collage and assemblage include Susan Howe's of philosophical texts, historical documents, archival manuscripts, personal letters, photographs, and art criticism; Charles Bernstein's of movies, business, computers, nursery rhyme, canonical literature, medical terms, popular song, and TV; and other Language poems that cannibalize elements of popular culture, as we will see in song-filled works by Armantrout, Michael Palmer, and Harryette Mullen. A large share of intergeneric criticism on contemporary poetry has concerned Language writing and other experimental forms. Marjorie Perloff hails a propensity in the twenty-first century toward ever greater "dialogue with earlier texts or texts in other media."[33] And indeed flarf poetry mines the Internet for found materials it copies, cuts up, and re-presents. Conceptual poetry often recycles language borrowed whole cloth from other discourses and media, enacting and thematizing a poetics of appropriation that updates the strategy of

Marcel Duchamp's ready-mades and other examples of found art. Vanessa Place's poem "Miss Scarlet," to cite one example of such transcriptive appropriation, consists entirely of quotations from Margaret Mitchell's enslaved character Prissy in *Gone with the Wind*, extracted and lineated partly as blank verse to reframe the novel and film's racist stereotype:

Miss Scarlett, effen we kain git de doctah
w'en Miss Melly's time come, doan you bodder
Ah kin manage. Ah knows all 'bout birthin.[34]

Instead of seeming to be created ex nihilo, transcriptive poems foreground contemporary poetry's willful enmeshment with received texts, sounds, and information, as seen below in works by M. NourbeSe Philip, Tracie Morris, and others.

Although "unoriginal" and "uncreative" poetry, as Perloff and Kenneth Goldsmith have wryly named such experimental writing,[35] is far from being alone in its dialogism, its conspicuously intertextual and intermedial dynamics can help alert readers to the dialogics of other kinds of poetry, including styles and schools often read monologically. Under the influence of modernism, experimentalism, media saturation, prose forms, and diminished genre hierarchies, even lyric styles have become increasingly dialogized, if not always overtly so. In our time, Moore's admonition not "to discriminate against 'business documents and // schoolbooks'" as *materia poetica* is observed across a range of poems that—whether lyric or antilyric, expressivist or antiexpressivist, "open" or "closed"—reverberate with extrapoetic discourses. Author of a poetic sequence written in a synthetic interlanguage, Cathy Park Hong also fuses in *Dance Dance Revolution* (2007) tourist-guide lingo with lyric, epic history with video game and pseudomemoir. Crediting the impact of Language writing, she lauds twenty-first-century poetry's "vital collision" and "mash-up," citing contemporary poets who "use collage as their modus operandi, whether it's plaiting their poetry with endocrinological data, passages of untranslated Tagalog, or mathematical equations."[36] Anne Carson's accordion-fold-out elegy for her brother, *Nox* (2010), dialogizes dictionary definitions, letters, photographs, and the essay.[37] Juliana Spahr's *Well Then There Now* (2011) examines the commercial expropriation of a Hawaiian beachfront, drawing on found texts and images, including signs, guidebooks, and legal documents.[38] Srikanth Reddy's *Voyager* (2011), though carved out of the language of a single text, former United Nations Secretary General Kurt Waldheim's memoir *In the Eye of the Storm*, reworks the Nazi collaborator's evasive prose by selectively erasing it three different times to fashion poetry in lyric, autobiographical, and narrative registers.[39] Paul Guest's *My Index of Slightly Horrifying Knowledge* (2008) deploys extraliterary forms such as the user's guide, the index, the to-do list, and the audio commentary, as if these templates were for the twenty-first-century poet what the sonnet, the ode, and the ballad were for earlier poets.[40] In some lyric poetry, "alien" materials are more thoroughly digested than they are in these examples, requiring more interpretive labor to disclose them. But whether lyric, experimental, or hybrid, poetry generated out of vigorous interactions with nonpoetry invites examination of its often strenuous refashioning of those materials. This book favors poems of many kinds that reward close reading, that weave sonic and verbal textures, tonal and formal intricacies, out of interchanges with their others. Within these limits, it investigates an array of modern and contemporary poems—from transatlantic modernism, the Irish Renaissance, and the Harlem Renaissance to objectivism, projectivism, personism, postconfessionalism, postcolonialism, Irish and English lyricism, and Language writing—that torque poetry's others and make something aesthetically new and rich out of their complex reworking of the nonpoetic.

In brief, from the modernist moment into the twenty-first century, poetry has dissolved itself into nonpoetry, parapoetry, even antipoetry. But in so doing, it has also paradoxically brought into view its specificities as poetry. A poem that almost becomes a novelistic fiction, a theoretical discourse, a legal brief, a news report, a prayer, or a musical song often distinguishes itself as poetry when on the verge of self-extinction. This book explores how poetry both blends with its others and distinguishes itself from them. By examining moments when poetry comes close to dissolving itself in other genres, we see how poetry expands its range and possibilities, at the same time that it flaunts its distinctiveness. Often missed in accounts of "appropriation" in contemporary visual arts, music, literature, and other forms is the counterimpulse in each medium—while giving itself over to its others—to be true to itself, even to assert itself over the others it incorporates. This double movement of self-annihilation and self-assertion may seem an impossible contradiction. But as Gary Saul Morson observes of what he calls "threshold" or "boundary works" that straddle two or more genres, "Transgressions *mark* boundaries."[41] And if this double movement is especially pronounced in contemporary works, it is part of a long-lived artistic equipoise. "Literary genres subsist in paradoxical balance," Herbert Tucker observes; "they sustain integrity by distinguishing themselves from the genres around them, even as they sustain vitality by drawing nourishment from exactly the same source."[42]

In modern and contemporary poetry, we take for granted analogous ways in which an individual work can move in opposing directions. Consider the paradox, for example, that John Ashbery, whose riotously agglomerative poetry is shot through with advertising, comic books, art criticism, travelogue, journalism, bureaucracy, and business, is also a poet who continually slips into the mode of ars poetica. From the frenzied collage of multiple intersecting discourses emerge lines that could almost be bumper stickers for poetry: "pure / Affirmation that doesn't affirm anything" is one of many such tags in "Self-Portrait in a Convex Mirror."[43] In "Soonest Mended," too, oblique self-definitions continually surface: "To step free at last, minuscule on the gigantic plateau— / This was our ambition: to be small and clear and free"; "a kind of fence-sitting / Raised to the level of an esthetic ideal"; "Making ready to forget, and always coming back / To the mooring of starting out."[44] Ironically, pastiche- and collage-based works by Language writers such as Bernstein, Howe, Armantrout, Palmer, and Mullen—seemingly extreme in their procedures of self-othering—frequently gesture toward their materiality and recursiveness as poems. As we will see in much greater detail in poetry's deep intersections with specific genres, it is possible for a poem to surrender itself to its others and at the same time to declare the poetry of its poetry.

This notion of poetry's self-consciousness of its difference may seem problematic in light of the literary-historical grand narrative of modernism and postmodernism as the triumphant emancipation of literature and culture from the supposedly dead hand of genre.[45] Indeed, I began writing this book as a consideration of poetry's dispersal into its others. But as I studied ever more examples of just such melding, I found time and again that poems reassert themselves as poems even in the moment of seeming to fuse with their others. If Eliot is right that poets, at the back of their minds, are "always trying to defend the kind of poetry" they are writing, and are in youth "actively engaged in battling for the kind of poetry" they practice, it stands to reason that this self-definitional drive would manifest itself not only in the poet's criticism, as Eliot maintains, but also in the poetry itself.[46] When we look at other genres as seen from within poetry, we often discover unexpected tensions, even when the other genre is held closest to the heart of a poem. Whereas Harold Bloom's theory of the anxiety of influence attributes vertical struggle to the relation of one poet to another, a no less intense horizontal agon can be seen in poetry's intergeneric rivalry with kindred discourses. Poems are enamored of, compete with, and steal from other genres. Even as they mimic a news report or a song or a philosophical system, they are sometimes involved in an existential struggle on behalf of poetry. Bakhtin claims that the novel "fights for its own hegemony in literature" and "gets on poorly with other genres. There can be no talk of a harmony deriving from mutual limitation and complementariness."[47] In my view, poetry's rivalry with other genres, its championing of its freedoms, forms, and prerogatives, even when devouring its others, may be still more intense than what Bakhtin ascribes to the novel. Prose fiction's cross-genre engagements are often more loosely assimilative than what happens within the compressed and highly charged space of many a poem.

If so, then this book needs to embark in two contrastive directions simultaneously, toward dialogic study of poetry's expansive absorption of closely related discursive forms and toward genre-specific analysis of poetry's persisting awareness of its difference, even when it welcomes multitudes. Navigating a third course between the pole of criticism that sets literature apart by virtue of its singularity and the pole that collapses all distinctions between literature and other media and genres, a dialogic poetics would be true both to the specificity of individual poems as poems and to their immersion in the welter of myriad cultural forms. At the same time that poetry incorporates various genres and discourses, it puts on display the compression, metaphoric density, self-reflexivity, sonic self-awareness, visual form, and other shifting features by which it differentiates itself from the others it internalizes.

For the purposes of this introduction, I consider poetry's ambivalent interactions with a few of its generic others—namely the novel, theory, and the law—before turning in succeeding chapters to fuller explorations of its self-inscriptions on the corpora of the news, prayer, and song. The term "genre" is thus extended to "heterogeneous" extraliterary discourses not on "a single common level," including philosophy, the law, the news, and prayer, as in Bakhtin's analysis of "everyday" or "speech genres," since their codes and conventions organize written and spoken utterances, as well as expectations of response.[48] As the New Critical model of the self-contained poem has come apart, critics have begun to address modern and contemporary poetry in relation to cinema, music, the visual arts, science, and the electronic media.[49] Although the novel, theory, the law, the news, prayer, and song are thus hardly alone as intergenres, I single them out because they are among poetry's closest cousins. Cohen writes of individual works, "Each member alters the genre by adding, contradicting, or changing constituents, especially those of members most closely related to it."[50] Poetry has many family resemblances with its near verbal relatives, raising the stakes, as in a real family, of its efforts at affiliative connection and self-distinction. How does poetry novelize itself even as it pursues strategies different from the novel? How does it theorize without turning into a philosophical treatise? How does it resemble legal testimony without belonging in a court of law? How do poets tell the news without writing texts that would be confused with journalism? How do they mimic prayer without writing sacred texts? How do they intercut their poems with song lyrics and techniques while differentiating their works from song? What differences emerge among varieties of poetry, as inflected by such extrapoetic enmeshments? Even as threshold poems call into question any essentialist notion of poetry, helping to disaggregate at least some of it into novelistic, theorizing, and testimonial varieties, into documentary, prayerful, and songlike kinds, close analysis of poetry's embrace of, and resistances to, its intergenres helps illuminate poetry's various self-understandings.

Focusing on a handful of areas of poetry's overlap with, and self-differentiation from, its generic others, I hope to develop a dialogic poetics that may have implications for poetry in relation to other interdiscourses: letters, biography, memoir, obituary, propaganda, criticism, politics, social networking, advertising, business, history, anthropology, psychoanalysis, biology, neurology, environmentalism, and so forth. The selection of poems in each intergeneric group is also kept small, to make visible the intricacies poems live by; hence, innumerable other relevant poems will inevitably come to mind—works for which I hope some of these observations may prove suggestive. My wager is that we gain insight into what poetry is, or at least what it understands itself to be, by examining closely its interplay with what it is not.

POETRY AND THE NOVEL

Even if Bakhtin's claim for the novel's hegemony may seem overblown, literary poetry had lost considerable ground to the novel by the early twentieth century. "Poetry at the start of the modern period," observes David Perkins, "had ceased to be the most important literary genre, its traditional place having been taken over by prose fiction"; poetry had become the focus of small but intense coteries.[51] Over the course of the twentieth century, especially with the waning of the privilege accorded poetic iconicity, complexity, and ambiguity in practical criticism and the New Criticism, poetry lost still more literary and academic prestige.

And whatever its cultural capital, its popularity was considerably less than prose fiction's. A few raw numbers might be illustrative. Near the end of the nineteenth century, whereas a novel such as Thomas Hardy's *The Woodlanders* enjoyed a first edition of ten thousand copies and his *Tess of the d'Urbervilles* burgeoned into seventeen thousand copies in four months, his poetry—to which he turned exclusively after *Jude the Obscure*—had more modest sales: *Wessex Poems and Other Verses* (1898), which included now canonical poems such as "Hap" and "Neutral Tones," appeared in a first edition of five hundred copies, and *Poems of the Past and the Present* (1901), with "Drummer Hodge," "The Darkling Thrush," and "The Ruined Maid," in a printing of a thousand, half for the British and half for the American edition.[52] In the early decades of the twentieth century, sales figures for collections of poetry by even the most prominent modernists now seem astonishingly modest: the press run of T. S. Eliot's *Prufrock and Other Observations* was 500, of William Carlos Williams's *Spring and All* 324 (largely unsold), of Marianne Moore's *Observations* 250, and of Ezra Pound's *Hugh Selwyn Mauberley* 200.[53] Most of Wallace Stevens's early and middle volumes appeared in runs of about a thousand, and W. B. Yeats, whose Cuala Press volumes usually appeared in runs of five hundred or fewer, was amazed at being able to sell two thousand copies of *The Tower*, "much the largest sale I have ever had."[54] Some modernist novels also had small initial print runs, but they occasionally became major hits and were massively reprinted—a fate that befell Claude McKay's best-selling *Home to Harlem*, its fifty thousand copies leaving his poetry collections far behind.[55] Although modernists sometimes deliberately restricted supply, as Lawrence Rainey argues, to turn their books into valuable art objects, this practice made sense only within the context of an already "limited demand for modernist literature."[56]

Just as most modernist poetry collections, whether published in limited, deluxe, or commercial editions, were hardly best sellers in the English-speaking world, nowadays Amazon's sales algorithms seldom elevate even the most acclaimed contemporary poets to the top. By the twenty-first century, the novel's readership had outstripped poetry's by a ratio perhaps as high as ten to one in America according to a 2007 Associated Press poll, or of four to one according to a 2004 report by the National Endowment for the Humanities.[57] Of course such figures don't account for the full range of people's exposure to poetry: there are many ways of reading or listening to it other than in books—settings that range from café performances and subway displays to journals and poetry websites. But poetry, having long been in its literary forms an art for limited and specialized audiences in the English-speaking world, became even more so after modernism made it still more difficult and forbidding, and even the abundance of slams and the explosion of online resources are unlikely to reverse its fortunes.

How has poetry responded to the challenge of the novel's "hegemony," albeit a hegemony increasingly diluted by other literary and extraliterary genres? Although an adequate treatment of this question would require a book of its own, I trace a thumbnail sketch of modern and contemporary poetry's divided response to the novel, in hopes that future literary histories will take up in fuller detail this surprisingly understudied question. In brief, poetry has in some ways become more novelistic, while in others, it has carved out especially nonnovelistic areas of attention and achievement. First let's consider poetry's novelization. Although Bakhtin dichotomizes poetry and the novel, he also allows that ever since the rise of the novel, poems such as Pushkin's *Eugene Onegin* have instanced the "novelization of other genres": "their language renews itself by incorporating extraliterary heteroglossia and the 'novelistic' layers of literary language, they become dialogized, permeated with laughter, irony, humor, elements of self-parody," and responsive to "contemporary reality (the open-ended present)."[58] While this is true of *Eugene Onegin* as well as other eighteenth- and nineteenth-century works (as critics such as G. Gabrielle Starr and Marshall Brown have shown), modernist poems still more obviously poach on novelistic terrain.[59] "In the effort of poets to write a less 'poetic' language," as Perkins observes, "the novel played its role."[60] Weary of what they felt were stale poeticisms and anxious to invigorate poetry's diction, syntax, and action, Thomas Hardy, E. A. Robinson, Robert Frost, Edgar Lee Masters, and other so-called low modernists imported into poetry the novel's interest in character, local setting, domesticity, social convention, verisimilitude, colloquialism, and psychological tension between individuals.[61] Bringing "a more prosy connotation" to poetry, Robinson, for example, carved out miniature novelistic sketches of ill-fated characters such as Richard Cory, who, though he seemed enviably fortunate, "one calm summer night / Went home and put a bullet through his head."[62]

Nor were the so-called high modernists immune to novelization. "Poetry must be *as well written as prose*," Pound declared.[63] Indeed, in the wake of experiments by Baudelaire, Rimbaud, and Mallarmé, many English-language modernists, such as Williams, Eliot, and Stein, wrote poems in prose, albeit, as Stephen Fredman states, these "would be difficult to mistake . . . for fiction or for purely discursive prose; they evidence a fascination with language (through puns, rhyme, repetition, elision, disjunction, excessive troping, and subtle foregrounding of diction) that interferes with the progression of story or idea, while at the same time inviting and examining the 'prose' realms of fact and anecdote and reclaiming for poetry the right to investigate the domain of truth."[64] Although many poets continued to write in lines, rhymes, and accentual-syllabic verse, the momentum toward loosening prosodic and stanzaic structures—with Pound and others insisting that poetry be composed "in the sequence of the musical phrase, not in sequence of a metronome"—lessened the gap between prose and verse.[65] Yeats, though no champion of prose realism, dismissed what he called the "poetical diction" of the Victorians and claimed that "in 1900 everybody got down off his stilts."[66] "Every revolution in poetry," wrote Eliot, "is apt to be, and sometimes to announce itself to be, a return to common speech."[67] Reacting like the Romantics against poetry's self-removal from everyday speech, its self-narrowing in both form and content, the modernists and their successors tried to reclaim the nonpoetic for poetry. As Michael André Bernstein writes, "poets like Pound, Williams, and Olson sought to recapture for verse the amplitude and inclusiveness of the novelist."[68] Building on the example of Robert Browning and other Victorian predecessors, twentieth-century poets, from Eliot, Pound, Frost, Robinson, Masters, and Sterling Brown to Okot p'Bitek, Robert Lowell, Richard Howard, Ai, Frank Bidart, and Carol Ann Duffy, turned to dramatic monologue, as well as what are sometimes called mask lyric and the persona poem, in part as a counterweight to the novel. They procured for poetry a novelistic character-and-plot interest in the psychological impact of sequentially unfolding events. Bidart's "Ellen West," for example, is built around painfully revealing episodes of an anorexic's disgusted fascination with other people's eating, intercut with a narrator-psychiatrist's comments, until her agonized, if suggestively poetic, attempts to sculpt her body culminate in suicide.[69]

Within this poetic drift toward novelization, specific novelists have had a direct impact on modern and contemporary poets. The archetypal patterning, polyglossia, stylistic heterogeneity, local-global compression, and multigeneric collage of Joyce's *Ulysses* cast a large shadow over a variety of ambitious poems—witness the "mythical method" of Eliot's *Waste Land*, the realism and compression of Pound's *Cantos*, the collage of newspaper, letter, lyric, and epic in Williams's *Paterson*, the ghostly colloquies in Heaney's *Station Island*, the cross-cultural layering of Walcott's *Omeros*, and so forth.[70] Henry James's transnationalism, conversational idiom, intricate syntax, social satire, subtlety, and difficulty were also generative for Pound, who called his *Hugh Selwyn Mauberley* "a study in form, an attempt to condense the James novel";[71] for Eliot, who considered James "the most intelligent man of his generation," with "a mind so fine that no idea could violate it";[72] and for Auden, whose Jamesian homage to James apostrophizes him, "O poet of the difficult," "Master of nuance and scruple."[73] If James's influence was one of refinement, modern and contemporary poetry's forays into low mimesis—brand names, technologies, mundane activities, bodily particulars, psychological extremes, and conversational idiom—also represent efforts to retake ground from prose fiction.

Not that this cross-genre appropriation works only in one direction. Even though the novel's eminence in the literary field has meant its influence on poetry has tended to be stronger than vice versa, at least some novels have been poeticized at the same time that poetry has been novelized. D. H. Lawrence's fiction, such as *The Rainbow*, sometimes syntactically ebbs and flows with anadiplosis and other resoundingly repetitive forms: "They took the udder of the cows, the cows yielded milk and pulse against the hands of the men, the pulse of the blood of the teats of the cows beat into the pulse of the hands of the men."[74] Virginia Woolf's novels can be read as much for their poetic patterning and lyricism as for plot and character, and few poems are richer in the "poetic" qualities of wordplay, paronomasia, or polyvalence than Joyce's *Finnegans Wake*. Toni Morrison's *Beloved* ends with incantatory passages that approach prose poetry, and A. S. Byatt's *Possession* invents long passages of poetry by her Browning-like and Rossetti-like authors.

Still, for all these indications of poetry's hybridization with the novel, it is perhaps too easy to assume that modern and contemporary poetry has merged with its prose other. It may seem, for example, that the strongest evidence for poetry's fusion with the novel is the proliferation of works that use verse forms to tell book-length stories, often called "novels in verse." Anticipated by Byron, Pushkin, the Brownings, and other nineteenth-century poets, these long poems include Vikram Seth's *The Golden Gate* (1986), Anne Carson's *Autobiography of Red* (1998), Les Murray's *Freddy Neptune* (1999), Bernardine Evaristo's *The Emperor's Babe* (2001), and Cathy Park Hong's *Dance Dance Revolution* (2007), perhaps as well as "epics" such as Walcott's *Omeros* (1990). Yet while these works adapt novelistic qualities, such as plot interest, character development, and social realism, they are richer in the inventive use of terza rima, octets, or Onegin stanzas, of densely layered wordplay, interlingual punning, and compressed code-switching. Sometimes their plots and characters seem like prosaic scaffolding erected to enable poetic construction or, to switch metaphors, novelistic hooks on which to hang the poetry. Although *The Emperor's Babe* and *Dance Dance Revolution* have engaging intercultural protagonists, these books devote more literary energy to creating dazzling verbal amalgamations—a tumultuous zigzag from street slang to high diction and foreign languages—than to freshly plotting the fate of their heroines. Indeed, many such works would probably be considered failures if seen only in light of novelistic expectations for richness, depth, and intricacy of character, scene, setting, and action. If so, then the terms "novel in verse" and "verse novel" may be misnomers insofar as they subordinate "verse" as descriptor to the substantive "novel"; given the disproportionately "poetic" emphasis of these works, "novelistic verse" might be more accurate. Just as Lawrence's, Woolf's, Joyce's, Byatt's, and Morrison's poetry-infiltrated fiction hardly abolishes the novelistic schemas they work with and against, the same could be said of these novelistic poems in relation to their poetic bearings, though over time the accumulation of such hybrid works creates new horizons of expectation.

The persistence of difference amid intergenre hybridization can also be seen in the vast array of modern and contemporary poems that turn not toward but away from the novel, shunning novelistic content and structure. Ever since the novel's nineteenth-century dominance, poets, Perkins notes, "had written with an anxious eye" on the competition, "which was seducing the audience of poetry and taking over many of its functions"; "it began to exert pressure on poets, forcing them to concentrate on subjects and uses of language that the novel could not easily appropriate" and producing poetry's "retreat into specializations (feeling, personal subjectivity, the lyric) that always occurs when a genre is on the defensive against its own past successes or against a developing new genre."[75] Although *Ulysses* informs *The Waste Land*, although Plath wrote *The Bell Jar* out of some of the same experiences that are the basis for lyrics such as "Lady Lazarus," and although Lyn Hejinian's *My Life* is predicated on the descriptive prose narrative sentences that it both scrambles and numerically straitjackets, these and other examples of modernist, confessional, and Language poetry would be impossible to adapt as novels—or at least they could not be as successfully adapted as, say, novels by E. M. Forster, Ian McEwan, and even Toni Morrison have been translated into films. Eliot's, Plath's, and Hejinian's poems, despite their partial novelization, strike out in various antinovelistic directions. Even in modernity and postmodernity, poetry's dissolution into the novel is far from complete. But what about writers who, like Plath, publish both poetry and prose fiction? Focused on poetry, the book you are reading sometimes uses the term "poets" for moderns such as Thomas Hardy, D. H. Lawrence, James Joyce, Gertrude Stein, and Claude McKay and for postwar figures such as Stevie Smith, Philip Larkin, Robert Penn Warren, James Dickey, Margaret Atwood, Michael Ondaatje, and Sherman Alexie; but they are more likely to be called "novelists" in critical books filed under the Dewey Decimal System's 813 or 823 (American or English fiction) instead of 811 or 821 (American or English poetry), as under the equivalent genre categories in the Library of Congress Classification (PN, PR, and PS). The scattering of these authors' works to different areas of the stacks may seem arbitrary and even violently distortive. But, perhaps surprisingly, the numerousness of such ambidextrous authorship may not always support the narrative of genre dissolution.

Consider the novelist of the style-shifting *A Portrait of the Artist as a Young Man*, the kaleidoscopic *Ulysses*, and the staggeringly polyglot *Finnegans Wake*. Although Joyce wrote lyric poetry, the novelist is sometimes unrecognizable in the Elizabethan song forms, sentimental lyricism, and static retrospection of *Chamber Music* and *Pomes Penyeach*. A poem in the *Chamber Music* sequence begins

> The twilight turns from amethyst
> To deep and deeper blue,
> The lamp fills with a pale green glow
> The trees of the avenue.[76]

In the delicate melodies and symbolist colorings of his lyric poetry, as a Yeats-haunted and -daunted Joyce understands the genre, there seems little room for the brash, booming, multiperspectival, and many-tongued heteroglossia of his novels. The satiric uncollected poems in rhyming couplets have more of his fiction's *non serviam* defiance ("Firm as the mountain-ridges where / I flash my antlers on the air," he writes in "The Holy Office") and impious, antidecorous physical humor ("This very next lent I will unbare / My penitent buttocks to the air," says the ventriloquized publisher in "Gas from a Burner");[77] but even they fall far short of his fiction's genre-expanding inventiveness. Hence Joyce's influence on poets from Eliot and Williams to Walcott has been through his novels, not his verse. Despite valiant critical efforts to read Joyce's poetry and prose as a seamless whole, they differ more than their authorship might lead us to expect.[78] Stephen's composition of a villanelle in *A Portrait of the Artist as a Young Man* may seem to exemplify intergeneric melding. But the poem's languor, conventionality, and monotone repetitiveness contrast with the vigorously multistylistic novel of which it is a part.[79] So too, the poetry of writers such as Lawrence, Stein, and McKay, despite numerous points of intergeneric contact, does not always resemble their prose fiction. At the risk of shoring up the Bakhtinian distinction between poetry and the novel that I have been trying to complicate (an issue returned to below), I would have to concede its provisional relevance in such cases. Notwithstanding the celebratory breakdown narrative of modernist and postmodernist genres, it may be too hasty to assume that intensified intergeneric traffic spells the postgeneric confluence of poetry and the novel.

The pressures that the early twentieth-century Western novel put on poetry both to assimilate it and to distinguish itself recurred later in another part of the English-speaking world, namely decolonizing Africa, birthplace in the 1950s and 1960s of some of the twentieth century's most important novels. First-generation postcolonial African poets sometimes responded to this challenge by metabolizing aspects of the novel. The Ugandan Okot p'Bitek, for example, adapted the novel's interpersonal dramatic tension, ethnographic content, conversational accessibility, and unrhymed and unmetered language in satiric book-length dramatic monologues such as *Song of Lawino* (1966). But another response was to write hyperpoetic works such as Christopher Okigbo's and the early Wole Soyinka's—that is, works that accentuate and exaggerate their poetic qualities, and that could never be mistaken for prose fiction, because they are so oblique, difficult, compressed, and stylized. It may be worth pausing over one such work in juxtaposition with a novel to see what light close analysis might shed on the hopelessly broad question of poetry's relation to prose fiction in the twentieth century.

When you think of the literary representation of the British colonization of Igboland, the most celebrated African novel, Chinua Achebe's *Things Fall Apart* (1958), is the work that is most likely to come to mind. Its historical and ethnographic content, cast in a limpid style, has helped to bring it worldwide attention and to place it, along with a handful of other novels, at the center of postcolonial studies. But what happens when much the same material—an innocent Igbo society, violent occupation, the destruction of Igbo religion—is projected through the lens of poetry that is emphatic about its identity as poetry? What distinctions and commonalities emerge? How does a poetic sequence digest some of the same material, yet insist on its specificity as poetry? A few years after the publication of Achebe's novel, Christopher Okigbo's sequence "Fragments out of the Deluge" (1962), which appeared first in the newly created African magazine *Transition* and then in a short Mbari-published book, *Limits* (1964), also evoked the colonization of Igboland. If Achebe is Africa's most famous novelist, Okigbo may be its most acclaimed anglophone poet, although, in a typical instance of the material consequences of the poetry-fiction divide, Okigbo's sales figures and popular currency have never reached a fraction of Achebe's. Because of the many commonalities in their lives and their subject matter, they bring into stark relief some of the divergences between poetry and its prose other. Like Achebe, Okigbo was born and grew up in southeastern Nigeria under British colonial rule. Like Achebe, Okigbo had Christian parents— though Achebe's family was Protestant, Okigbo's Catholic. Both Achebe and Okigbo were sons of teachers. Both attended Umuahia Government College for secondary school and proceeded to University College, Ibadan. Some years after Okigbo was killed as a combatant in the Nigerian Civil War, Achebe coedited a literary memorial for his friend and fellow founder of Citadel Press, the anthology of poems *Don't Let Him Die* (1978). Okigbo appropriates some elements from Achebe's revered novel, which he read in manuscript;[80] but the difference in his poetic handling of similar material is enormously suggestive.

If historical and cultural background and subject matter were primary in literary works, as sociohistorically sophisticated but formally naive studies of postcolonial literature sometimes assume, we might well expect Achebe's fiction and Okigbo's poetry to mirror one another. But when we set "Fragments out of the Deluge" and *Things Fall Apart* side by side, the generic frameworks within which they are written spawn profound differences. Surely, at the most basic, referential level, there are connections. The eighth and tenth lyrics in *Limits*, of which "Fragments out of the Deluge" is the second half, tell of the arrival of the colonizers and their destruction of Igbo religion and culture—a historical story that is also central to Achebe's novel. The "us" in the tenth poem is clearly marked as an indigenous Igbo community ("And to us they came"), in contradistinction to the "they" who ominously "scanned" and "surveyed" and "entered into the forest."[81] In the eighth lyric, a sunbird—an Igbo religious symbol—recounts the arrival of a "fleet of eagles" and their holding "the square / under curse of their breath":

> Beaks of bronze, wings
>   of hard-tanned felt,
> The eagles flow
>   over man-mountains,
> Steep walls of voices,
>   horizons;
> The eagles furrow
>   dazzling over the voices
> With wings like
>   combs in the wind's hair (47)

Like Achebe's missionaries Brown and Smith, who personify the gracious and severe faces of religious colonization, these eagles seem, as suggested by Okigbo's diction and figurative language, potentially inviting ("felt," "wings like / combs") and frightfully rigid ("Beaks of bronze," "hard-tanned"). They threaten dominance and terrifying destruction, but they also allure—"dazzling," "Resplendent . . . resplendent" (47, ellipsis in original). We may infer that as in Achebe's novel, the Igbo are at once attracted and repelled. Okigbo tersely suggests the vulnerability of the indigenous people and of their religious symbols: "And small birds sing in shadows, / Wobbling under their bones . . ." (47, ellipsis in original). Like Achebe's ambivalent characters, the Igbo in "Fragments out of the Deluge" feel vulnerable for good reason. In the tenth lyric, the sunbird that sang much of the eighth poem is abruptly "killed" (49). The intruders are said to find and break "the twingods of the forest," glossed by Okigbo's note as the "tortoise and the python" (49). The eaglelike colonizers swoop down and destroy Igbo gods:

> And the ornaments of him,
> And the beads about his tail;
> And the carapace of her,
> And her shell, they divided. (49)

Readers of Achebe's novel will recognize these religious and folkloric images. In *Things Fall Apart*, a Christian convert kills the sacred python and, seemingly as the result of divine retribution, soon falls ill and dies.[82] In an inset etiological beast fable, after the trickster Tortoise falls from the sky, a medicine man fits the shell fragments back together: "That is why Tortoise's shell is not smooth."[83] Moreover, the long-drum that resonates through *Things Fall Apart* silently heralds, in Okigbo's sequence, the death of these and other Igbo gods:

> And the gods lie in state
> And the gods lie in state
> Without the long-drum. (50)

Igbo religious imagery, the people's ambivalence toward a Janus-faced colonizer, and a narrative of European colonial destruction of indigenous religion—this much Okigbo's poetic sequence has in common with Achebe's novel. "Fragments out of the Deluge," writes Okigbo, renders retrospectively "the collective rape of innocence and profanation of the mysteries" (xxiv). The same could be said of *Things Fall Apart*.

But the poetic sequence's divergences from the novel even on this shared terrain highlight some specificities of poetry as a medium, even when "novelized." When you first turn from Achebe's novel to Okigbo's "Fragments out of the Deluge," it is the absences that are the most striking. In comparison with a novel, the abstraction of lyric poetry may seem, as Helen Vendler writes, "impoverished, existing as it does without much of a plot, and without any significant number of dramatis personae."[84] In Okigbo's tenth lyric, for example, there are no characters—figures like Okonkwo and Obierika, clearly distinguishable from one another by action, speech, and personality—but only an implied Igbo community ("us"), the poet or "protagonist" (xxiv), and the eaglelike "They," who figuratively evoke but do not realistically depict the European colonizers. There is no plot, except for the barest implied narrative of colonization and religious destruction—surely nothing like the flawed Okonkwo's strongly plotted tragic fall. There is no historical framework in which the literary story takes place, except as abstracted and internalized—again, nothing like the finely drawn fictional village of Umuofia near the start of the twentieth century. Indeed, to make sense of Okigbo's poem and extract a narrative from it, you have to know already the history of European colonial destruction of Igbo religion and traditional society. It is almost as if Okigbo assumes you have read *Things Fall Apart*. Achebe's novel's historical and social fullness and its temporal and spatial delimitation and coherence are likely to be more heuristically effective than is Okigbo's poetry in attempts to teach what life might have been like for the Igbo during the initial phase of European colonial settlement. Little wonder it has become a staple of high school and college syllabi, whereas Okigbo's sequence is known by only a tiny subset of the already small numbers of readers of difficult poetry.

If poetry is *less* in all these respects—condensed, stripped down, abstracted, as well as inaccessible to many readers—how could it at the same time still be *more*? Could there be plenitude in this poverty? Although Okigbo's colonizers are not Achebe's seemingly flesh-and-blood British missionaries or district commissioner, Okigbo's densely figurative language and allegorical mode of representation evoke the awesome power and violence of the arrival of the colonizers in strikingly few words:

> Their talons they drew out of their scabbard,
> Upon the tree trunks, as if on fire-clay,
> Their beaks they sharpened;
> And spread like eagles their felt-wings,
> And descended upon the twin gods of Irkalla (49)

The freedom of poetic syntax and the accentuation by line breaks build up the terror of this arrival. The syntactic inversion in the strophe's first line ("Their talons they drew out of their scabbard") spotlights at either end the birds' dangerously swordlike claws, and in the ensuing lines ("Upon the tree trunks . . . / . . . they sharpened") the ominous whetting of their beaks. The middle line ("Upon the tree trunks, as if on fire-clay"), punctuated by two spondees, floats ambiguously between two parallel lines inverting subject and verb, and so seems to connect syntactically with both (i.e., is it "Their talons they drew out . . . / Upon the tree trunks" or "Upon the tree trunks . . . / Their beaks they sharpened"?). The magnificent spreading of wings suggests the horrifying splendor of this exercise of colonial power. The anaphoric, anapestic, and other kinds of repetition suggest a relentless destructive menace that recurs as if in a dream, over and over, not the once-only chronology of realist fiction. Okigbo's sequence is more insistently artificial than anything in Achebe's seemingly plainspoken novel: "Fragments out of the Deluge" is replete with high diction, syntactic contortions, dense metaphoricity, and other denaturalized uses of language. Its "brazenness" and "strangeness" recall the artificiality that Jonathan Culler attributes to poetic apostrophe and by implication to poetry more generally.[85] A teacher of literature may often have to work to remind students that a novel like Achebe's is a construction, not a mirror held up to history, that the characters are fabricated, the diction crafted, the story plotted, whereas the reverse challenge may arise with poems such as Okigbo's—namely, helping them see the affective and social worlds embodied in poetry's formal contrivances.

This poetic sequence's alliterations, figurative condensation, and musical cadences suggest the iterative dreamtime of myth, and indeed Okigbo annotates his reference to Irkalla, which recalls "the twin-gods of the forest" two strophes earlier, as the "queen of the underworld" in "Sumerian myth"—most notably in the ancient epic *Gilgamesh*, one of the sequence's persistent intertexts (49). The python and the tortoise thus make their second appearance as Sumerian gods of the underworld, Mesopotamian myth refracting Igbo myth, in accordance with the modernist syncretism Okigbo knew well in Yeats, Pound, and Eliot. Despite the authorial wink in the Yeatsian title of *Things Fall Apart* and despite the novel's Christian shaping of some plot elements, Achebe sharply delimits his referential field, never leaving the reader in doubt as to the Igbo village setting and as to the author's self-exclusion from the diegesis. In Okigbo's sequence, obtrusive transnational quotation, allusion, and superposition call attention to the shaping authorial hand and palimpsestically layer other worlds on the Nigerian landscape of oilbean and bombax trees. "*Malisons, malisons, mair than ten—,*" intones the tenth lyric (49), the beginning of a Scottish malediction on anyone who hunts the wren ("*That harry the Ladye of Heaven's hen!*"), cited in James Frazer's influential *Golden Bough* as an example of pagan belief in sacred animals that cause suffering and death if killed.[86] The Igbo sunbird is collocated with the Scottish wren, just as Sumerian and Igbo deities are superimposed. To a much greater extent than *Things Fall Apart*, Okigbo's sequence—abruptly and mysteriously shifting registers and skidding transcontinentally on its references—intermaps the British assault on Igbo beliefs and lives with violent acts in other times and places, from *Gilgamesh* to Picasso's *Guernica*, the latter named and annotated in the sequence's final lyric and thus paralleling Okigbo's fragmentary lament over violent destruction with that of a Spanish-born modernist painter. In the magazine version Okigbo's epigraph from Eliot's *Waste Land* drew another transnational parallel with a high modernist: "These fragments I have shored against my ruins."[87] Although poetry is often assumed to be far more locally or nationally rooted than the novel, Okigbo's sequence shows poetry to be no less nimbly cosmopolitan, and sometimes even more so, than prose fiction.

Pace Bakhtin's distinction between poetry's monologism and the novel's dialogism, Okigbo's poem is dialogic in its interplay of viewpoints from discrepant times and places, heteroglot in its mixing of different discourses and registers. Other cultural voices abruptly cut across the poet's lyricism—most obviously the Scottish chant, but also, at the level of style and image, Euroclassical technique and modernist syncretism. Yet, as we saw in Joyce, Bakhtin's distinctions are not wholly inapplicable. Okigbo's poems submit scattered references, allusions, and discourses to the centripetal pressure of a singular subjectivity. The rich music of his cadences and repetitions, the highbrow references and stylization of the language, the inversions and torsions of the syntax—these and other features of the poems are unavoidably stamped "Okigbo." Instead of disappearing, as does Achebe, behind a panoply of characters of different backgrounds and social classes in conversation with one another, Okigbo annotates figures such as Eunice as "My childhood nurse known for her lyricism" (48), leaving no doubt that the sphere of his experience is the poem's magnetic field, if drawing together heterogeneous filaments. Admittedly, there are also many postcolonial and postmodernist novels that "lyricize" the novel, smearing the mimetic windowpane with illusion-blocking authorial palm prints. And there are examples of nonlyric African poetry that are less inwardly focused and more historically mimetic than Okigbo's work, such as Okot p'Bitek's dramatic monologues. But there are also lyric poems, if Okigbo's sequence is any indication, that, while hetero- and polyglot, dialogic and cross-cultural, counterbalance fragmentation with inwardness, compression, and stylistic patterning.

Although Bakhtin thought it was the novel that "fights" for

its place and "gets on poorly with other genres," Okigbo's poetic sequence demonstrates that poetry may be at least as territorial and even combative. It absorbs novelistic qualities but insists on its capacities, freely wielding metaphor and syntax, layering time frames and compressing allusions. None of these qualities is exclusive to poetry, but taken together and in relation to the novel, they are a reminder of how vigorously even novel-inflected poetry plays with and against poetic norms. A poem influenced by the novel makes use of the forms' shared imaginative basis, even if it is thinner in plot, character, and social mimesis, thicker in syntactic, figural, and allusive play than many a novel. Partly novelized, poetry since modernism has often been penetrated by the novel's historicity, low mimesis, colloquialism, psychological realism, and other features; but partly resistant to novelization, works such as "Fragments out of the Deluge" have at the same time shown off poetry's linguistic and formal range, its compression and intensity, its flexibility and artifice.

POETRY AND THEORY

While the novel has pulled some strands of modern and contemporary poetry in the direction of greater sociohistorical detail, another of poetry's discursive others has tugged the genre toward greater abstraction. In current usage in literary studies, "theory" is a speculative, generalizing mode of analysis,[88] related to philosophy but less disciplinarily circumscribed and more capacious in its reflections on culture, society, and psychology. Theory today can be seen as picking up where philosophy left off before analytic philosophy narrowed its purview. Poetry's age-old struggle with philosophy—both to take it in and to differentiate itself from it—continues today with theory, another impossibly large but inadequately examined topic about which I offer a few preliminary observations.[89]

Lest the blending of poetry and philosophy in the twentieth and twenty-first centuries be seen as unique, we need only remember that already in antiquity poetry and philosophy sometimes fused to produce hybrid works, from Anaximander's *On Nature* to

Lucretius's *On the Nature of Things*. Ancient philosophers famously disagreed over whether philosophy and poetry were incompatible or affiliated. Although Plato thought poetry's fake mimicry and knowledge-deficient emotionalism were at odds with the truth, warranting the banishment from the republic of all but hymns to the gods and odes to great men, Aristotle suggested an affinity between the discourses, calling poetry "more philosophical" than history, "for poetry tends to express the universal, history the particular."[90] Many subsequent critics and philosophers have modified this account, seeing poetry as the mediating term in Aristotle's implied discursive spectrum: it has often been thought to fuse universality with particularity, as in John Crowe Ransom's adaptation of Hegel and especially of Kant in the concept of the "concrete universal."[91] But as is widely acknowledged in the wake of poststructuralism, even when philosophy has considered itself poetry's antithesis, it has hardly been able to keep clean of poetic figuration, as in Plato's supposedly antipoetic allegory of the cave, and despite the dream of representational transparency, its language has been tinged with poetry, most self-consciously in the work of poet-philosophers such as Nietzsche, Kierkegaard, Heidegger, and Derrida, the last of whom deconstructs philosophy into the fictiveness, rhetoricity, and metaphoricity of literature.[92]

Conversely, modern and contemporary poets, like such nineteenth-century poets as Coleridge, Shelley, and Arnold, have not hesitated to philosophize and theorize, although few philosophers have seen poetry as conceptually groundbreaking or analytically rigorous. A handful of modernist poems explicitly engage with academic philosophy. T. S. Eliot, a graduate student in philosophy from 1911 to 1916 and author of a technical dissertation on F. H. Bradley's philosophy, quoted Bradley in a note to explain the "prison" of consciousness in *The Waste Land*: it is "a circle closed on the outside," so that "every sphere is opaque to the others which surround it."[93] As an undergraduate at Harvard, Eliot had studied with the pragmatist George Santayana but claimed he "never liked Santayana" or his writing, finding some of it "exceptionally bad," whereas Wallace Stevens, also a Harvard student, partly embraced Santayana's philosophy.[94] His elegy "To an Old

Philosopher in Rome" pays tribute to the enlarging capacities of the imagination, honoring Santayana's ability (and the poet's) to transform poverty into splendor, depletion into riches, everyday sounds and smells into something more: "The newsboys' muttering / Becomes another murmuring; the smell / Of medicine, a fragrantness not to be spoiled . . ." (ellipsis in original).[95]

Yet such modernist poems aren't merely mouthpieces through which poets voice philosophical abstractions. Albeit directly marked by philosophy, even these poems are less interested in making conceptual statements dressed up in colorful metaphors and catchy rhythms than they are in devising innovative forms and vocabularies for an experience that includes philosophy, inter alia. Eliot believed that a poet's mind is "constantly amalgamating disparate experience," such as falling in love and reading Spinoza, and that poets at their best can "feel their thought as immediately as the odour of a rose."[96] In strong acts of poetic thinking, the thinking and the poetry are inseparable. Charles Simic criticizes

> the assumption . . . that the poet knows beforehand what he or she wishes to say, and that the writing of the poem is the search for the most effective means of gussying up these ideas.
>
> If this were correct, poetry would simply repeat what has been thought and said before. There would be no poetic thinking in the way Heidegger conceives of it. There would be no hope for poetry having any relation to truth.[97]

Instead of performing a preexisting conceptual script, the poetic enactment of ideas can develop or change them—or even create them anew.

Besides, despite their debts to Bradley and Santayana, both Eliot and Stevens pushed back against the philosophies that influenced them—Eliot against professional philosophy's narrowness, Stevens against Santayana's fact-dissolving aestheticism.[98] Although Eliot nearly became an academic philosopher, he feared that "all philosophising is a perversion of reality," because it imposed a "complete consistency" on a "confused and contradictory world" more amenable to the unsystematic, amalgamative procedures of poetry.[99] The refusal of philosophy's ironing out of experience also plays a role in Marianne Moore's poetry. Explicitly contending with ancient Greek philosophy in one of her most ambitious poems, "An Octopus," she evokes the untamable ruggedness and uncontainable variety of Mount Rainier's sublimity partly by contrast with the Greek aesthetics of the beautiful: the ancients "liked smoothness, distrusting what was back / of what could not be clearly seen."[100]

Such overt references in Moore, Stevens, and Eliot are, of course, a small part of the picture of modernist poetry's engagements with philosophy. A modernist poem compounds usually unnamed, often contradictory philosophical presuppositions about the world, the self, language, and experience. Modernism's intense self-scrutiny made it increasingly difficult to believe that the poet is, in Richard Rorty's words, the performer of "unmediated woodnotes," "a naive producer of literature whose jaw" would drop on learning that poetry is "supported by philosophical oppositions."[101] At a more general level, modern poets and philosophers can be seen as working to some extent in parallel. Whether citing a specific philosophy as foundation or foil or seemingly ignoring philosophy, the modernists brought to poetry a philosophical ambition to reconceive the grounds of existence, knowledge, time, perception, language, and identity, their notorious difficulty resulting in part from their refusal to remain comfortably nested within inherited preconceptions. Like philosophers, modernist poets had the from-the-ground-up drive to rethink. Yet however influenced by Bradley or Santayana or the ancient Greeks, by Nietzsche's tragic fatalism, Henri Bergson's *durée*, William James's stream of consciousness, or Bertrand Russell's axiom of reducibility, their poetry does not follow the ratiocinative procedures of canonical Western philosophy. The modernists' metaphoric leaps, wrenchingly disjunctive surfaces, linguistic self-obsessions, affect-charged diction, and sometimes violent and unexplained juxtapositions and digressions may owe something to modern ontology and epistemology, but the poets part company with many of philosophy's characteristic protocols, such as systematic argument, syllogistic ratiocination, step-by-step logic, exhaustive explanation, and self-effacingly transparent conceptual language (protocols also breached, of course, by poet-philosophers such as Nietzsche).

In modernism's aftermath, many poets have been strongly informed by philosophy and theory, from Louis Zukofsky and George Oppen to Jorie Graham, John Koethe, and J. H. Prynne. Conceptual poetry, by virtue of its name, may seem as close as poetry gets to theory. "Conceptual writing," according to Kenneth Goldsmith, "is more interested in a *thinkership* rather than a readership. . . . Conceptual writing is good only when the idea is good; often, the idea is much more interesting than the resultant texts." So far, conceptual poetry may sound more like philosophy or theory than poetry as usually understood. "And yet . . . ," Goldsmith continues, appealing to aesthetic principles that have long been more closely associated with poetry than with theory, "there are moments of unanticipated beauty, sometimes grammatical, some structural, many philosophical: the wonderful rhythms of repetition, the spectacle of the mundane reframed as literature, a reorientation to the poetics of time, and fresh perspectives on readerliness."[102] Despite the pressures of both deconstruction and experimental writing on distinctions between poetry and theory or philosophy, it may be easier to blur than to void them, as indicated when Goldsmith, though favoring "ideas" over "texts," summons "the shocking amount of beauty" to be discovered even in conceptual poetry's rhythms, repetitions, defamiliarizations, and reorientations.[103] However "poetic" we may think the writings of Derrida, Foucault, and Heidegger, or those of Richard Rorty, Luce Irigaray, and Judith Butler, if their essays were reprinted in a poetry anthology or if we were to teach them in a poetry class, we would be hard pressed to defend their achievements as poetry even on Goldsmith's expansive terms ("moments of unanticipated beauty," "wonderful rhythms of repetition," etc.), let alone on the basis of their metaphoric daring and reach, imaginative reinflections of the poetic line, vigorous remaking of literary forms, affective impact and subtlety, or other such achievements. There are no hard-and-fast lines between the poetic and the philosophical, and yet some of the conceptual and aesthetic energy that poet-philosophers and thinker-poets generate in their work comes from their darting across such presumed lines, however indistinct and unstable.

Critics have surveyed a variety of instances of the interplay between twentieth-century poetry and theory or philosophy, from modernism and objectivism to the New Criticism, feminism, and Language writing, so I concentrate here on a few illustrative works by a modern poet and a contemporary poet who, though they have not yet figured in the overviews, can help us explore significant areas of intergeneric exchange and difference.[104] Although Yeats is sometimes seen as a poet of closed lyricism, I turn to his intergeneric openings here and in each subsequent chapter, hoping to complicate the standard picture of his supposedly monologic poetics. His ambivalences toward philosophy are exemplary of the divided response in much modern and contemporary poetry: sometimes his work blends poetry and philosophy, at others it times sets them fiercely against one another. He famously cites Goethe's remark "[A] poet needs all philosophy, but he must keep it out of his work."[105] If this were the totality of Yeats's views, there would be little more to say on the subject. Instead, in an essay that quotes Goethe's aphorism, "The Symbolism of Poetry," Yeats characteristically argues both sides of the question of whether philosophy nourishes or impoverishes poetry. Abstract critical thought has always been important for the formation of "great art," he claims, echoing Arnold in "The Function of Criticism at the Present Time," and its paucity in England, "where journalists are more powerful and ideas less plentiful than elsewhere," may help explain why such art "is perhaps dead in England."[106] Philosophy is seen as an important counterweight to journalism's day-by-day, hour-by-hour, low-mimetic particularism. Yeats's critical reflections on art and his immersion in Western philosophical texts by Vico and Nietzsche, in the non-Western philosophies propounded in the *Upanishads* and elsewhere, indicate a more philosophical inclination than we usually attribute to lyric poets. At the same time, Yeats regards images too obviously burdened by ideas as mere "intellectual symbols," images subordinated to and overmastered by an abstraction, such as "a cross or a crown of thorns" for "purity and sovereignty."[107] In the earlier discussion of poetry and the novel, we saw that Vendler and other critics deem lyric "abstract" by comparison with prose fiction, but in comparison with philosophy, it is surely less so. If poetry is more theoretical than the novel, it is often more novelistic than theory. For Yeats, as for other symbolist-oriented modernists, philosophical, religious, and other forms of abstraction must not pinion images or rhythms, which should participate organically in the subtle moods they evoke. While *A Vision* is the later culmination of Yeats's efforts to construct an abstract "system," an eccentric theoretical amalgam of various forms of mysticism and traditional philosophy, his poems reanimate both sides of the debate in what Plato was already calling the ancient quarrel between poetry and philosophy.

Yeats illustrates the dangers he warns against when he allows his poetry to serve as versification of his system: in a poem such as "The Phases of the Moon," poetry and philosophy, system and style, struggle against and stifle each other. But even this poem includes the supposed singing of a song, and in so doing calls attention to the gap between its blank-verse didacticism and its inset musical performativity. In his more persuasive dramatizations of the tensions between philosophy and poetry, Yeats enacts a longing for abstraction, only to turn against it and embrace the sensual immediacy of embodied thought. Philosophy is a systematic defense against our vulnerabilities, he suggests in "Nineteen Hundred and Nineteen," in a passage that metonymically displaces human anxiety onto a personified "night":

> The night can sweat with terror as before
> We pieced our thoughts into philosophy,
> And planned to bring the world under a rule,
> Who are but weasels fighting in a hole.[108]

Philosophy, as suggested by the verb "pieced," represents the drive for totalization, for making whole by mending or patching together fragments. The abstract rules of logic and philosophical system are conflated with governmental "rule," philosophy appearing here as an almost imperial mastery and manipulation of reality. Yeats reproaches would-be philosophers like himself for disguising their tooth-and-claw power struggles, "weasels fighting in a hole." What precedes this self-reproach for self-deluded philosophizing is one of the most horrifying images in Yeats's poetry, based on the report of a brutal killing of a woman by British ex-servicemen known as the Black and Tans: "a drunken soldiery / Can leave the mother, murdered at her door, / To crawl in her own blood, and go scot-free."[109] The immediacy of this image of a mother shot and crawling in her blood contrasts jarringly with the pat comfort of thoughts as philosophical puzzle pieces, fitted together into a coherent whole. Large ideas here function as shields to affect, as distancing generalizations. But a particular person's death ruptures the philosophical whole. Her singular death can't be seamed together with others, stitched into a conceptual totality. Reflecting on his own mortality in "Among School Children," Yeats mocks the philosophies of Pythagoras, Aristotle, and Plato, the latter of whom "thought nature but a spume that plays / Upon a ghostly paradigm of things"; they are impotent to stay the relentless truth of aging: "Old clothes upon old sticks to scare a bird."[110] In its powerful rhythms and sensual images, poetry keeps closer than philosophy to the truths known in the body.

Yeats's critique of the aspiration "to bring the world under a rule" recurs in the first lines of the sonnet "Meru":

Civilisation is hooped together, brought
Under a rule, under the semblance of peace
By manifold illusion . . . [111]

But now it is civilization that imposes comforting deception, not philosophy. The phoneme "man" tears out of the word "manifold" to name the subject of the relentless drive to pierce through illusion:

but man's life is thought,
And he, despite his terror, cannot cease

Ravening through century after century,
Ravening, raging, and uprooting that he may come
Into the desolation of reality . . .

In "Nineteen Hundred and Nineteen," philosophy was a defense
against the terror of violence; here "thought" plunges us, despite
our "terror," into a bare, extracivilizational reality. In contrast
with the view that a staid and falsely integrative philosophy is
a defense against reality, thinking here is represented as a propulsive force that smashes through all barriers. As in Heidegger's
account, the task of thinking is "to rip away the fog that conceals
beings as such"; genuine thinking is "the torn condition—the torn
consciousness," and "[p]oetry is the saying of the unconcealed-
ness of what is," or *alētheia*.[112] *Ravening*—devouring or plunder-
ing—comes into English from the French *ravenir*, to stream, rush,
or furrow (e.g., the earth) with gullies;[113] *raging* may recall King
Lear on the heath bidding nature to unleash total destruction;[114]
and *uprooting* completes the alliterative participial triplet that associates thinking with ongoing violent, boundary-shattering forces
of nature. Yeats also sounds out this relentless, form-breaking
energy in his rhythms: repeating the hammering dactylic start
of the previous line, "Ravening," he packs the strongly enjambed
line's five stresses with eight unstressed syllables ("Ravening, raging, and uprooting that he may come"). Here "civilization," not
"philosophy," is the totalizing and falsifying ideology that dis-
guises our similarity with nature's violence, and philosophy deliv-
ers us into the real. The permanence sought by Yeats's Hindu
hermits is beyond the confines of culture: they bare their bodies to the ferocious cold as if to merge with an ultimate reality.
Ironically, it is through the highly cultivated form of the sonnet
that Yeats tries to think through and beyond cultivation, so that
the "glory" and "monuments" imagined as "gone" presumably
include this very poem, imperiling the poetic exceptionalism of
Horace's "Exegi monumentum" and Shakespeare's sonnet 55. But
this Shakespearean sonnet's knowing participation in long-lived
lyric traditions, even as it overruns them rhythmically, syntactically, intellectually, and stanzaically (Shakespearean rhyme yet a

Petrarchan *volta*), qualifies its anticivilizational and even antipoetic impulses.[115] It associates genuine poetry with the philosophical quest for truth, not with artful consolation or illusory contrivance. Its enactment of such thinking in art-disrupting art, with a rush of extra syllables, propulsive enjambments, hybrid stanzaic form, and tumbling syntax balanced against a closing couplet, lyricizes the philosophical drive for disclosure. "Man can embody truth but he cannot know it," Yeats asserted in a letter a few weeks before he died; "The abstract is not life and everywhere draws out its contradictions. You can refute Hegel but not the Saint or the Song of Sixpence."[116] Embodying truth in its prosodic, metaphoric, and sonic enactments, Yeats's "Meru" is no more vulnerable to refutation than is a nursery rhyme.

In criticism on contemporary writing, the intersections between theory and poetry that have been most frequently remarked are those in the work of experimental poets indebted to poststructuralism, such as Goldsmith, Bernstein, and Palmer. By some accounts, "[o]ne of the major results of this mingling of the lyrical with the philosophical . . . was the emergence" of Language poetry.[117] Less noticed has been the role of theory in postcolonial and diasporic poetics, even though theory itself has garnered, along with fiction, sustained attention in postcolonial studies. Close analysis of a poem saturated with postcolonial theory may help illustrate how poetry can at one and the same time interfuse with theory and diverge from it. Tobago-born, Trinidad-raised, Toronto-based writer M. NourbeSe Philip's poem "Discourse on the Logic of Language" is celebrated in part because it shares in the widespread postcolonial theorization of the colonizer's violently imposed language as leaving the (post)colonized subject verbally wounded and struggling to give utterance to a non-European experience. "It was in language that the slave was perhaps most successfully imprisoned by his master," Kamau Brathwaite speculates, "and it was in his (mis-)use of it that he perhaps most effectively rebelled."[118] From Brathwaite and Ngũgĩ wa Thiong'o to *The Empire Writes Back*, countless essays and books have discoursed upon such linguistic maiming and revolt.[119] But just as traditional lyrics expounded the paradoxes of death and desire without being reducible to their thematic content, we need to ask, what is distinctively poetic about how Philip's poem explores this familiar concept? Although theory is often applied to decode such works, how does the poem work with theory and at the same move beyond it? What can it do that theory can't?

With a title that seems to enfold the poem within theoretical abstraction, Philip's "Discourse on the Logic of Language" begins:

> English
> is my mother tongue.
> A mother tongue is not
> not a foreign lan lan lang
> language
> l/anguish
>   anguish
> —a foreign anguish.[120]

Like the title, the reliance on the copula "is" in these first two sentences highlights the poem's intersection with the definitional and analytic discourse on which it draws. But the dryly declarative language quickly devolves into agitated stutters and slips. Instead of merely stating that the foreign language both impedes and enables expression, the poet realizes this paradoxically expressive deformation in emotionally tumultuous sentences that fracture grammatically and words that splinter into puns: the phrase "foreign lan" shows up the alienness of a European language in a colonized land, and the ensuing lines tease the words "languish" and "anguish" out of the imposed "language." The poet's dissolving of the English language and of the very word "language" into words expressive of that language's injuries exemplifies postcolonial subversion of the imperial standard. Seemingly impeded from univocal statements by the language through which she seeks expression, Philip uses the resources of poetry to mark formally the postcolonial imprisonment within, and transvaluative "(mis-)use" of, an imposed English.

Exploiting poetry's recursive sounds, enjambments, flexible syntax, and relative freedom from grammatical norms, Philip personifies English as a "father tongue" and evokes postcolonial disinheritance in this alien language:

I have no mother
tongue
no mother to tongue
no tongue to mother
to mother
tongue
me (56)

Philip's enjambment momentarily evokes total disinheritance ("I have no mother") before allowing the seeming substantive to morph into a modifier of "tongue." Her line splitting of the dead metaphor "mother / tongue," followed by modulation of the noun "tongue" into a verb ("no mother to tongue") and then by chiastic inversion ("no tongue to mother"), infuses an abstraction with bodily concreteness, enabling her to begin to repossess the nonmother tongue as her own. Owing a debt to the propositional discourse of postcolonial theory, Philip also diverges from it in her compressed verbal enactment of what it feels like to speak and stutter from within an alien language. The sonic slide in ensuing lines from "dumb-tongued" to "dub-tongued" (as in African Caribbean "dub" or performance poetry) is emblematic of the transformation of silencing into indigenized expressivity (56). Here poetry coincides with theory in conceptualizing the postcolonial subject's relation to language; but instead of abstractly propounding the idea, it inventively and urgently dramatizes this verbal suppression and subversion in puns, repetitions, consonances, metaphors, and personifications, grafted onto telling line breaks, vivid typographical juxtapositions, and syntactic disruptions, inversions, and parallels.

Some of these techniques spill over from Philip's lineated poetic text ("English / is my mother tongue") to the vertically printed prose poetry in the left-hand margin, which at first seems to be a naturalist description of a newborn child of indeterminate species whose "MOTHER'S TONGUE" is said to have "TONGUED IT CLEAN" of the mother's amniotic sac. Unlike the fractured mother-daughter relation in the stuttering lineated poem, the prose poetry represents intergenerational continuity between mother and child. But this poetically recursive and oblique prose text, which crosses naturalism with *écriture feminine*, also amplifies the lineated text's literalization of "mother tongue" (56). On a subsequent page, the description further plays on this literalization by inverting it, remetaphorizing this lingual relation when the mother is said, in a vision of unbroken intergenerational continuity, to blow words—"HER WORDS, HER MOTHER'S WORDS, THOSE OF HER MOTHER'S MOTHER, AND ALL THEIR MOTHERS BEFORE—INTO THE DAUGHTER'S MOUTH" (58). Philip's vertical and horizontal texts evoke and undo oppositions between prose's particularist realism and poetry's reverberating metaphoricity.

But even though these prose passages echo and reinforce the lineated poetry, the poetry also sharply separates itself from other discourses. Running alongside the poetic text and the prose poetry are two other kinds of texts, as emphasized visually by font and layout, in one case shifting to italics and in another to a multiple-choice format. "[C]ramping the space traditionally given the poem itself" and "forcing it to share its space," Philip's juxtaposition of voices in various typefaces makes materially visible the pressure on the poetic text of scientific and legal discourses.[121] Though split-page interdiscursive juxtapositions appear in works by Derrida and other theorists, they have an especially dramatic place in poetry, where every detail, including the typographic and visual appearance of texts on the page, contributes significantly to the signifying processes. In the margins to the right of the lineated poetry, Philip prints two italicized edicts, cast in the voice of British colonial authorities before emancipation; indeed, in a powerful audio recording of a performance of the poem, this part of the text is delivered in a genteel male British voice, while Philip intones the lineated poetry and prose poetry (another male, North American voice recites the science history).[122] The first edict demands that slaves be mixed with other slaves who do not speak their language, thereby preventing their speaking to each other to *"foment rebellion and revolution"* (56). *"Every slave caught speaking his native language,"* according to the second edict, *"shall be severely punished,"* including *"removal of the tongue"* and its monitory display (58). These edicts historically contextualize the significance of the postcolonial speaker's longing for an absented mother tongue, her estrangement from the very language she is using, and her aggressive wringing of unexpected meanings and puns out of words. Also lending resonance to her creative assault on English is another intertext on the first facing page—a seemingly scientific, analytic passage about speech-related parts of the brain, named after the nineteenth-century doctors Wernicke and Broca—the latter of whom sought to prove white males "superior" to "women, Blacks and other peoples of colour" (57). At the end of the poem, the discourse of scientific knowledge is cast in the form of multiple-choice questions about the tongue, except that unexpected counterdiscourses interrupt, as when a man's tongue is defined as an organ of (a) taste, (b) speech, (c) "oppression and exploitation," or "(d) all of the above," and spoken words are said to require

(a) the lip, tongue and jaw all working together.
(b) a mother tongue.
(c) the overseer's whip.
(d) all of the above or none. (59)

The imaginative deviations and leaps of poetry disrupt the neutral sheen of scientific language.

Philip's poem struggles with and against the scientific and legal languages it incorporates. "Discourse on the Logic of Language" provides evidence of poetry's cross-generic contamination by its others yet also of poetry's urge to differentiate itself. Its form-overflowing forms, its intently purposive playfulness, its witty and turbulent paronomasia are set against the analytic discourses it encompasses within its "discourse." In this regard, Philip's poem is exemplary of much contemporary poetry's simultaneous intergeneric porosity and self-definitional intensity: the "poetic" text that runs down the center of the page, reinforced by the vertically printed prose poetry, is formally, graphically, and semantically distinguished from the prose kinds that surround it, even though the entire collection of texts, including imperial edicts and multiple-choice questions, is ultimately subsumed to a multivocal and multigraphic poem.

Though Philip incorporates within her properly "poetic" lineated text the analytic discourse of postcolonial theory's conceptualization of language in relation to oppressed and marginal subjects, her text isn't merely warmed-over theory. Opening fractures between words for the "torn consciousness" that Heidegger attributed to thinking, her poem demonstrates a thought-rich inventiveness that is less propositional than it is formal, linguistic, and typographic. Although poetry and theory are often seen as irreconcilable opposites—lyric particularity and feeling as against inhuman abstraction—Philip, Yeats, and other modern and contemporary poets reveal the complex ways in which poetry both is and is not its theoretical other. They show us how poetry is interanimated with theory even as, to a greater extent than theory, it vigorously and extravagantly stretches language, rhythm, syntax, metaphor, typography, and other formal resources in rethinking experience from the ground up. Poetry that draws on theory highlights poetry's kinship with its more abstract cousin, ripping "away the fog that conceals beings as such," at the same time that it exhibits poetry's greater materiality, visuality, and formal embodiment, its nonsystematicity and conceptual plurality.

POETRY AND THE LAW

As an intergenre to poetry, the novel is especially rich in sociohistorical detail, while theory and philosophy are especially powerful in conceptual abstraction, so that poetry's incorporation of each allows it to extend itself in opposite directions. Somewhere between these discursive poles, a third discursive system, the law—the body of rules governing society and enforced by the state—synthesizes abstract principles and social reality. Lawyer-poet Archibald MacLeish went so far as to compare the law's dialectical nature to poetry's: "The business of the law is to make sense of the confusion of what we call human life—to reduce it to order," while "the business of poetry" is "to make sense of the chaos of our lives" and "compose an order which the bewildered, angry heart can recognize."[123]

But the law's "order," its way of mediating between the abstract and the concrete, isn't the same as poetry's, as suggested by the collision between these two different orders of order in the poems discussed below. After all, if it were the same, less ingenuity would be required to connect the preeminent modernist lawyer-poet's unpeopled and imagination-flush poems to his Hartford practice as an insurance lawyer, and the interpretive yield of doing so would be more substantial.[124] That said, poems by lawyer-poets other than Wallace Stevens more directly engage the sometimes vexed relation between poetry and the law. Formally trained as a lawyer who practiced law for seven years, until 1983, M. NourbeSe Philip writes poetry interfused not only with theory but also with the law, as already seen in the use of edicts in "Discourse on the Logic of Language." Like another legally trained poet, the objectivist Charles Reznikoff, Philip bases some of her poetry directly in juridical documents.[125] But whereas Reznikoff condenses American courtroom narratives from 1885 to 1915 in *Testimony* and edits down and compresses material from the records of the Nuremberg and Eichmann trials in *Holocaust*, Philip massively expands the short legal text on which she bases her book-length poetic sequence *Zong!* (2008). Another lawyer-poet, a criminal defense attorney specializing in rape and other sex-offense cases, Vanessa Place gives this transcriptive practice a conceptualist twist in what she calls "self-appropriations, in which I pick my own pocket, such as repurposing my legal briefs in *Tragodia*."[126] All three writers twin poetry with the evidentiary particularity of legal texts to expose excruciatingly difficult material for maximum impact while limiting the ethical risks of aestheticization, of aesthetically profiting from other people's suffering and loss. Even poets without legal training sometimes directly appropriate legal documents to similar effect. Muriel Rukeyser's long documentary sequence "The Book of the Dead" interweaves congressional testimony on the outbreak of lung disease in West Virginia's coal fields with ancient spells of the Egyptian *Book of the Dead*, and Robert Hayden, building on Rukeyser's work, evokes the *Amistad* incident and other moments in the slave trade in "Middle Passage," a poem that splices legal depositions by slave traders from the *Amistad* and other court cases with ship log, memoir, prayer, hymn, and lyric effusion. But while Philip follows Hayden and Rukeyser in her poetic use of found legal documents, she, like Reznikoff, restricts the words in her long poem largely to those in her chosen legal intertext (she adds African names at the bottom margin of the page).

The language of *Zong!* is drawn almost entirely from a 1783 legal decision, *Gregson v. Gilbert*, rendered after the owners of the slave ship *Zong* sued insurers to collect damages for the "loss" of between 130 and 150 slaves. In an atrocity that strengthened the argument in Britain for the abolition of the slave trade, the enslaved Africans had been thrown overboard to die in the sea because the captain believed that the insurers would be liable for "cargo" unloaded to preserve the remaining crew and slaves, whereas nothing could be collected from the insurers if the enslaved people died onboard because of illness. In the surviving legal decision, which Philip reprints at the end of *Zong!*, the enslaved Africans are assumed to be "property," the captain's action a mere "throwing overboard of goods," in part "to save the residue."[127]

"Law and poetry," Philip comments, "both share an inexorable concern with language—the 'right' use of the 'right' words, phrases, or even marks of punctuation; precision of expression is the goal shared by both" (191). While she acknowledges the desire for "precision" in legal language, Philip also sees "the legal report of *Gregson v. Gilbert* masquerading as order, logic, and rationality," part of a discourse that "promulgated the nonbeing of African peoples," its order hiding disorder, "its logic hiding the illogic" (197). For her, poetry contests the fearful power of the law to constitute subjects and to void them. *Zong!* is immersed in the regulative language of the British legal decision, but the book's dispersal, fragmentation, and even violent shredding of those words accord with Philip's view of poetry as pushing "against the boundary of language by engaging in language that often is neither rational, logical, predictable nor ordered," in the way of the law (197). "While a concern with precision and accuracy in language is common to both law and poetry," she writes, "the law uses language as a tool for ordering; in the instant case, however, I want poetry to disassemble the ordered, to create disorder and mayhem so as to release the story that cannot be told, but which, through not-telling, will tell itself" (199). At the same time that she recognizes the kinship between poetic and legal discourses, Philip, despite MacLeish's near equation of poetic and legal order, intercalates the dispassionate, coercive order of legal language with her poetry's gaps and perturbations, its inverted hierarchies and disruptive energies, to unmake that precise order from within.

Take "Zong #24," the diction of which is from *Gregson v. Gilbert*:

evidence

is
sustenance
is
support
is
the law (41)

The diction of legal reasoning ("evidence," "support," etc.), the anaphora formed by a neutral-seeming and unvarying copula, "is," the ordering of a stanzalike unit with a seeming heading ("evidence," later "the ship," "the perils," etc.) that subordinates the right-hand substantives, all seem close cousins with the order, hierarchy, and rational procedures of legal language. Its alternate lines braced from above and below by "is," the poem persists with seemingly definitional and evidentiary claims about the ship as the captain and crew, about the perils of the rains and seas and currents, until it ends on an abrupt twist:

the case

is

murder (41)

In the 1783 judicial opinion the word "murder" is used, but, astonishingly, not in relation to what happened to the enslaved people, who are mere "goods," but by way of analogy to prove a legal principle: "Every particular circumstance of this averment need not be proved. In an indictment for murder it is not necessary to prove each particular circumstance" (211). Another judge quibbles with this fanciful comparison, but again, not because the drowning of the enslaved people was murder, but because the "argument drawn from the law respecting indictments for murder does not apply" (211). The legal text uses the word "murder" only by way of analogy. Philip's emphatic ending to her poem reveals this figurative usage, in a bizarre legal quarrel over niceties of argumentation, as a kind of Freudian slip: through it, the slave killings well up in the judicial text that tries legally to rationalize them into a loss of cargo. The legal text speaks "murder," but only in an apparently unconscious acknowledgment. Philip's poem recognizes its family resemblance to the law, but by energetically rearranging and deranging law's ostensibly rational language, it reveals what is sometimes concealed by law's seemingly authoritative logic. The poems in *Zong!* may constitute, in Philip's term, an "antinarrative" (204), disrupting narrative order and fluency by their spacing and stuttering, but they also function as a counternarrative, telling a story of colonial atrocity that, because of its sheer enormity and lack of adequate documentation, "cannot be told yet must be told, but only through its un-telling" (207). The law is also often seen as a tissue of narratives, though these are ultimately intended not to renarrate the past for purposes of enlightenment but, as Paul Gewirtz puts it, "to invoke the coercive force of the state on one's behalf."[128] Poetry lacks any such governmental power of enforcement. Because it stands outside mechanisms of regulative authority, it has the freedom to question and disrupt the legal norms that have sometimes legitimized the dehumanization of subject peoples. In broken sentences and large white spaces, Philip's sequence opens up silences in which the humanity denied by the subject-effacing force of the law has a chance of being heard.

Another poem that retells without telling the history of slavery in the Caribbean, Jamaican poet Lorna Goodison's "Annie Pengelly" closely intertwines poetry and the law, with profound implications for our understanding of the relation between these discourses. Although Goodison's lyric style looks nothing like Philip's experimental disjunctiveness and collage of found texts, her poem is also permeated by legal discourse, even as it, too, explores its difference from the law:

> I come to represent the case
> of one Annie Pengelly,
> maidservant, late of the San Fleming Estate
> situated in the westerly parish of Hanover.[129]

At the start, the speaker's formal and authoritative voice seems very much like that of a lawyer. To "represent" her subject in a poem, the poet suggests, is akin to representing her in a court of law: in both realms, a surrogate speaks for a silent plaintiff and tells her untold story. Annie Pengelly is defined formally and factually by her name, work, and place of work (San Fleming Estate fictionalizing San Flebyn Estate),[130] though the adjective "late" starts to hint at difference: this plaintiff is long dead. In poetry, unlike law, there are no statutes of limitation. Annie Pengelly, we learn from an account that reaches back to before the 1838 abolition of slavery in the West Indies, is the pseudonym of an enslaved girl forced by her unhappy lovelorn mistress to "lie draped, / heaped across her feet / a human blanket" (29), and keep her warm in the cold of winter. When the insomniac mistress sang and danced, she commanded Annie to applaud. She kept Annie awake by sticking

her with a pin, slapping her, or, worst of all, making her *"cut-up /
to throw-away"* piles of old newspaper—dubbed by the poet "the
paper torture" (30).

Setting the scene in both place (northwestern Jamaica, where
the mountains rear up in "the shape of a Dolphin"s head" [27])
and time (the Middle Passage "journey in long, mawed ships, / to
drogue millions of souls" [27]), the poem at first plays along with
conventions of trial law, while code-switching into nonstandard
diction ("this need . . . that cause" [27]) and long-historied scene
setting, and so running counter to law's formality, antidigressive
narrative methods, and foreshortened time horizons:

> So now you are telling me to proceed
> and proceed swiftly.
> Why have I come here representing Annie? (27)

The judge's voice echoes in the poet-lawyer's repetition and
address, but the poem, while evoking through dramatic monologue the oral give-and-take of a trial, refuses the judge's demand
for narrative linearity, for what have been called law's "institutional requirements" of "brevity and relevance"—and the law's
customary injunction to tell nothing but the truth.[131] The speaker,
it turns out, has been telling and yet slyly refusing to tell the plaintiff's story:

> Well this is the first thing she asked me to say,
> that Annie is not even her real name.
> A name is the first thing we own in this world.
>
> We lay claim to a group of sounds
> which rise up and down and mark out our space
> in the air around us.
> We become owners of a harmony of vowels and consonants
> singing a specific meaning. (27–28)

So much for legal efficiency and representation: this lawyer-poet
refuses to disclose even the plaintiff's real name. Remarkably, in

the plantation context, Goodison presents naming not as someone else's forcible imposition—a slave master's—but as self-
possession, in her self-reflexively "poetic" description of a name
as a unique musical signature, a verbal fingerprint that no one can
erase. Annie's "real name was given to her / at the pastoral ceremony of her outdooring" (28)—a West African naming ritual that
provides communal grounding for her self-identity, as reenacted
in turn by the poet's incantatory verses.

Appropriately for a tale of colonial servitude, the words "own"
and "owners," in this poem's "harmony of vowels and consonants," will echo to the very ending. Goodison richly mines poetry's phonemic recursiveness and semantic ambiguity—features
of poetry that invert the law's emphasis on discursive linearity,
transparency, and clarity. Several words beginning with *o* repeat
and interact in the poem's vowel-enwound tissue of sounds: *own*,
owe, *O*, *Oh*, and *one*. *Own*: in retelling her story, the speaker would
restore a kind of self-ownership to a girl once owned by a cruel
slavemistress; the verbal self-possession of poetry supplants the
dispossession of slavery. Though having been deprived of the
ownership of her body, the girl can, at least in this civil-trial-by-
verse, own a name as a locus of identity. The word "own" thus
points in two contrastive directions, as a signifier of both European
legal rights to owning black bodies in slavery and poetic rights to
nominal self-ownership in the naming ritual of verse. So too, the
word "one" ripples through the poem in two opposite senses. It
is a marker of Annie's subjugation to the status of property, or
chattel, as when the speaker grimly lists "one small African girl"
(29) after an anaphoric list of objects owned by the slavemistress
that begins, "One pair of tortoiseshell combs, / one scrolled silver backed mirror" (28). Enslaved people were, as Colin Dayan
indicates, civilly dead, like things or animals, even if they were
persons in law in the highly restricted sense of being accountable
for crimes.[132] "One" thus recurs in Goodison's poem in the sense
of what the *OED* calls an "[e]mphatic numeral" to mean "one
only,"[133] suggestive of the evidentiary particularity of the courtroom—a listing bleakly resumed in the phrase "One pile of newspapers" (30). But at the trial-like beginning of the poem, "one"

appears in another sense familiar from the courtroom, as an indefinite pronoun in apposition to the plaintiff's name, here meaning "some one, a certain one, an individual, a person":[134] "I come to represent the case / of one Annie Pengelly" (27). In contrast to her being legally a *no one* under colonialism, mere property, "one small African girl," the lawyer-poet emphatically redefines her in her singularity, as a some*one*. Retrospectively restoring to Annie a human self-sameness negated by laws that permitted slavery, the poem clangs these two legal meanings of "one" against each other to acknowledge Annie's degradation and yet replace one kind of oneness (property), protected by the law, with another (human uniqueness), protected in this instance by the lawlike poem.

Recounting Annie's abuse, the speaker makes an appeal to collect symbolic damages, transmuting an unjust history of *owning* into the nearly homophonic poetic-legal demand for *owing*:

> So I come to say that History owes Annie
> the brightest woolen blanket.
> She is owed too, at least twelve years of sleep. . . . (29)

At the poem's end, the speaker insists again that "history owes Annie" (31), lists the damages sought, and concludes:

> Annie Pengelly O.
> I say, History owe you. (31)

The poem's climactic juncture between two *o* sounds, achieved in part through creolization of the verb (used in its uninflected West Indian form), encapsulates the relation this work has been developing between legal and poetic discourses. The final lines shift the speaker's addressee from the imaginary judge, who has by this point disappeared entirely, as well as from a bidder on Annie and the slavemistress: poetry's vocative O is directed to the dead Annie Pengelly, who can hear this address only by the poetic fiction of apostrophe. Goodison has been trying to rhyme poetry with justice, the imaginative *O* with the legal *owe*. Like a lawyer, she has been seeking redress for injustices to Annie in part by telling her story before the court of contemporary opinion. But while hitching its apostrophic *O* to the judicial *owe*, the poem also points up the difference between the coercive capacity of the law, which by virtue of being vested with the authority of the state could bring about material and social reparation for past injustices ("It is so ordered"), and the imaginative and rhetorical authority of poetry: long-dead Annie can benefit only in the sense of latter-day recognition of her abuse. There is no governmental power vested in poetry, as in law, for the redress of grievances, for defining rules and realities of *ownership*, for compelling the injuring party to repay anything to the *one* who may be morally *owed*. Hence the self-unmasking fancifulness of the reparation she seeks, including "thousands of nights / of sleep upon a feather bed" (31). Yet by its own procedures of *re*-presentation, which include magical sonic junctures between antitheses and imaginative reparation for irreversible losses, poetry can aspire to address (*O*)—maybe even figuratively redress (*owe*)—past injustices and grievances (*Oh*) that sometimes lie beyond the reach of the law.

This poem's counternarrative of suffering and abuse is part of an oral family tradition, one of the poet's mother's stories. Goodison directly places her white great-grandfather in the poem, George O'Brian Wilson, "Shoemaker and Sadler," formerly "bruk Sailor" (28)—the same sailor who mated with Goodison's African great-grandmother in the poem "Guinea Woman," both of whose stories are told in Goodison's memoir *From Harvey River*.[135] By the poem's mention of the historical figure of Lady Nugent, this living African Caribbean oral tradition is implicitly set against the written European tradition. In her published journal—another of the poem's intergenres—Lady Nugent takes her cultural bearings from Britain and Europe, vividly documenting Jamaican society from the perspective of a colonial administrator's spouse resident on the island from 1801 to 1805. At the time of her wedding, for example, she assembles all the "black servants" dressed in white muslin: "Their wish was, that General N. and I might live happy together, till our hair was as white as their gowns. They don't know what snow is, or I suppose they would have said snow, rather than gowns."[136] Goodison inverts Lady Nugent's assumption that European experience and language are normative: in "Annie Pengelly," she recounts how, during the season when the slavemistress made Annie lie across her feet because cold winter winds blew, the "transplanted" planters were confused by the weather,

> Causing them to remember words like "hoarfrost" and
>   "moors"
> from a frozen vocabulary they no longer had use for. (29)

During her first fall in Jamaica, Lady Nugent complains of feeling "the cold quite uncomfortable"; "the squalls of wind are so powerful, that they pervade everything" (46).

Whether Lady Nugent knew that the slavemistress at a Hanover estate used an African girl as a human water bottle, she does not say, but she did witness and deplore the abuse of other enslaved people. Despite her participation in the colonial enterprise, her narrative—though Eurocentric—is sympathetic with the fate of the often physically and sexually abused "blackies" and thus gives limited voice, perhaps surprisingly, to an anticolonial counternarrative. In Lady Nugent's journal, sugar production is at first described as "very curious and entertaining" (85), but the Englishwoman does not suppress her horror at learning, when first touring a Jamaican sugar mill, that "negroes" were forced to work monotonous and arduous twelve-hour shifts over boiling cauldrons. The overseer, she says, "owned to me that sometimes they did fall asleep, and get their poor fingers into the mill; and he shewed me a hatchet, that was always ready to sever the whole limb, as the only means of saving the poor sufferer's life! I would not have a sugar estate for the world!" (86). Partly by virtue of her gendered position both as colonial participant and as subject of a patriarchal colonial system, Lady Nugent recognizes that the enslaved Africans are cruelly abused, physically and sexually. To the extent that her colonial narrative and others embed within themselves an anticipatory counternarrative, they differ from legal narratives that function as argument subordinated to the necessity of winning a case.[137] So too Goodison's poem, despite its primary drive to "represent" the plight of the colonized, also gives voice to suffering on the other side of the colonial divide, and in this regard it cuts across the binary logic (guilty-innocent, true-false) and adversarial procedures (defense-prosecution) of the common law system, let alone colonialism. Amid its many internal echoes, the poem lexically links the gender-based "servitude" (31) of the slavemistress to the race-based oppression of her "maidservant" (27). The poem's split sympathy separates it from one-sided legal argument, since the poet-lawyer's concession could undo the case against the accused slavemistress in a court of law:

> and poor Missus enslaved by love
> fighting her servitude with spite. (31)

Annie's tormenter is herself tormented, we learn, despite the speaker's disavowal of salacious gossip about the colonial planting class:

> With all that birthday show of affection
> Massa never sleep with missus.
> But I am not here to talk about that,
> that is backra business. (29)

When she acknowledges that Missus is "enslaved" by patriarchy, just as Annie Pengelly is enslaved by colonialism, the speaker risks giving ammunition to the other side and seeming to explain or even justify the slavemistress's abhorrent abuse of the claimant. In an astonishing lexical choice, the word "slave" or "enslaved" does not appear in the poem except, ironically, in reference to the slavemistress's bereft subjugation to her loveless master. This vernacular perspective on "backra business" cannot be straitjacketed within what Philip calls the "order, logic, and rationality" of the law. Goodison borrows rhetorical maneuvers from the law, building an evidentiary basis for her plea for reparation. But in her cross-cutting narratives and echoic binding together of antitheses, she forsakes the discipline and singular directedness of legal argument for poetry's polyphony, its multiperspectivism. She acknowledges that law and poetry share a great deal, even as she, like Philip, uses a legal language that ultimately turns the law on its head.

The short poem "On the Death of a Poem" by A. K. Ramanujan, built around the relations between the poetic sentence and the judicial sentence, plays on the family resemblances between poetry and law.

> Images consult
> one
> another,

begins the poem. The next stanza shifts from tenor (the images in a poem) to vehicle (the jury), personifying images as

> a conscience-
> stricken
> jury,

before the final stanza represents the convergence of the twain:

> and come
> slowly
> to a sentence.[138]

Both the poetic and the judicial sentence involve a dialogic process of deliberation, except that in a poem various possibilities internalized within a poet's mind commingle, while members of a jury give and take views among themselves. Both poetic and judicial sentences also involve a certain finality—a permanent decision after a process of debate and consolidation. Yet the ending of the idiosyncratic act of poetic creation, like the ending of the sentence in a poem, has an aesthetic finality, while a death sentence handed down by a jury has the force of the state behind it and results in an execution. The inner deliberation of the poet, the aesthetic collision of different images in a poem—Ramanujan reminds us of a poetic polysemy that persists, despite being aesthetically rounded out by a poem's ending, long after a poem's paradoxically deathlike birth into publication. By contrast, once judge or jury has made the decision to execute and the state steps forward to carry out the verdict, the law attempts to shut down tensions and deliberations, the multiple contending views that meet in the arena of the courtroom. Poetry—suggest Ramanujan, Goodison, and Philip, Reznikoff, Rukeyser, and Hayden—resembles the law in its precision, narratives, and suasive rhetoric, but its extravagant open-endedness, even in its aesthetically finished state, encompasses narratives and counternarratives, logic and illogic, guilt and innocence; it brings together history and imaginative fancy, the quest for redemption and the acknowledgment of irredeemable loss. Poetry can seek to address ("O") and perhaps even redress ("owe") histories of unimaginable death and cruelty, extending the reach of justice well into the past and making use of poetry's elasticity and multifariousness to reopen what may have seemed a shut case. None of its sentences will be final verdicts that have the force of law; but if poets ever approximate "unacknowledged legislators of the world," in Shelley's famous phrase, it may be by virtue of their ability to lift "the veil from the hidden beauty" in persons negated by the law; to unlock silences and disclose what has been legally suppressed; to retell narratives that include their own counternarratives; to restore a multidimensionality to the past, even when arguing, with an almost legal purposiveness, for the dignity and worth of a humanity that the law had rendered invisible.[139]

For all the differences between poetry and theory and between poetry and the novel, we've seen that poetry's sense of its difference from the law is often stronger. When two lawyer-scholars gathered legally related poems for an anthology, *Poetry of the Law: From Chaucer to the Present* (2010), many more examples of intergeneric contention than of communion were to be found: poems that, like John Donne's, attack lawyers for their greed and deceit or, like D. H. Lawrence's, accuse judges of ignorance and hypocrisy, or, like those of Walt Whitman, Edgar Lee Masters, and Martín Espada, bemoan the fate of citizens trapped in or abused by the legal system.[140] Poets such as Goodison and Philip can piggyback on the law because they share law's preoccupation with verbal precision, testimony, and long-memoried awareness of precedent, but they also distinguish their poems from the law by their polyphony, incantatory recursiveness, self-reflexivity, and graphic arrangements on the page. Despite the mutual emphasis in poetry and in law on verbal exactitude and life experience formally ordered, poetry's impatience with the binary logic, linearity and formality, and argumentative single-mindedness that it sometimes sees in the law results in friction, even in poems that base themselves in judicial decisions, testimony, and settings.

•

By examining poetry's jostling with and against other genres, we glimpse implied self-definitions with a range of interlinked family resemblances. These are not static or universal but situational, contextual, shifting depending on the other engaged—whether the novel, which makes poetry seem abstract; theory, against which it looks concrete; or the law, in relation to which it seems neither abstract nor concrete but idiosyncratically disruptive and imaginative. Other emphases emerge, as we will see in ensuing chapters, when poems rub shoulders with the immediacy and transparency of the news, a heavily capitalized, empiricist, informational discourse; with the ritualism, oral performativity, and self-subordination of prayer, frequently as sanctioned by religious institutions; and with the voice-ingrained music of song, the genre with which poetry has perhaps the most in common. Poetry is swayed by, but breaks with, the seductive powers of these others in a variety of ways. In documentary or newslike verse, as in novelized poems, poetry turns the dial toward mimesis but defines its news as other than news reporting partly by accentuating recursiveness, performance, and sonic density. These features of poetry cannot, however, serve the same self-definitional function in relation to prayer or song, since those genres tend toward even greater repetition and oral performativity than poetry. By the same token, a song-enriched poem that amplifies poetry's sonic qualities also sometimes draws attention to the difference between a song and a poem on the page—say, by manipulating the effects of visual textuality. Again, this difference may help distinguish a poem from a song but not necessarily between a poem and a newspaper story. Poetry may often seem more personally and emotionally expressive than the law or the news but not song. The reflected light that these contrasts shed on poetry is partly shared and partly discrepant across intergeneric fields—a variety that, with each pivot of the dialogic compass, helps demonstrate poetry's elasticity and multiplicity.

Pound's oft-repeated distinctions among different kinds of poetry as *melopoeia*, *phanopoiea*, and *logopoeia*, recast in Northrop Frye's Aristotelian triad of *melos*, *opsis*, and *lexis* and his humorous dyad of "babble and doodle," represent a venerable way of mapping poetry that may have some bearing here.[141] Poems infused with song or prayer can be expected to tend toward *melopoeia*, in which the words are charged with music; when informed by the novel or the news, toward *phanopoeia*, in which images are paramount; and when interlaced with theory or the law, toward *logopoeia*, the vaguest of these terms, implying an emphasis on the language as language. But these inexact alignments should not be pushed too far, lest they occlude countervailing qualities in each group—the emphasis on *melos* even in a seemingly *phanopoeic* news-based poem or on *opsis* even in a seemingly *melopoeic* song-inflected poem. To supplement and multiply these standard coordinates may be helpful, because poetry twists and turns in different formal and discursive directions across a kaleidoscopic range.

Probing poetry's dialogue with a discursive cousin one at a time for the sake of argumentative clarity, I am well aware that a poem usually engages more than one simultaneously, as seen in Philip's reframing of theory, the law, and science, and Goodison's of the law and memoir, let alone Ashbery's protean shifts, line by line, among many generic interlocutors. In news-based

poems I note overlays of prayer; in prayerlike poems we sometimes hear overtones of song; and in song-inspired poems there
are occasional nods in the direction of theory. But by separating
out specific areas of intergeneric exchange for focused analysis, I
try to suggest what may be at stake in each case—slices of attention that subsequent criticism can reintegrate to explore a single
poem's often multivectored dialogue with its others. I concentrate
on threshold works that are more obviously intergeneric than
most poetry, hoping to shed light on the dialogic qualities of
seemingly monogeneric poems. To make audible its dialogic overtones, poetry often requires close attention to its minutiae, especially when enormous aesthetic pressure has transformed its
extrapoetic ingredients almost beyond recognition.

Despite Bakhtin's privileging of the novel as the ultimate cross-
generic genre, poetry—while perhaps neither as rich in sociohistorical mimesis as the novel nor as analytically astute as theory,
neither as enforceable as law nor as informative as the news, neither as devotionally pitched as prayer nor as musically and orally
resonant as song—borrows from its generic others to create fresh
formal amalgamations that make it new. Even if poetry's specificity is always bleeding and blurring into other forms, poets lay
claim to its varied aesthetic particularity. They take from, and
then send their works back into, the larger universe of colliding
and ever-mutating genres. Sticky-fingered, modern and contemporary poetry is enriched by long-memoried and widely scattered
genres, tropes, and linguistic inheritances. Though poetry, it is
dialogized by nonpoetry, and though modern, it is entangled in
the premodern. Its tentacles spread far and reach deep.

2

POETRY
AND THE NEWS

PROBABLY THE MOST famous comment on the relation between
poetry and the news appears in William Carlos Williams's "Asphodel, That Greeny Flower," which implicitly defines poetry by placing it in an intergeneric context:

> It is difficult
> to get the news from poems
>   yet men die miserably every day
>   for lack
> of what is found there.[1]

One way of understanding poetry, it seems, is as antigenre to the
news. Williams identifies "despised poems" with emotional and
spiritual nourishment, as against the information conveyed by the
more popular news media. His declaration of poetry as the soul-
sustaining opposite of the news inverts the usual configuration

of poetry as a leisure option, the news as essential for modern citizenship. When news media cite these lines, as they often do, they ironically remind themselves of their limitations and of the spiritual vitality they concede to poetry as beyond their ken. Yet among the many genres that constitute the discursive field out of which poems are carved, the news has a particular power and pervasiveness; in John Hartley's words, "journalism is *the* textual system of modernity."[2] Quickly read, easily disposed of, the news has been one of the most potent generic others against which modern and contemporary poetry has defined itself.

Despite differences with Williams's "anti-poetic" aesthetic,[3] Wallace Stevens also sees poetry as pitted against the news—in the sense both of information about current events and of their media representation. Noting the "extraordinary pressure of news," coming from America but also from "Europe, Asia and Africa all at one time," he characterizes poetry in part by its power of "resistance to this pressure" of reality that, during World War II, is "physically violent for millions": "It is a violence from within that protects us from a violence without. It is the imagination pressing back against the pressure of reality."[4] In response to the news media's encoding, purveying, and even amplifying of an overwhelming empirical reality, poets as different as Williams and Stevens have imaginatively proliferated alternative worlds and challenged journalistic assumptions. Since the Industrial Revolution, poetry's quarrel with the news has often been even more vociferous than its long-standing quarrel with philosophy.

"Every morning brings us the news of the globe," laments Walter Benjamin, "and yet we are poor in noteworthy stories."[5] Benjamin's argument in "The Storyteller," theorizing the newspaper as the generic opposite of storytelling, has often been brought to bear on prose fiction, but it also has implications for poetry. In his analysis, the news is shallow and ephemeral, whereas the traditional story is, like Auden's "memorable speech," strongly oral, mnemonic, and grounded in a long tradition:[6]

> The value of information does not survive the moment in
> which it was new. It lives only at that moment; it has to sur-

render to it completely and explain itself to it without losing any time. A story is different. It does not expend itself.
It preserves and concentrates its strength and is capable of
releasing it even after a long time. . . . [A] story from ancient
Egypt is still capable after thousands of years of arousing
astonishment and thoughtfulness. It resembles the seeds of
grain which have lain for centuries in the chambers of the
pyramids shut up air-tight and have retained their germinative power to this day.

There is nothing that commends a story to memory more
effectively than that chaste compactness which precludes
psychological analysis.[7]

Concentrated, compact, durable, memorable—these are qualities also frequently invoked to characterize our expectations of
poetry, a discourse with "an amplitude that information lacks."[8]
Whereas the storyteller, like the poet, seeks to instill thoughtfulness and reflection, Benjamin writes in a short piece, "The Newspaper," that "impatience is the state of mind of the newspaper
reader," an "all-consuming impatience," a "longing for daily nourishment" by fragmentary and disconnected facts.[9] The newspaper,
in Benjamin's analysis, commodifies information, "the scene of
the limitless debasement of the word."[10] If transience, impatience,
disconnectedness, and linguistic debasement seemed to characterize newspapers in the 1920s and 1930s, the rise of electronic
and digital news media since that time has only exacerbated these
features of the news, which have ever more thoroughly saturated
our lives.[11] In contrast, poetry and storytelling depend on long
traditions to legitimize their far-fetched imaginings, their stretch
and amplitude. They are examples of what Benjamin calls "crafts-
manship" or "an artisan form of communication," which instead
of trying to convey objectively "the thing, like information or a
report," "sinks the thing into the life," so that "traces of the storyteller cling to the story," and of the poet to the poem, "the way
the handprints of the potter cling to the clay vessel."[12] Despite the
"Impersonal theory of poetry" held by T. S. Eliot and in various
forms by other modernists and postmodernists, a poem, unlike a

news report, is often as much about the handprints that cling to it as it is about the information it contains.[13]

Like Benjamin, Ludwig Wittgenstein asserts the difference of literary from informational discourse, warning that the resemblances are misleading: "Do not forget that a poem, although it is composed in the language of information (*der Sprache der Mitteilung*), is not used in the language-game (*Sprachspiel*) of giving information."[14] If we take our cues from Wittgenstein and Benjamin, Williams and Stevens, one approach to the impossibly general question we began with, "what is poetry?," is an almost equally general answer: under modernity, poetry is what it is by virtue of not being the news. Compared with the news, poetry seems compressed and memorable, phonetically patterned and figuratively rich, if also slow and often counterfactual; compared with poetry, the news seems instantaneous and transparent and dense with information, if also ephemeral, denotative, and flat.

Even so, these distinctions need to be modulated. Poetry and the news take many different forms, some of which are less starkly divergent, and the circulation and exchange of poetry in salable books and other commodified forms implicate it like the news in the market economy, albeit on a far more restricted scale.[15] More important, poetry is sometimes shot through with the news. If we turn to close analysis of some threshold poems that open onto the news, we see that poetry dialogically incorporates and resists journalism in a fascinating variety of ways. After all, pace Williams, if we tried to get the news of the last century or so from poems, we wouldn't come up empty handed. In English-language poems, we would read about the world wars, especially the first; the Great Depression; the decolonization of the British Empire since Ireland's Easter Rising; changes in gender and sexuality; the civil rights movement; the rise of new technologies; the assassinations of world figures; the Spanish Civil War, the Vietnam War, the Salvadoran Civil War, the Gulf Wars, and so forth. Early in the twenty-first century, the news event that may have outstripped all others was the September 11 destruction of the World Trade Center, my starting point in analyzing individual poems in relation to the news. Poems on the borderline between these genres showcase their differences and convergences, pressing the question, how can poetry tell the news without becoming the short-lived information vehicle that is journalism?

Recent criticism on poetry and the news has focused on the "information-age database poetics" of "documentary poetics," "docupoetry," or "poetry of information"—contemporary American poetry that steeps itself in journalistic data and reportage.[16] Such works, often made up of found texts, seem to push poetry as far as it can go toward journalism. One example may hark back to Tristan Tzara's instructions for how to make a dada poem—cut up a newspaper article, shake the words in a bag, and copy them out diligently: Kenneth Goldsmith's *Day* (2003) transcribes the *New York Times* of September 1, 2000, omitting photos, design graphics, typeface variations, and other structuring visual cues, as it runs together the newspaper's text as a massive collage.[17] More overtly political than Goldsmith's wryly conceptualist reframing of newsprint, Mark Nowak's *Coal Mountain Elementary* (2009) samples reports of coal-mining disasters in the United States and China, basing itself in West Virginia testimonies and reports from Xinua News Agency, Reuters, and other outlets.[18] But even "docupoetry" that seems to merge with the news all the more vividly draws attention to deep-seated genre differences that it both transgresses and shores up. Well before reaching page 836 of Goldsmith's *Day* (the end of the conceptual poem and of section F's classified ads), a perhaps inhumanly patient reader will have noted scattered moments of unexpectedly "poetic" juxtaposition, built on the collagelike adjacency that Benedict Anderson discerns in newspaper layout;[19] but this same reader will have been reminded thousands of times how different our expectations are of poetry and the news, even when the genres seem to have been collapsed. And Nowak's transnational rhyming of American and Chinese reports performs a poetic conjuncture that, while having the look of standard news, metaphorizes these media accounts (*metapherein*, to carry across). To take at face value the supremacy of information in such poems and infer a seamless "docupoetic"

fusion may be to overestimate the cross-genre affinities they demonstrate and to underestimate the broader tensions between the
news and poetry. In a period that witnessed a massive burgeon-
ing of the news media, the larger story of twentieth- and twenty-
first-century poetry's intertwining with newswriting is often both
affiliative and agonistic, and it still needs to be told. While a com-
prehensive narrative exceeds the scope of this chapter, we can
perhaps fill in a few key episodes by examining some exemplary
news-based poems written in England, Jamaica, Ireland, and the
United States, and in forms as various as ode, elegy, epigram, ballad, poetic journal, satire, occasional poem, ekphrasis, lyric, epic,
prophecy, and prose poetry, whether raw or polished, transcriptive or vatic, collage or confessional, demotic or high literary.

POETRY AND JOURNALISM

Seamus Heaney's "Anything Can Happen" might seem an odd
example of the information-age newsy poem, since among the
many poems about the September 11 attacks, it reworks a two-
thousand-year-old Latin ode by Horace (*"after Horace, Odes I,
34"*).[20] But this very fact tells us something important about poetry
and at least one of its approaches to the news:

> Anything can happen. You know how Jupiter
> Will mostly wait for clouds to gather head
> Before he hurls the lightning? Well, just now
> He galloped his thunder-cart and his horses
>
> Across a clear blue sky. It shook the earth
> And clogged underearth, the River Styx,
> The winding streams, the Atlantic shore itself.

The "just now" of Horace's poem (*"nunc"*) is renewed, doubling
as the now of the ancient past and the now of the immediate
present, unlike the once-only "now" of the news. To reiterate and
adapt Benjamin, poetry "does not expend itself. It preserves and

concentrates its strength and is capable of releasing it even after a long time." Heaney's poem evidences poetry's delayed-release capacity by reawakening an ancient poem, highlighting its surprisingly strong resonances with the contemporary (the cloudless sky, the shaking earth, the rivers and shore, the inversions of fortune). It represents itself as an overlay on an earlier poem, showing poetry to be, in words quoted above from Benjamin and perhaps especially appropriate for an ode, "still capable after thousands of years of arousing astonishment and thoughtfulness." One part of our experience of Heaney's poem is the power of its compact and eerie evocation of the 9/11 attacks; another is our wonder at poetry's transhistorical durability and transnational adaptability: "It resembles the seeds of grain which have lain for centuries in the chambers of the pyramids shut up air-tight and have retained their germinative power to this day." Poet and reader encounter the "news event" through a cross-historical and cross-cultural detour into literary antiquity, responding simultaneously to an ancient text and to current reality.

By first publishing the poem, then titled "Horace and the Thunder," in the *Irish Times* on November 17, 2001, Heaney emphasized the poem's intersections with the news, but in so doing he also accentuated the difference between poetry's often slow, layered, and indirect way of telling the news and much of what is found in the newspaper. It is worth repeating Benjamin's insight into the temporality of the news media: "The value of information does not survive the moment in which it was new. It lives only at that moment; it has to surrender to it completely and explain itself to it without losing any time." This is what Benedict Anderson calls the "obsolescence of the newspaper on the morrow of its printing."[21] Encapsulating the sped-up temporality of the information age, John Guillory explains: "Information demands to be transmitted because it has a shelf life, a momentary value that drives the development of our technologies in their quest to speed up, economize, and maximize the effectiveness of transmission."[22] Many of us remember feeling after the 9/11 attacks that "all-consuming impatience" for news about who, what, when, where, why, and how as we scoured newspapers and radio, TV and the Internet. Heaney's poem adds nothing to this store of information. It participates in an old technology that is slow, measured, and ceremonious—the Horatian ode. And yet it has "an amplitude that information lacks."

Anything can happen, the tallest things

Be overturned, those in high places daunted,
Those overlooked regarded. Stropped-beak Fortune
Swoops, making the air gasp, tearing the crest off one,
Setting it down bleeding on the next.

By intertwining with an ancient poem in another language, Heaney's lyric openly declares the transhistorical and transnational dependence of poems on other poems and, more generally, of thoughtful understanding on wide time horizons and vast contexts often absent from the news. Instead of aspiring like the news to what Benjamin calls "prompt verifiability," Heaney's poem isn't "understandable in itself": you have to know something not only about the Twin Tower attacks but also about Horace, Jupiter, the River Styx, and classical Fortune; you have to have some context for the poem's literariness and difficulty, its classical mythology and elevated diction ("Stropped-beak," for example, meaning a beak strop-sharpened like a razor). The poem acknowledges its deep embeddedness within literary tradition, instead of presenting itself as a history-free report of current reality. Like Yeats's "Leda and the Swan," it sees current upheaval as the recurrence of a birdlike assault on the human by the divine. It has, as Heaney says of poetry and Benjamin suggests of storytelling, "a touch of the irrational," "a soothsaying force."[23] With its news orientation and yet also its unpredictable deities, swooping Fortune, and hurled lightning, the poem is true to our divided experience of such horrific events, in Heaney's words, "partly as assimilable facts of day-to-day life, partly as some kind of terrible foreboding, as if we were walking in step with ourselves in an immense theatre of dreams."[24]

As memorable speech that remembers prior memorable speech, and yet that also evokes contemporary reality, the poem freely translates Horace to point up references to 9/11, dropping Horace's first stanza and adding a new final stanza:

> Ground gives. The heavens' weight
> Lifts up off Atlas like a kettle lid.
> Capstones shift, nothing resettles right.
> Smoke furl and boiling ashes darken day.

The last line's syntactic complexity ("furl" used not as a verb but as a noun) and its echo of Auden's "In Memory of W. B. Yeats" ("The day of his death was as dark cold day")[25] complete a poem that has built up intensity by deploying a variety of poetic resources, including apostrophe ("You know . . ."); enjambment (emphasizing "just now" at the end of one line and "Across a clear blue sky" after a stanza break); mixed formal and colloquial registers ("Well . . ."); asyndeton (Styx, streams, shore); chiasmus ("those in high places daunted, / Those overlooked regarded"); tension between iambic pentameter and Latinate caesurae; metaphor ("the air gasp") and simile ("like a kettle lid"); and alliteration ("Ground gives"). Poetry isn't the news. But when it tells the news, it tells it slant. It mediates contemporary history through a transnational thicket of long-memoried aesthetic structures that entwine the news with alternative temporalities.

Heaney's poetry was often quoted in the days after 9/11, but a still more widely circulated poem was Auden's "September 1, 1939," for reasons made obvious by the opening stanza, in which the speaker sitting in one of Fifty-Second Street's "dives" observes that

> Waves of anger and fear
> Circulate over the bright
> And darkened lands of the earth,
> Obsessing our private lives;
> The unmentionable odour of death
> Offends the September night.[26]

That Auden's poem was set in New York City, that it was dated September, that it evoked the onset of violent catastrophe, all seemed, like the Horatian thunderbolt in a cloudless sky, an uncanny anticipation of the Twin Tower attacks—another poetic seed that germinated long after composition. Confirming that even an occasional poem bearing a calendrical title could reverberate across a sixty-year gap, many news consumers turned to Auden for a reflective and humanly vulnerable ("Uncertain and afraid"), public yet personal expression of historical calamity (86).

Toward the end of the poem, which recalls the trimeters and public-private fusing voice of Yeats's "Easter, 1916," Auden sets his poetry in opposition to newspapers:

> All I have is a voice
> To undo the folded lie,
> The romantic lie in the brain
> Of the sensual man-in-the-street
> And the lie of Authority
> Whose buildings grope the sky . . . (88)

The "folded lie" of the newspaper, as of various ideologies, contrasts with the openness of the poet's demystifying voice. The newspaper, associated here with the deceptions and dishonesties of romantic love, commerce, and the state, may seem plainer than poetry, but its unsuspected convolutions, like the folds of the human "brain," can conceal and distort more than they reveal. This poem joins other "Ironic points of light" that flash affirmatively, despite the overwhelming "Negation and despair" (89). Brightly lit with irony and resonant with orality, poetry is seen as affording liberating affiliations among poets, and between poets and readers, in contrast to newspaper-supported political power, with its blindly lustful and coercive "grope." An Englishman in New York, addressing the German invasion of Poland and drawing on Irish, Greek, Russian, and other cultural sources, poetically embodies a world that, like that of Heaney's "Anything Can Happen," is complexly enmeshed across national borders.

Figured obliquely in the kenning of the "folded lie,"[27] the newspaper is overtly thematized in other poems. Two years earlier, another of Auden's topical public poems, "Spain," encompasses its frontline report on the urgent present within a panoramic global vision that extends back to ancient China and prehistoric Northern Europe and looks ahead to a utopian future, including "Poets exploding like bombs."[28] This vast timescale is one of the many differences between the poem and a standard news account, newswriting glanced at in the depiction of "the poor in their fireless lodgings, dropping the sheets / Of the evening paper."[29] They find in the newspaper no delivery from their constraining circumstances. Like "September 1, 1939," "Spain" incorporates news discourse but is anxious to assert its difference from it—broader temporal and cultural horizons, utopian longings and admissions of guilt. A few years earlier, Auden's *The Orators* (1932) included a scathingly satiric attack on newspapers, addressed to "Beethameer, Beethameer, bully of Britain," a conflation of the press barons Lord Beaverbrook and Lord Rothermere, the latter of whom subsequently supported Hitler, Mussolini, and the British Blackshirts in his *Daily Mail*:

> In kitchen, in cupboard, in club-room, in mews,
> In palace, in privy, your paper we meet
> Nagging at our nostrils with its nasty news,
> Suckling the silly from a septic teat,
> Leading the lost with lies to defeat . . . [30]

Newspapers permeate every corner of modern experience, like a false and deceitful god that appears in both private and public spaces, both inside and outside the body. With the recent explosive growth of digital media, the ubiquity of the news has, if anything, been still more fully realized since Auden's riposte. A pretend "prophet," a deceiving "Savior," the press is—as in "September 1, 1939" and in Benjamin's skeptical account—a tool of power, commerce, and the nation-state: "I advertise idiocy, uplift, and fear, / I succour the State, I shoot from the hip" (87). Like "September 1,

1939," which links poetry with both love and irony, this poem associates a poetic "awareness of difference" with "love" (75) but sees newspapers as a crushingly homogenizing force: "Newspapers against the awareness of difference" (86). "The newspaper is an instrument of power," writes Benjamin. "It can derive its value only from the character of the power it serves; not only in what it represents, but also in what it does, it is the expression of this power."[31] Despite its revolutionary potential, the newspaper, in Benjamin's view as in Auden's, "belongs to capital."[32] This poem's postscript satirically declares the poet's competition with the information ephemera reproduced by the mass press: "10,000 Cyclostyle copies of this for aerial distribution" (87). Poetry can't compete with the mass appeal of the news, nor has it the coercive power of the press's commercial and political allies, but Auden attributes to it, because of its relative personal freedom, the power to ironize and demystify.

Despite Auden's defiance of what he represents as the hegemonic news media, he, like Heaney, is much more of a public writer than many modern and contemporary poets. He even remarked, "[I]n literature I expect plenty of news," and he recommends that the writer take an "interest in objects in the outside world." An artist has to be "a bit of a reporting journalist"—that is, someone for whom "the first thing of importance is subject"— although Auden also warns that too much journalism "can and frequently does kill" the "sensibility."[33] Many of his most celebrated poems would have been impossible without journalism. If even Auden's poetry, including news-inflected public poems such as "Spain" and "September 1, 1939," draws on journalism and at the same time pits itself against the discursive norms of the newspaper, purchased daily at that time by 69 percent of the British public,[34] then the large bulk of modern and contemporary poems, most of which have no such direct relation to public events, can also be seen as carving out discursive alternatives to the news media, though often less overtly so. To write poems, whether about love or nature or grief, as in many "mainstream" lyrics, or about contemporary language's infestation by commodity discourse, as in many "experimental" poems, is at some level to propose another way of telling the news of our outer and inner lives.

A very different kind of poet can also help measure poetry's relation to journalism, since her work, like Auden's, constantly makes use of and rubs up against the news, yet might otherwise seem to share little with Auden's and Heaney's high literary verse. A news announcement of sorts, "What a joyful news, Miss Mattie," begins Jamaican Creole poet Louise Bennett's best known poem, "Colonization in Reverse."[35] Bennett's career was entwined with the news media and with newspapers in particular, much more so than that of most significant modern or contemporary poets. Initially, she published many of her poems on a weekly basis in the Jamaican newspaper the *Sunday Gleaner*, and their popularity, despite the editor's initial reluctance, was a boon to the paper's fortunes. Whether published in newspapers, magazines, or books, or aired on the radio, many of Bennett's topical poems vernacularize the headline news, such as the 1958 West Indies Federation and Jamaica's 1962 independence, wartime scarcities and victories, public water problems and overcrowded trams, emigration and race relations and the women's movement, even visits by politicians such as Adlai Stevenson and Creech Jones and singers such as Marian Anderson and Paul Robeson. It isn't difficult to get the local and global news from Bennett's poems of the 1940s, 1950s, and 1960s.

But does this mean that her poems, initially bound up with the production and circulation system of a national newspaper, approximate Benjamin's characterization of the news—short lived, lacking amplitude, exhausted in the moment of its telling? After all, they are more topical than most modern and contemporary poems, have little of the high literary allusiveness of Heaney's and Auden's poems, and don't ground themselves in a slow-germinating writerly tradition that goes back to antiquity. But because of their strongly marked oral and narrative texture, Bennett's ballads are perhaps even more like Benjaminian storytelling than are Heaney's and Auden's poems. Written and performed in a robust Jamaican Creole that contrasts with the Jamaican newspapers' Standard English, her poetic narratives are propelled by the tetrameter rhythms and alternating rhymes of the ballad quatrain. They recontextualize news fragments, situating them within balladic narratives about women's lives and gossip.

Many of these orally coded stories, which are as much about the local human impact and circulation of the news as about the news itself, begin in a reading or overhearing of journalism, such as "bans o' big headline" in "Invasion," about the Allied successes toward the end of World War II (102). Elated by the news of Nazi and Japanese defeat, the speaker of "Peace" seizes on it to warn two gossips about the danger of deceit and lies:

> Two-face Muriel teck me warnin
> Check yuh wutless 'ceitful way,
> Faas-mout Edna clip yuh long tongue
> Lie an back-bitin noh pay. (106)

Hybridizing Jamaican oral tale telling, global news reporting, and the British ballad, Bennett shows her characters turning impersonal and faraway news into moral and social meaning, despite the comically disjunctive fit between global and local, public and private. In these transnationally stretched poems, Bennett's speakers make use of journalism's global information field, but they also don't hesitate to transgress the news's compartmentalizations by making local use of foreign news, rhyming their private lives with global events. Such poems build semantic bridges among sites often segmented in the news media.

Bennett's news poems are metanews poems, telling stories in which the material reception and human appropriation of the news is itself the news. In this they differ from the seemingly transparent and objective apprehension of events in the news media, albeit with the occasional authenticating story about the quest for, and impact of, the news. The speaker of "Big Tings" (1947) has comically partial and impaired access to the news, pressing her ears to a hole in the wall ("Mi kotch me aise a one li-hole") to hear about a local election ("Miss Mum son dah-read newspapa") (150). The verbal physicality of poetry, as emphasized by Bennett's sonic metaphors of insistent rhymes, jaunty rhythms, and tight ballad stanzas, accentuates the bodily circumstances of news retrieval and transmission, as opposed to the frequent aspiration to non-corporeal anonymity in syndicated reports. Another speaker also has access to the news through a hole, in a poem about the V-Day Parade in London, written while Bennett was there at the end of World War II. The speaker of "Victory" is trying to witness the unfolding of this momentous news event, including a marching contingent of "coloured bwoys," but a woman's hairdo (a "high upsweep") comically blocks her view:

Me teck time teck me finga bore
One hole eena de hair,
An t'rough the gal upsweep me spy
De whole parade affair! (107)

As sonically underscored by rhyme, the news "affair" is, for this speaker, inextricable from a woman's upswept "hair." Her vision is swept up, as it were, in the social fabric. The little hole she has to bore through the woman's hairdo represents her vision as partial, limited, physically located, a parodic and poetic inversion of reportorial objectivity and immateriality. Although most news accounts transmit information as if the journalist had impartial access to the truth, in Bennett's epistemology the news is insepa-rable from the bodily perception of it, as dramatized by the indi-visibility between meaning and poetic sound.

Bennett's readers and hearers are not passive consumers of the news; they physically reembody it. In "'Sir,'" the speaker ridicules by phonetic repetition the newspapers' usual "bus-fuss / An de cuss-cuss an abuse" and "foo-fool / Letta to de edita" and claims she almost "never read de news" (148). But in another kind of mir-roring, a self-recognition gently ironized by the poem, she is elated to see the picture and report of a black man, a preindependence finance minister, who has been knighted, suddenly legitimizing the blackness that had been a source of shame. "Nayga man tun eena 'Sir'!" she exclaims, adding, "Lawd me pride an head a-swell up" (147). News of public recognition has changed her relation to her own racial body, which is flushed with newfound self-esteem, and toward the social body: she berates her friends for having devalued the hair and noses of their black lovers. If the news is a public space through which we mediate our relation to our psychological, physical, and social selves and communities, a poem like Bennett's, tracking this public-private interplay, opens a space for ironic reflection on it.[36]

When Bennett's speakers try to conjure for themselves the newspaper's huge and impersonal events, they reimagine them embodied on a human scale. In "Italy Fall," we learn that "Po' Italy kick puppa-lick, / Newspapa say she fall!" (103). That is, Italy has somersaulted and fallen, showing upturned buttocks that seem ready for a father's ("puppa") spank ("lick").[37] The poetry physically metaphorizes and sonically indigenizes large events to make them comprehensible in terms of the known world. Regarding Mussolini's disappearance, the speaker remarks: "Soh maybe him dah-hide wey eena / Italy boots toe" (104). The clichéd image of Italy as bootlike, ominous under Fascist rule, is imaginatively revitalized in the speaker's cartographic fantasy of Mussolini hiding in Italy's toe. Lamenting Italy's degradation by its alliance with Hitler, the speaker concludes with a proverb about the dangers of consorting with turkey buzzards or carrion crow: "ef yuh fly wid John Crow, yuh / Wi haffe nyam dead meat!" (if you fly with John Crow, you will have to eat dead meat; 104). Whereas Auden's and Heaney's lyrics are grounded in a Western literary tradition that self-consciously traces itself back to antiquity, Bennett's poems are less visibly indebted to this tradition, but they, too, have a deeper time than the news: they reanimate the compressed repositories of "folk" wisdom and wit not only in the British ballad but also in Jamaican proverbs, by which she creolizes foreign news. As Benjamin puts it, a proverb "proclaims its ability to transform experience into tradition."[38] Even popular, topical poetry like Bennett's can exceed its occasion. Through proverb, allusion, rhyme, metaphor, and other devices, poets plunge the molten moment into a colder, deeper time that hardens it into something that can last.

Although the language of poetry is often thought of as being elevated, Bennett's distinguishes itself, paradoxically, by its lowly register, the supposedly subliterary register of West Indian Creole—the use of which delayed her recognition as a poet for decades. But the vividly imagistic physicality and phonetic vibrancy of Bennett's poetry set it apart less from other kinds of poetry than from the disembodiment of the newspaper English she parodies. Instead of being impersonal and immaterial, information is incarnate. The speaker of "Big Wuds" is baffled by a woman's lumbering abstractions, "dem big wud" like "'New Nation,' 'Federation,' 'Delegation,'" until she realizes she is parroting news reports about plans for the West Indies Federation: "Oh, is newspapa yuh readin / Meck yuh speaky-spoky so!" (164, 165). But in the story woven around this tension between discourses, soon the speaker, too, is seduced by big words from the newspaper, such as "development" and "improvement," "delegation" and "population," taking to them with zeal (165). They make her feel learned. There is one potential problem. To speak in abstractions of political unity is ironically to risk breaking ("bus") her own body:

Me like sey de big wuds dem, gwan like
Me learnin is fus rate;
But me hope dat me jawbone noh bus
Before we federate. (165)

The newspaper diction is made to seem lifeless and clichéd by comparison with richly poetic Creole descriptions of jawbones in danger of rupture, like the federation that will come apart in a few short years. Another poem that quotes "bans o' big wud" from the news (102), "Invasion" punningly turns on its head empty news rhetoric by way of explaining the impossibility of anyone with self-respect siding with the nasty Nazis:

For ef yuh cuss nayga "naasy"
Dem get bex an feel shame,
But German bawl out tell de whole worl'
"Naasy" is dem name! (103)

Bennett's bilingual pun on Nazi ("Naasy") and nasty ("naasy"), comically compressing and bridging transnational distances, exemplifies the sonic association and semantic friction that poetry so readily elicits from words, in contrast with the transparent one-dimensionality and ephemerality of most news reports. Her physical reembodying, narrative reembedding, ironic rethinking, and transnational creolizing of the news show up poetry's difference from the news, even when poetry comes closest to it. After Bennett's initial newspaper contributions, she went on to create popular radio and TV shows, working within changing forms of the popular media while continuing to remake their norms.

Exploring what poetry is not—in this case, the news—may seem an oddly roundabout way of getting at our starting question of what it is. But whether overtly or not, all genre definitions depend on contrast, if always complicated by exceptions: a tragedy is a noncomedy, except of course in tragicomedy; epic is neither lyric nor dramatic, though epics can incorporate lyrics and plays can tell epic stories; and so forth. For poetry, the news is an especially pressing other under modernity, when the media's assumptions about time, information, language, nation, and representation are everywhere—assumptions that, as we've seen, poets often contest. Not that poetry is pristinely uncontaminated by the news. As we've also seen, poems often bespeak a newslike consciousness of the historical now, even when, as in Heaney, they embed themselves within a slow-germinating aesthetic with wider time horizons than those of the news, or, as in Auden, they wield an ironic and disenchanting discourse meant to undo state and capitalist ideologies, or, as in Bennett, they deploy a vernacular, physically rich, proverb-laden language to renarrate and creolize public circumstance within lived social experience. Poetry's vigorously transnational energies, forms, and affiliations, observed in all three examples, sometimes make use of journalism's global reach but often confound the nationalist imperatives and geographic compartmentalizations of the news. Poetry's attention to the material embodiment and intersubjective shaping of knowledge, its self-consciousness of its verbal and formal embeddedness in long traditions, its slowing down and compression of the language through which it transmits thoughts and feelings about the changing world—these and other qualities distinguish its way of telling the news from journalism's ever-faster, objectifying, and dematerializing procedures. Poetry will never be satisfactorily defined, but as Williams declares, and as these three poets' odes, lyrics, satires, occasional poems, and ballads demonstrate, under modernity the news is one of the major discursive others with and against which it defines itself.

As the legible face of modernity, the news is a powerful and highly capitalized discourse that has broadly shared commonalities in America, Britain, Ireland, and Jamaica. Hence the pertinence of Benjamin's remarks about the news not only for early twentieth-century Germany and France but also for English-speaking countries and colonies in the British Isles, the Caribbean, North America, and elsewhere, even well into the twenty-first century. "In most cases," as Barbie Zelizer summarizes, "the texts of journalism have agreed-upon features—a concern with certain events . . . , recency or timeliness, and factuality." Even so, US journalism for many years has tended toward "an uncritical gravitation to the middle of the road on issues of contested public interest," thereby diverging somewhat from journalism in certain other parts of the world—albeit a difference perhaps less marked since the new millennium.[39] Distinctive histories, recurrent crises, and cultural norms shape journalistic practices in different regions. For these reasons it may be useful to branch out to case studies of poetry and the news in different countries, namely Ireland and the United States. In doing so, we must bear in mind that—as Benjamin, Zelizer, and Anderson have taught us, along with Heaney, Auden, and Bennett—the deep grammar of the news media cuts across these national differences. Whatever Irish or American specificities we may impute to news-engaged poems are greatly complicated by travel and long residences abroad, by the global circuits and reach of the modern news media, and by the transnational energies and confluences of poetry.

IRISH POETRY AND THE NEWS

"The bad news is that I buy a newspaper every day." So begins Paul Durcan's two-line poem "Newsdesk" (2007). "The good news," it humorously concludes, "is that I do not read it."[40] Like Williams's famous quote with which I began, this antinews news report implicitly defines poetry as the opposite of newswriting, although it also concedes the poet's reliance on newspapers. Durcan's epigrammatic turn encapsulates something of poetry's ambivalent relation to the news media in Ireland. The attraction is surely there. In "Tribute to a Reporter in Belfast, 1974," Durcan celebrates Liam Hourican, a reporter for Raidió Teilifís Éireann (RTÉ), for scrupulously chip-carving "each word and report" about the sectarian violence of the Troubles; his "verbal honesty" is especially welcome "in a country where words" have been exploited for sectarian ends "by poets as much as by gunmen or churchmen."[41] Notwithstanding this tribute, in which the news bests poetry, Durcan more frequently parodies journalism. Many of his poems lead off with wittily contorted headlines for titles, such as "Wife Who Smashed Television Gets Jail," "Minister Opens New Home for Battered Husbands," "Margaret Thatcher Joins IRA," and "Irish Hierarchy Bans Colour Photography"—this last a mock news report in which the Irish Hierarchy bans color pictures because they contradict the "innate black and white nature of reality."[42] While ridiculing clergymen and politicians, such poems parrot journalistic technique and slide from realism to surrealism to implicate news stories in the injustice, absurdity, and even violence that are sometimes passively and unquestioningly reported.

More than a century after Joyce's Leopold Bloom "wiped himself" with the story he'd been reading in a popular weekly, Irish writers are still puzzling over the relationship between literature and the news.[43] Novels such as *Ulysses* have often been seen as replete with journalistic discourse, but little has been said about the vexed to-and-fro between Irish poetry and the news media. *Ulysses*, in Declan Kiberd's view, "can be read as a slow-motion alternative to the daily newspaper of Dublin for 16 June 1904. Given that most inhabitants of cities by 1922 read only newspapers by the time of its publication in 1922, it might be construed as an artist's revenge, a reappropriation of newspaper methods by an exponent of the threatened novel form."[44] The novel, from the Latin *novus* or "new," bears more etymological and generic resemblances with the present-minded prose of newspapers than poems have with the news: "poem" comes from the Greek *poiein*, to make or construct, and so names works of artistic making or deliberate shaping. By contrast with the short-lived value of information, the news's immediate obsolescence, its need to be transmitted and consumed rapidly, poetry's time horizons are much wider, as we've begun to see, because of its capacity to germinate over many years, its slowing down of the reading process, its frequent metaphoric abstraction of the mundane, its layering of different moments, its suspension in phonemic materiality, and its being imbued with long-lived verse traditions, thematics, and vocabularies, setting up stronger contrasts between poetry and the news than between the novel and the news. Poetry's modern struggle with the news helps to cast in relief its age-old quest to cross the temporal with a deeper time, to stitch the flutter of the moment into a longer-lived and longer-living fabric.

The extraordinary pressure of the news in Ireland, particularly during the Troubles both early and late in the twentieth century, has given a special urgency to the partnership and quarrel between the news and poetry. Within this news-heavy context, some Irish poets have even doubled as journalists. According to Kiberd, "What set the Irish modernists off from their Continental counterparts was their marked willingness to engage with newspapers," as instanced by "Yeats's voluminous journalizing."[45] After Yeats, major Irish poets spent significant parts of their careers working for the news media, both Louis MacNeice and Paul Muldoon as employees of the British Broadcasting Corporation. A recent literary editor of the *Irish Times* has claimed that Irish "poems are linked to the newspaper's lifeblood: News."[46] Already by the 1890s in Ireland, according to a historian, the newspaper had entered its golden age as "an important passport to entry into the modern world,"[47] making it a master discourse that poetry had to respond to, absorbing, questioning, and resisting it. Under modernity, writes Christopher Morash, Ireland was no longer merely "a geographical entity" but "an informational field," "part of a modern informational order" made possible by technologies of instant communications and the news media they proliferated.[48] At the head of the media revolution and ever since have been regional and national newspapers, many of them openly sectarian. How have Irish poets echoed and incorporated newswriting? How have they defined and defended themselves against it? What implicit self-understanding can be teased from their poetry in relation to journalism?

Already at the start of the twentieth century, Yeats was deeply involved with newspapers and periodicals, and yet he strenuously refused to be dominated by their terms. "The newspaper is the roar of the machine," he declared in a 1909 diary entry.[49] Machine and mechanization were anathema to Yeats, as they had been for Blake and other first-generation Romantics. The "roar of the machine" includes the rotary press cylinders that rapidly spun off mass printed newspapers, in contrast to the painstaking craft of hand-printed book publication in his sisters' Dun Emer and Cuala Press. In context, Yeats is distinguishing between the motives behind newspaper and book production, in particular newspapers' loud "clash of interests" or "contest of interests," arguments waged or lost on behalf of what are now labeled interest groups, as against what Yeats, implicitly allying himself with Kant on the aesthetic, calls books' "slight separation from interests."[50] Little wonder that he, as a young man, declined a job at a unionist newspaper.[51]

Not that Yeats was aloof from political engagement. During such public controversies as the Hugh Lane affair (whether a bridge gallery should be built for a collection of Impressionist paintings) and the Dublin lockout of 1913 (whether tens of thousands of workers should have been locked out to prevent unionization), Yeats took positions in public speeches, poems, and journalism, sometimes directing his wrath at the newspapers themselves. As quoted by R. F. Foster, Yeats said during the Lane affair, "In Ireland we have a most ignorant press & a priest created terror of culture," and during the lockout: "When I think, however, of the press of Dublin which is owned by one of the parties to this dispute, and remember how the nationalist press has printed open incitements, publishing the names of working men and their wives for purposes of intimidation, and that the Unionist Press—with the exception of one article in the *Irish Times*—has been disgracefully silent, I find no words to express my contempt." At the time of the lockout, Yeats defended working-class labor rights against incitement by the "press of Dublin with the plain connivance of the Castle and the Castle police."[52] He charged that money, imperial and administrative power, and religious sectarianism perverted journalism's disinterestedness. Yeats would have endorsed Benjamin's remarks that the "newspaper is an instrument of power" and "belong[s] to capital."[53] Still, the newspaper's representational dominance had to be acknowledged. In a note for *Poems Written in Discouragement* (1913), Yeats reflects on the controversies over Parnell, Synge's *The Playboy of the Western World*, and the Lane gallery: "In the thirty years or so during which I have been reading Irish newspapers, three public controversies have stirred my imagination."[54] The introductory prepositional phrase concedes that newspapers are a primary arena for engagement in public life. Accordingly Yeats published some of his signal public poems in their pages, such as "Mourn—and Then Onward!" (an elegy for Parnell) in *United Ireland* and "September 1913" (partly about the lockout) in the *Irish Times*.[55]

During the controversies over the Lane pictures and the Dublin lockout, Yeats's principal antagonist was the press baron William Martin Murphy, proprietor of the *Irish Independent* and the *Evening Herald*. In a history of Irish newspapers, Murphy's *Irish Independent* is said to have "won respect and admiration for its scorning of sensationalism and for the honourable, impartial treatment it gave to every school of thought in Ireland";[56] but Yeats had an entirely different view. Having been attacked in print by Murphy, Yeats reduces him to the synecdoche of "an old foul mouth" in "To a Shade," a poem that apostrophizes Parnell and voices Yeats's critique of Murphy in particular and of the press in general.[57] "To a Shade" revolves around the contrast between the freedom and nobility of the arts and the press's ignorance, trickery, and mob mentality. A man of Parnell's "own passionate serving kind" (Hugh Lane) has offered a gift (his Impressionist paintings) that could have instilled in future generations ("their children's children") an artistic sensibility ("loftier thought, / Sweeter emotion"). The arts and their patrons look toward the distant horizons of the future; the newspapers are fixated on the now. While Yeats's disagreement with Murphy and the press may start in differences of class, politics, and sect (middle class vs. would-be aristocracy, Catholic vs. Protestant, Parnellite vs. anti-Parnellite, etc.), it also involves fundamentally divergent genre assumptions about time and representation. In other Irish poems, whether Catholic, Protestant, or neither, working-class, elitist, or neither, the constricted timescale of the news is a recurrent point of contrast with poetry's wider temporal horizons and its relative freedom from the imperatives of the immediate present. As against the ever-youthful energies of the arts, Murphy's mouth is "old," and as against the benefactor's singular nobility, Murphy incites the mob like wolves ("the pack"). By superimposing the Lane affair on the Parnell affair (Murphy had attacked both men), Yeats exploits the reiterative structure of poetry for figures of thought—the type or paradigm of the unappreciated hero recurring across time.

Yeats's "To a Friend Whose Work Has Come to Nothing" also associates newspapers with the pursuit of power and self-interest, as against the noble disinterestedness of the arts. The synecdochic reduction of Murphy to another organ of speech, a "brazen throat," again suggests, like "old foul mouth," journalism's competitive threat to the voice of poetry. Yeats asks a friend (Lady Gregory) how she and other supporters of the arts can "compete, / Being honour bred, with" a shameless liar. To "turn away," to be "secret and exult," is harder than mere "Triumph" of the kind pursued by the ruthless newspaper magnate.[58] Losing the competition with soulless, sales-driven journalism, friends of the arts are counseled to retreat, their interiority their final defense. Yeats champions poetry's freedom, nobility, interiority, and *longue durée*, as against what he sees as the newspaper's shallow present-mindedness and its mastery by power and money interests. Although these contrasts are hardly impartial—Yeats was, after all, implicated in systems of patronage, book production, and prestige—they signal his struggle to protect a less sectarian, a larger and longer visioned, discursive alternative to the news, a powerful rival he saw as dangerously divisive and short sighted.

Yeats contends with the news even in poems that don't refer directly to newspapers or their owners, as indicated by occasional poems titled with the dates of current events, such as "September 1913," "Easter, 1916," and "Nineteen Hundred and Nineteen." "Easter, 1916" reports on the most consequential Irish revolt against British rule and the ensuing execution of its leaders, providing names of the Rising's leaders, the date of the event, brief biographies, and political context—information of the sort one could also find in the *Irish Times*, the *Irish Independent*, the *Freeman's Journal*, the *Evening Herald*, and other newspapers (though most Dublin papers were initially shuttered by proximity to the fighting). The elegy even ventures policy predictions, such as the possibility that Britain might implement Home Rule. But if Yeats makes some concessions to the age of the newspaper, he also claims alternative procedures for poetry. Instead of representing his text as a day-after report on the event, he dated the poem's composition at five months afterward and even withheld broad publication for four more years, when it could resonate with the Irish War of Independence, and printed it not in a Dublin paper but in London's *New Statesman*. The elegy was hardly a newsflash. Moreover, if we approach the poem not already knowing that nearly 1,600 Irish Volunteers and 200 members of the Citizen Army took over buildings and a park in Dublin, that the rebellion was crushed after six days, that 15 leaders were executed, that 450 people died during the insurrection, we would be hard pressed to extract this information from the poem. Despite its names and dates and portraits and parliamentary politics, "Easter, 1916" functions poorly if read for news delivery. Its iterations and inversions ("All changed, changed utterly"), mind-divided oxymorons ("terrible beauty"), deictic pronominal adjectives ("That woman's," "This man," "This other"), embedded pastoral parable ("The stone's in the midst of all"), mixed perfect and slant rhyme (*name/come, death/faith, verse/Pearse*), performative rhetoric ("I write it out"), abrupt mixing of tenses ("He had done," "I number him"), elegiac delay in naming the dead, and other poetic manipulations of language are information poor but aesthetically rich.[59] They formally embody as a repeatable linguistic performance a poet's and perhaps a society's complexly ambivalent apprehensions of a major historical event.

If the poem doesn't aspire to objective news reporting, as signaled first and foremost by the prominence of the lyric "I," does it at least resemble an editorial or leader, since both editorials and poems acknowledge being partial? "Easter, 1916" brilliantly internalizes and articulates multiple conflicting viewpoints—that the heroes were both heroic and antiheroic, both comic and tragic, bathetic and noble; that their sacrifice resulted from both monomaniacal political fixation and something like romantic love; that their actions would issue in the birth of a free Ireland and may have been an unnecessary waste of life. By its tumultuous movement back and forth between these differing viewpoints, its fracturing and complicating of nationalist and antinationalist views of the Rising, the poem inverts the "opinion" piece, editorial, or leading article, in which room is usually made for one and only one strongly partisan argument, certainly in Irish and English newspapers at the time, such as Murphy's *Irish Independent*, which vehemently denounced the "insane and criminal" insurrection by "unfilial ingrates" and endorsed the execution of the rebel leaders.[60] The poet punctures or interrogates or qualifies his views, parading doubts, uncertainties, and internal divisions of the sort seldom heard in editorial or opinion journalism. Whether in its role as objective purveyor of information or as partisan rallying cry, the newspaper is—explicitly in "To a Shade" and "To a Friend Whose Work Has Come to Nothing," implicitly in "Easter, 1916"—a discursive other against which Yeats's lyric poetry defines its complex aesthetic, affective, and political calibrations.

Yeats was hardly alone among Irish poets in his struggle with print journalism. The year of Yeats's death, fellow Anglo-Irishman Louis MacNeice published *Autumn Journal* (1939), a long poetic meditation on the fall of 1938, when the world, not only Ireland, was swamped with news. Two years later, MacNeice published a critical book on Yeats and launched a career as writer and producer for the BBC. A member of the 1930s generation, for which documentary was a prominent genre, MacNeice was in some ways more open to journalism than Yeats was. In *Modern Poetry: A Personal Essay*, he lists "a reader of newspapers" as among the first qualities he expects of the modern poet,[61] and the plainspoken style of *Autumn Journal* veers closer to journalism than does Yeats's more highly wrought verse.

But although MacNeice, like Auden, welcomes into poetry aspects of modernity that Yeats had shunned, the news—in the dual sense of both reporting and new information—is seen in *Autumn Journal* as insidiously pervasive, a threat to human agency. In canto 5, people struggle to comprehend "posters flapping on the railings" with news of Hitler's speeches but "cannot take it in," going to their "Jobs to the dull refrain of the caption 'War' / Buzzing around us as from hidden insects."[62] Surrounding and even "bombarding" people, the news seems to harm human subjects and confine them in both space and time, as suggested by the rhyme of "War" with "before" (22). Another rhyme sonically encodes the invasion of external news into the body:

No, what we mean is Hodza, Henlein, Hitler,
    The Maginot Line,
The heavy panic that cramps the lungs and presses
    The collar down the spine. (23)

In this vivid imagery of the body squeezed by the news (of Czechoslovakia threatened and annexed by the Nazis), MacNeice shows the modern subject physically and psychologically pressed by globally mediated events. Yet another enjambment of "presses" links the word's use as verb (i.e., squeezes) with its meaning as noun (i.e., printing machines):

And when we go out into Piccadilly Circus
    They are selling and buying the late
Special editions snatched and read abruptly
    Beneath the electric signs as crude as Fate.
And the individual, powerless, has to exert the

Powers of will and choice
And choose between enormous evils, either
Of which depends on somebody else's voice.
The cylinders are racing in the presses. . . . (23)

In this capitalist hell of mechanical buying and selling, newspapers
are seen as having the inevitability of classical fate. Overbearing
electric signs and demonically whirling cylinders in rotary printing presses represent the impersonal menace of the news as both
medium and message. Underworld associations accrue in Mac-
Neice's diction: "Who can control his fate?" asked Othello, imagining a day in hell when "fiends snatch at" his soul (*Othello* 5.2.265,
275). Having depicted people as automata, the canto stumbles in
search of agency: first the strained moral assertion that the individual "has to exert" free will, but then, stuttering between "choice"
and "choose," the concession that the only choice to be found in
the newspapers is "between enormous evils." Choiceless choice,
powerless power, voiceless voice—MacNeice's paradoxes reveal
the constraints on the democratic ideal of a free and informed
citizenry; here, the news seems to constrict freedom instead of
enlarging it. As the speaker tries to fall asleep, listening to the
mechanical inevitability signaled by an up-shifting car and a chug-
ging train, he wonders "what the morning / Paper will say," before
realizing it's already morning, "the day is to-day" (25). Bracketing
life between the late edition and the morning edition, the news
relentlessly defines and delimits temporal succession.

But the back-and-forth ruminations of *Autumn Journal*, its loop-
ing back to the personal past and the histories of Britain and Ireland, its allusive layering of the present with classical myths and
literary intertexts, and its speculations on the future, differentiate
the temporal horizons of this poetic journal from those of journalism. No doubt MacNeice's journal is utterly dependent on journalism for information about the global events of his time. The
speaker dwells and speaks from within the unfolding present. But
that present is multiplied, echoed, and stretched into the past and
future by poetic form and memory, including sonic echoes and
figurative twists in rhyme, alliteration, and metaphor. "Time is a

country," writes MacNeice toward the end of the sequence, "the present moment / A spotlight roving round the scene" (93). If newspapers are locked within the narrow-visioned present, the poet must look farther. "We need not chase the spotlight," he affirms. "The future is the bride of what has been" (93). Although the poet must respond to the now, live in touch with historical change, and so cannot dispense with the news, poetry's wit and formal play, rhymes and metaphors also cannot merely be chained to the moment; they link it to time past and future, playing across literary memories and inventive possibilities. When Pound declared a few years earlier, "Literature is news that STAYS news," he cited as example how the "news in the Odyssey is still news."[63] Although *Autumn Journal*'s focus on the news of 1938 illustrates the deep penetration of journalism into poetry, MacNeice creates news that stays news by hybridizing the genres of prose journal and lyric, the syntax of colloquial statement and formal rumination, the tenses of long literary memory and present-awakened commentary. Formally and humanly expansive, poetry permits Mac-Neice to register how world historical news threatens to narrow time and constrain agency, even as poetry also enables him to push back against these limits.

Just as Yeats, MacNeice, and others in the first half of the twentieth century write into poetry the Easter Rising, the Irish War of Independence, the Irish Civil War, and World War II, later Irish poets engage or deflect the cataclysmic news of the post-1968 Troubles over several decades, sometimes in newspapers and other media, at other times against them, often both at the same time. Among the most celebrated examples of news-inflected poems is one that, published in the *Irish Times* on Saturday, September 3, 1994, marked the suspension of hostilities between armed Catholic and Protestant groups in Northern Ireland. That day's newspaper was busy with news of the first assurances and doubts, hopes and suspicions, attacks and political maneuverings just a few days after the Irish Republican Army ceasefire on August 31. The *Irish Times* reported on unionist and republican political responses. One article began, "The IRA will not retaliate against loyalist attacks on Catholics, and the cessation of its campaign will not be broken by provocation, the Sinn Fein president, Mr Gerry Adams, has said."[64] Another stated: "The DUP leader, the Rev Ian Paisley, yesterday announced plans to try to organise an alternative pan unionist convention in the North" and "launched a vitriolic attack on the Taoiseach," in which he described "Mr Reynolds as 'the petty little Fuhrer in Dublin.'"[65] It was amid these news stories, bifurcated along Northern Ireland's sectarian divide, that Michael Longley's poem "Ceasefire" appeared. The newspaper marked the work's identity as poetry by sealing it in a box on page 8, leaving much white space around the text, and printing it in a font larger than that of the book reviews surrounding it.[66]

How does the poem coincide with and diverge from news reports of this momentous event? As in Yeats and MacNeice, Longley's title marks the poem as having a family resemblance to journalistic reports, a textual index of the now. But this is also where the twain part, for the story the poem tells isn't new but the oldest in Western literature:

> Put in mind of his own father and moved to tears
> Achilles took him by the hand and pushed the old king
> Gently away, but Priam curled up at his feet and
> Wept with him until their sadness filled the building.

The immediate present is there, but only as seen through the lens of the ancient past. Instead of representing each event, newslike, in its atomistic isolation, the poem understands the now through its resemblances with a story told long ago in another language in a faraway country—parallels that suspend the immediate pressures of sectarianism. Writing about allusion, Andrew Welsh observes that poetry reaches for "the timelessness of myth and fable, to archaic models which can be integrated into the present moment and lift that moment out of the linear flow of historical time into timelessness."[67] Poetry integrates a discrete news event into the imaginative space of literature's perpetual return. Longley's formal measures also enlarge the moment. Twinning Homeric epic with a modified Shakespearean sonnet, in quatrains limited to one rhyme (very slant in "might" and "sighed"), the poem reanimates an old lyric form's language of physical beauty and erotic love.

Unlike the news reports that day, this poem understands the event through a nexus of resemblances: the poet sees the ending of the Trojan War in the ending of the Irish Troubles; so too the Greek Achilles sees his own father, Peleus, in the Trojan Priam (in Longley's Homeric source, Priam repeatedly calls on Achilles to remember his father).[68] Resemblance crosses the divide between enemies, and grief unites the two men in a microcosmic cross-cultural union, signaled by the plural possessive adjective "their." Simile generates further resemblances in the next stanza, between Hector's dead body and the gift it has strangely become—washed, dressed, "ready for Priam to carry / Wrapped like a present home to Troy at daybreak." Having been reimagined as father and son, their physicality highlighted, the protagonists come still closer through their figuration as lovers:

> When they had each eaten together, it pleased them both
> To stare at each other's beauty as lovers might,
> Achilles built like a god, Priam goodlooking still
> And full of conversation, who earlier had sighed:

> 'I get down on my knees and do what must be done
> And kiss Achilles' hand, the killer of my son.'

Whereas the news reports in the *Irish Times* function as transparent windows onto the objectively apprehended reality of the cease-fire, minimizing their identity as texts, the poem foregrounds its linguistic remaking of the story it retells. At poem's end, the jangling alliteration of "kiss" and "killer," braced within the full couplet rhyme of "done" and "son," sonically and semantically encapsulates the inversion of violence in reconciliation. Even the poem's first lines, rather than objectively report, had peered into Achilles's consciousness as he remembered his own father. The imprinting on the scene of the poet's singular imagination and language, mediating his ancient precursor's, cannot be overlooked.

News reports are said to tell us who, what, when, where, why, and how, a framework that can help us measure the distance between this newspaper poem and the news. Who and what? The poem's ontology is oblique, seemingly about conciliation between Greeks and Trojans but ultimately also about Irish Catholics and Protestants. When? The poem's temporality is likewise ambiguous, suspended between ancient Troy and present-day Northern Ireland. Where? The poem is set in ancient Troy but by its title refers to (and it was printed in) Ireland, floating translocally in between, unmoored in either site. Why? To explain why he humbles himself before Achilles, Priam says he does "what must be done," turning on its head a phrase sometimes used to justify killing as obligatory; but his and Achilles's motives, as well as the causes of wars modern and ancient, are left indeterminate. How? The how of the poem, its elegant verbal texture, its intricate play of resemblances, its formal and figurative echoes of Homer and of the sonnet tradition are as much what it is about as the how of the events it relates. It revitalizes an ancient poem's story of reconciliation, using it both to place the day's news in a larger context and, after so many years of bloodshed, to set an ethical standard of peacemaking against which the ceasefire can be measured. Like Yeats and MacNeice, Longley makes powerful use of the cross-temporal, transnational, cross-sectarian potentialities of poetry.

Another contemporary Irish poet who has made the news one of his major subjects, as we've already seen in his September 11 poem, has also himself been a prominent news subject. "As a journalist," said Olivia O'Leary of the BBC in introducing Seamus Heaney, "it was wonderful to come across a great poet who thought that what we did was important." Borrowing poetry's prestige, O'Leary presupposes the genre's difference from the journalism it flatters with attention. But her next sentence assimilates the most public contemporary Irish poet to her profession: "We were conscious all the time of someone who reads all the papers, who keeps up with the current affairs debates, who's as interested in news as any journalist, because maybe he feels he needs to know constantly the context in which he's writing.

And we quickly realised that that attic in Sandymount is no ivory tower."[69] While it is true that Heaney's poetry, like the work of most public Irish poets, has been heavily reliant on the news, he has been more circumspect about journalism than journalism has been about him. The bifurcated structure of his most famous and controversial volume, *North* (1975), embodies poetry's long-running ambivalence toward journalism. The collection divides between a first part, intensely lyric poems that could scarcely be less journalistic, and a second part, poems that openly adapt and engage news rhetoric. Heaney conceded that "Whatever You Say Say Nothing," a poem initially published alongside prose accounts of the Troubles in the *Listener* and later in part 2 of *North*, was "journalistic, happily and I'd hope unpejoratively so," written in a "looser, more documentary style" than his "more inward, brooding" poems,[70] to the extent that, in Blake Morrison's view, some of the lines "might almost have been taken from the journalistic prose alongside" them in the *Listener*.[71] But the poem can also be seen as evidencing one of *North*'s two main methods for resisting journalism, and so of modern and contemporary poetry's sometimes internalizing, sometimes externalizing approaches to the news: like other poems in part 2, it journalistically incorporates journalism as ambivalent other against which poetry defines itself, whereas the poems in part 1 resolutely exclude journalism from their lyricism, as externalized alter ego.

"I'm writing just after an encounter / With an English journalist in search of 'views / On the Irish thing,'" begins "Whatever You Say Say Nothing," placing its language in a competitive relation with the journalism it implicitly tags as alien, external, and clichéd.[72] Despite Heaney's statement about his "journalistic" poems and O'Leary's claims about Heaney as a would-be journalist, this poem's verbs and verbals associate the news media—"sniff and point," "coiled," "Litter"—with dogs, guns, snakes, and pollution (57). In an indirect ars poetica, the poem affiliates itself with earlier works of literature, implicitly vaunting poetry's deep transnational memory, here by allusion to *Hamlet*, as distinct from the

national biases ("an English journalist") and temporal shallowness
of the news:

> The times are out of joint
> But I incline as much to rosary beads
>
> As to the jottings and analyses
> Of politicians and newspapermen (57)

Another self-definitional strategy is to link lyric with the ritualistic and recursive performance of prayer, as contrasted with the
rapidly written and consumed "jottings" of journalists, hastily
"scribbled down"—a distinction encapsulated in the contrastive
rhyme of news "leads" with "beads." The harsh internal echo
of the spondaic "'Backlash'" with "'crack down,'" inverting the
phoneme /ka/ in "'escalate,'" embeds these clichés in a staccato
patter that suggests newswriting's depersonalization of suffering
and violence. Suddenly breaking free of satire, the poet defiantly
reclaims lyric voice: "Yet I live here, I live here too, I sing" (57).
Jamming three independent clauses into one line, the poet stakes
his right to the local and global, to the deictically defined "here" of
Northern Ireland and the transnational lineage of poets from Virgil to Whitman. By contrast with journalism's clichés and ephemerality, poetry must try "To lure the tribal shoals to epigram / And
order"; that is, even when a poem is imprinted like this one by
journalistic topicality, syntax, and rhetoric, its richly condensed
and shaped language must aspire to be, in the Horatian boast,
more lasting than bronze, "*aere perennius*" (59).

Instead of incorporating the journalistic rhetoric they war
against, like poems in the book's second half, poems in the first
half cloak themselves in an intense lyricism that largely shuts out
news discourse. And instead of writing about the immediate present, quickly recorded for rapid consumption and disposal, Heaney
reflects on bodies preserved for thousands of years in the acidic,
cold, deoxygenated water of peat bogs—their preservative qualities akin to poetry's in creating verbal monuments more lasting
than bronze. "The Grauballe Man" concerns an especially well-

preserved Iron Age body, first encountered by Heaney in P. V. Glob's archaeological study *The Bog People* (translated from Danish in 1969). The Grauballe man, his throat cut from ear to ear, was deposited in a Danish bog, probably in sacrifice to a fertility goddess to ensure the coming of a fruitful spring, but he was so well preserved that two thousand years later he could still be fingerprinted by the police. While the news of killings by loyalist and republican extremists hovers around the poem's edges, this lyrically self-engaged work is both a poem and a metapoem. Its first words, "As if," announce the poem as poem, an imaginative thought experiment, a speculative excursion stretching beyond the literal: "As if he had been poured / in tar." The word "seems" ("and seems to weep // the black river of himself") also foregrounds the poet's associative work of imaginatively remaking the body, as do the tropes of fluidity—*poured, weep, river*—that figuratively liquefy the bog man (35). His body presented as the product of his grief over his sad fate, the bog man is imagined as self-created, and as such, his beauty illustrates the relative autonomy of the aesthetic, his body and the poem's self-returning melancholy body mirroring one another. Instead of suppressing its figurative properties in favor of newslike transparency, the poem runs wild with similes and metaphors, even remaking the blazon tradition that likened the beloved's parts to fruits and flowers and animals. In the poem's ekphrastic meditation on photographs in Glob's book, parts of the dead man's body are "like bog oak" and "like a basalt egg," or they're as "cold as a swan's foot / or a wet swamp root," or they're metaphorized as "the ridge / and purse of a mussel" and "an eel arrested / under a glisten of mud," or they're reimagined as "a visor" and a "vent" and "a dark / elderberry place" (35–36). Along with its figurative extravagance, the poem's sonic materiality—for example, the consonants *g* and *b* in *Grauballe* repeated in the word cluster *black, grain, bog, ball, basalt,* and *egg,* and "swan's foot" rhymed with "swamp root"—call attention to the poem's dense artifice.

Wordsworth defined lyric poetry as "emotion recollected in tranquility," and Heaney, saying of the Grauballe man that "now he lies / perfected in my memory," implicitly compares his lyric labor with the bog's preserving, curing, eternizing the object of its reflection (36). Twice enjambing "he lies"—a phrase that in context recalls the "here lies" or *hic jacet* of tombstones—the poem signals its epitaphic function. Just as the bog does violence to the body in effecting its preservation ("twisted," "bruised"), so too the poem has had to twist and trope the body as various figurative others (another sense of "he lies"), perhaps even bruising it in the process of lyricization (36). In so doing, it has made possible the bog man's rebirth into this poem ("bruised like a forceps baby"), but it worries about the cost of its having aesthetically "perfected" him (36). The dead man is likened to a famous statue in the Capitoline Museum, and implicitly the poem also considers whether it has cramped the dead man within the aesthetic: he is

> hung in the scales
> with beauty and atrocity:
> with the Dying Gaul
> too strictly compassed
>
> on his shield,
> with the actual weight
> of each hooded victim,
> slashed and dumped. (36)

The poem has largely resisted news discourse, foregrounding instead of effacing its artifice, commemorating not a contemporary but an ancient killing, and focusing intently not on "whodunit" but on the dead body. But the words "arrested," then "slashed," then "corpse" and "body" insinuate a news lexicon into the poem that culminates in the final words about a "hooded victim, / slashed and dumped." Such words still appeared years later in news reports, such as the *Irish Times* obituary for a mid-1970s victim of the notorious UVF Shankill Butchers: they "slashed his arms and wrists. Believing him dead, they dumped him in the alleyway," where he was found alive the next day.[73] But when the phrase "slashed and dumped" appears at the end of Heaney's poem, in contrast to news reports, it shocks as much because of its thudding sonic materiality as by its referential transparency. By virtue of *not* being overtly about the victims of the IRA or the UVF, by dwelling on a preserved ancient body and on its own poetic body spun out of a profusion of figurative similitudes and sonic clusters and syntactic parallelisms, the poem all the more powerfully evokes the specificity of the Troubles' victims—people whose killings exceed the compass of both aesthetic and journalistic representation. Heaney was harshly criticized for mythologizing and archetypifying the victims of the Troubles in *North*. But his indirect approach—evoking contemporary news by modernist mythical analogy with news thousands of years old—is news that stays news because of the eddying resonances between now and then, between poetry's material body and the victim's bodies. Ethically self-scrutinizing, "The Grauballe Man" well understands the critique that it has "too strictly compassed" victims of contemporary Northern Irish political violence in an artificial parallel between them and ancient sacrificial Danish bog victims. But its wager is that poetic resemblance, even when transnationally and transhistorically stretched, makes possible forms of attention and understanding occluded by more denotative, atomistic, newsy forms.

Whereas the news of sectarian violence is unmistakably present as a shaping force in Heaney's poetry, more interpretive labor is required to uncover the Troubles in Paul Muldoon's early verse, where they lurk in analogies between American Indians and the Irish, in a poem such as "Meeting the British," or are embedded in the psychoanalytic parable of a violently punished schoolboy turned IRA volunteer in "Anseo." Muldoon's approach to news of the Troubles is still more oblique than Heaney's, his skepticism toward journalism still deeper than his former tutor's, despite—or perhaps because of—Muldoon's having worked for thirteen years as a radio and TV producer for the BBC in Northern Ireland. From early on, he was well aware that his poems seemed to have little to do with the news. In "Lunch with Pancho Villa," he disarms criticism for fiddling while Belfast burns by voicing it within the poem:

'Look, son. Just look around you.
People are getting themselves killed
Left, right and centre
While you do what? Write rondeaux?
There's more to living in this country
Than stars and horses, pigs and trees,
Not that you'd guess it from your poems.
Do you never listen to the news?
You want to get down to something true,
Something a little nearer home.'[74]

The Mexican revolutionary-turned-journalist Pancho Villa, whose naively ocular epistemology is encapsulated in the command "Look," upbraids the poet for writing rondeaux: their formal circularity and pastoralism impede rather than afford access to the news of contemporary urban violence. But Villa subverts his own advice. He deploys the deictic "this" to root his mimetic writing in a specific place, but where is "this country"? Is it Ireland or Mexico? In the writer's backyard or "a thousand miles away / From here" (42)? As often in Muldoon, and still more aggressively than in Heaney, place is questioned as stabilizer of identity and truth. Having privileged the immediacy of firsthand sight, Villa reveals that he means mediated secondhand overhearing: "Do you never listen to the news?" The "something true" that the poet is supposed to embrace rhymes slant with "rondeaux," and "from your poems" with "nearer home," evidencing how the telling irresistibly mediates and skews the "true." After he unveils the poem's narrative as no more than a stage set, a front door that opens "Directly on to a back yard" (41), the poet is asked, "'When are you going to tell the truth?'" (42). But it turns out the naively titled book *How It Happened Here* may not exist, despite Villa's claims to have coauthored it. Perhaps to tell the truth is to admit that the news fabricates its seemingly uncomplicated and unmediated facts, as in Jean Baudrillard's simulacra theory of the news media. In this poem's constructivist account of even supposedly transparent language, Muldoon questions news realism as a sham and implicitly defends the poet's more self-conscious playing with forms and deliberate reimagining of the real, even at a time of large-scale violence. The news is seen as an indexical genre, based in an unsubtly positivist epistemology in which representation is but reproduction. Questioning journalism's nonperformative and nonconstructivist self-conception, Muldoon ramps up poetry's avowal of its madeness, its active shaping of its world.

To trace some of modern and contemporary Irish poetry's engagements with journalism is not to suggest that poetry's news stays news only when it is about current public events. Many poems turn poetry's discursive dial even farther from the news. Medbh McGuckian, a self-described "threader / of double-stranded words,"[75] writes in a note to the poem "Drawing Ballerinas": "This poem was written to commemorate Ann Frances Owens, schoolfellow and neighbour, who lost her life in the Abercorn Café explosion, 1972. The French painter, Matisse, when asked how he managed to survive World War II artistically, replied that he spent the worst years 'drawing ballerinas.'"[76] During the Troubles in Belfast, to write poems about the body, flowers, and slips of the tongue was McGuckian's equivalent of drawing ballerinas. War is not present in Matisse's ballerina drawings or most of McGuckian's sensuous word paintings, except by virtue of its exclusion. Her poetry's basic operating procedures are the reverse of what we look for in journalism. Action is indefinite or altogether absent. Sentences dilate, continually deferring meaning in interlocking syntactic ambiguities. Pronouns such as "you" and "she" and "they" appear and disappear without referents. Objects blend, one person blurs with another, and contrary ideas dissolve into each other. Metaphorical chains of evocation proliferate and interlink. From Yeats to Durcan, as we've seen, many other poets contend with journalistic rhetoric, referentiality, and present-mindedness, but McGuckian's *écriture féminine* is—in its opacity, self-referentiality, and sensuous verbal surfaces—perhaps the poetry least like journalism.

Not that the Troubles are altogether absent. Having been left out of Frank Ormsby's anthology of poems about the Northern Irish Troubles, *A Rage for Order* (1992), McGuckian cited Picasso's remark about World War II for the epigraph of *Captain Lavender*:

"I have not painted the war . . . but I have no doubt that the war is in . . . these paintings I have done."[77] Then, from the mid-1990s on, once the pressures of the Troubles began to recede, war figured more overtly in her poems: as she writes in "Life as a Literary Convict," "Signs of the still recent war / creep among the people like a plague, / dressed as Phoebus."[78] McGuckian implicitly contrasts her art with photojournalism, "printed black on white"; her role is instead to "wander about in search of the dead," to mourn those killed in the still lingering war, though the living emerge as an overwhelming presence. "Everything that ended in gunshots / and news of massacres / and third-class funerals" has threatened to become routinized and domesticated,

> . . . the clockwork life of the unchanging
> street, and the uninterrupted houses in rows
> neutralised the lava of war
> to a normal part of winter
> at an enormous cost.

Amid memories of relentless violence and arbitrary killing, McGuckian wants emphatically not to neutralize the lava of war. The unpredictability and difficulty of her poems, their opaque way of engaging the Troubles, preclude any comfortable domestication. The daily printing of photos and stories in newspapers, the nightly airing of radio bulletins, the relentless production of TV news shows all were thought to bring the Troubles closer, but McGuckian wonders whether this simulacrum instead led people to think they understood a catastrophe that was beyond rational comprehension. Unsettling and estranging, McGuckian's poetry forbids our feeling we can consume and normalize the reality of viciously inflicted death, suffering, and loss.

•

When poetry is examined in relation to the information field that has largely defined how we've understood living history since the start of the twentieth century, differences emerge that may be worth baldly encapsulating again, despite the many exceptions and points of intergeneric convergence. The news is quickly read; poems are slow, difficult, and repeatable. Poems luxuriate in their verbal surfaces and sounds, making their linguistic texture inescapably complicit in their co-creation of reality; the news media aim the bulk of their representational energy beyond their linguistic surfaces to public events. Newswriting is focused on the now; poems are long memoried, built out of vast transnational storehouses of figure, rhythm, and sound. Many twentieth-century Irish poets other than those I've been able to discuss, including Thomas Kinsella, Patrick Kavanagh, Derek Mahon, Paula Meehan, Eavan Boland, Seamus Deane, Ciarán Carson, Rita Ann Higgins, and Nuala Ní Dhomhnaill, take various approaches to journalism, sometimes parodying it, sometimes rigorously excluding it, sometimes drawing it within. From Yeats and MacNeice, to Longley and Heaney, to Muldoon and McGuckian, Irish poets have pursued an ever more oblique approach to public events, tying the civic tongue in ever more knots (with Durcan something of an exception). By the time Durcan and Muldoon are writing, in contrast to Yeats's aureate artifice, the high-low, literary–mass media divide has eroded. But despite these and other differences, poetry's engagement and struggle with journalism—"an old foul mouth" and "brazen throat," "jottings and analyses" and "*How It Happened Here*"—has been vigorous, perhaps especially on an island where news of public events has been insistent and ubiquitous. News discourse has been for Irish poetry a shadow self, a shaping counterforce. It has pushed poetry to define itself in its difference from the newspapers and other media forms that many poets, for all their misgivings, "buy every day."

AMERICAN POETRY AND THE NEWS

This chapter began with Williams's observation about the difficulty of extracting the news from poems, and having explored how poets from Ireland, as well as from England and Jamaica, respond to recurrent features of the news, I return to Williams, along with other modern and contemporary American poets, to ask what further light their work might shed on poetry's inter-generic engagements with the news. The sectarian-straddling capacities of poetry, which emerged as one of its more important dimensions for Irish poets from Yeats to Heaney and Longley, tend to be less significant for American poets, who nevertheless resemble Irish and other poets we've explored in counterposing poetry's *longue durée*, linguistic and sonic density, and self-reflexivity against the news's mimeticism, presentism, positivism, and transparency. Such distinctions lurk in Williams's acerbic comments on the news. "What is the use of reading the common news of the day," he asks in his *Autobiography*, "the tragic deaths and abuses of daily living," since such news is "trivial fill-gap," unlike the "profound language" of poetry?[79] Newspapers "reveal nothing whatever, for they only tell you what you already know,"[80] and their "headlines die in less than twenty four hours and become meaningless," "too short lived a mode for serious thought."[81] With the turn-of-the-century development of mass-circulation daily newspapers in rapidly expanding cities, their publication enabled in part by the increasingly efficient rotary press and ever cheaper pulp, the newspaper had become, as Alan Trachtenberg observes, a dominant form of reading and experience in America. "Unlike the printed page of a novel," or, we might add, a page of poetry, "the newspaper page declares itself without mistake as good only for a day, for this reading only: as if today's history of the world has nothing in common with yesterday's or tomorrow's"; "the daily newspaper deadens memory."[82] Williams was disturbed by the newspaper's discursive dominance, a position strangely strengthened by the form's built-in obsolescence (as identified by Trachtenberg, Benjamin, Anderson, and other theorists of journalism). In London, Ezra Pound also railed in *Hugh Selwyn Mauberley* (1920) against Fleet Street and the press's displacement of cultural memory and high art with the crass short-term values of the marketplace, even if his imagist principle of "direct treatment of the 'thing'" and his series of abrupt, collagelike juxtapositions could be seen as co-opting for poetry the immediacy and adjacency of the news.[83] For Williams, as for fellow modernists Pound, Stevens, and Eliot, the news is shallow, ephemeral, and predictable, while poetry can, at its best, claim durability, profundity, and unexpectedness.[84] Against the relentless pressure of the news, Stevens lays claim to the poet's "ecstatic freedom of the mind."[85] As already seen with Yeats in the Anglo-Irish context, in the first half of the twentieth century this modernist understanding of poetry's specificity is shaped by the genre's contention with the more intensively capitalized and more pervasive discursive form for representing living history.

But if the news and poetry take sharply divergent approaches to the representation of public events, then why does Williams paste newspaper stories and clippings into his poetry, especially in his urban epic *Paterson*, a work often cited as a key progenitor of experimental documentary poetry? Why does his epic poem draw on the juxtapositional layout of the newspaper, in which unrelated events and voices are shoved up against one another? At the very least he must believe he can incorporate the newspaper within modernist poetry's heteroglossia without degrading it. Despite his objections to the transience and shallowness of the newspaper, Williams does not exemplify Andreas Huyssen's "great divide,"[86] scorning popular journalism as beneath notice; instead, like later documentary poets, he thinks the poet uses "the same materials as newsprint, the same dregs."[87] Williams seems less anxiously elitist about the newspaper as genre than his preeminent Irish contemporary, and the more patterned poetic forms of Irish verse have been slower to admit raw journalism than have "open" American forms. Even so, this national and formal distinction shouldn't be overdrawn, since Williams no less than Yeats believes the poet, etymologically a maker, does not "hold the mirror up to nature" but makes something distinctive from these materials—"a new thing, unlike any thing else in nature, a thing advanced and apart from it."[88] By contrast with the seemingly passive mediation of current events by the reporter, the poet's use of language and form must actively re-create the historical present, an imaginative event that recurs perpetually in the sustained present of poetry's inventiveness.

For Williams, the main attraction of the newspaper lies in its immersion in locality, akin to the role of Irish folklore and place-names in Yeats's poetry. The modern newspaper as a genre has been conceptualized as helping "create and sustain Americans' sense of local community," a sense of locality rooted in what appear to be "factual, immediate, commonsensical, and authentic" stories—a locality more important in early twentieth-century newspapers than it is today.[89] In his comments on *Paterson*, Williams emphasized the poet's need "to write particularly," not "in vague categories," trying "in the particular to discover the universal."[90] Adapting John Dewey in the claim "The local is the only universal, upon that all art builds," Williams wished the city Paterson in his poem to "be as itself, locally, and so like every other place in the world."[91] In "Americanism and Localism," a 1920 essay in the *Dial* ironically sandwiched with Pound's extravagantly transnational fourth canto, Dewey had argued that "the newspaper is the only genuinely popular form of literature we have achieved" because it "has revelled" in localism and so provides the "depth or thickness" lacking elsewhere in American literature.[92] Sympathetic to American nativism after World War I, Williams refused what he saw as Pound and Eliot's "conformist" cosmopolitanism, their "rehash, repetition" of their European masters.[93] In *Paterson* he seized on the urban newspaper as intergenre to help curb poetry's pull toward abstraction, seeking instead to indigenize the foreign forms of epic and of poetry more generally by making them responsive to the local experience of American landscape, language, and history.[94]

Trying to absorb the newspaper's local "depth" and representational "thickness" into poetry, Williams gleaned news of gruesome child deaths and other local stories from issues of the newspaper *The Prospector* published in 1936:[95]

> Old newspaper files,
> to find—a child burned in a field,
> no language. Tried, aflame, to crawl under
> a fence to go home. So be it. Two others,
> boy and girl, clasped in each others' arms
> (clasped also by the water) So be it. Drowned
> wordless in the canal. So be it. (98)

Williams grounds his American epic in the local specificity of such news items, even thematizing appropriation of the news into literary form ("Old newspaper files," "amazed from the reading") (98). But in the process of generic metamorphosis, instead of remaining purely "local," these stories are abstracted as synecdoches for tragic news stories—"a child," "boy and girl." In this long series in *Paterson*'s library episode, moreover, Williams punctuates the news items with a refrain, "So be it," once an English rendering of "amen" that archaically places the adverb "so" before the verb, a phrase that goes back hundreds of years in English literary history.[96] Williams was anxious to assign this English "chant," with its "sense of almost liturgical formality" (in Louis Martz's phrase),[97] an American provenance, telling Pound, "[T]he 'so be it' I copied verbatim from a translation of a Plains Indian prayer."[98] But in a translation that substitutes a venerable English equivalent for Hebrew and Native American postprayer interjections, the indigenous and the foreign have become inseparable. Other repetitions, such as the children's being figuratively "clasped" by the water, weave the news's denotations into poetry's metaphoric texture. Meanwhile, Williams retells these stories in lines that approach English blank verse, building on Milton's example in irregular rhythms, cannily end-stopped lines ("a child burned in a field, / no language"), and violent and sometimes mimetic enjambments ("to crawl under / a fence"; "Drowned / wordless in the canal").[99] Ultimately, he bends the newspaper's present-minded localism and linear American realism in the direction of prayer's recursiveness and ritualism. Rather than holding the mirror up to current events, he fashions a cross-cultural and intergeneric amalgam that is "a new thing, unlike any thing else." Its fingers reaching deep into the language and across traditions, *Paterson* deploys—despite Williams's putative nativism—literary and liturgical resources that ritualize and transnationalize the ephemeral stories commodified by local journalism.

Williams saw the news as offering "the precise incentive to epic poetry, the poetry of events,"[100] and his epic poem incorporates large chunks of prose taken from or summarizing newspaper stories, in a newslike collage with personal letters and other forms of textual materiality. In the first long news story that Williams includes in *Paterson*, set off typographically like subsequent passages by its small typeface, as well as its plain-style prose, Williams condenses two different events.[101] A shoemaker is said to have found pearls in "mussels from Notch Brook near the City of Paterson" and sold them, including one known as "the 'Queen Pearl,' the finest of its sort in the world today," starting a nationwide search, with mussels "destroyed often with little or no result"; one pearl that "would have been the finest pearl of modern times, was ruined by boiling open the shell" (9). Though journalistically grounded in the city of Paterson and its environs, this narrative's locality is entwined with transnational flows and geographies. The local news travels far beyond New Jersey—"News of this sale created such excitement that search for the pearls was started throughout the country"—as emphasized by the ensuing verse lines about Paterson's worldwide "communications" (9). Trade circulates the pearls nationally ("sold to Tiffany") and even globally ("and later to the Empress Eugenie") (9). Even in the poem's deployment of the news as signifier of locality, the local is enmeshed in global trade and communications.

Williams's remaking of the story further stitches it into webs of what Édouard Glissant terms "le poétique de la Relation" (relational, or cross-cultural, poetics).[102] Echoes between the prose passage and the encompassing poetry resonate beyond the news story's emphatically specific geography—"Notch Brook near the City of Paterson." The pearls, fastidiously quantified as being worth "$900" or "$2,000" and "weighing 400 grains," reverberate across networks of poetic figuration: they are made to echo the metaphorical and unquantifiable pearls in the lines of poetry immediately preceding the prose news passage, lines in which Williams metaphorizes the mountain's base as "Pearls at her ankles" (9). The resonance implicitly contrasts the poet's benign figuration of nature with the destructive commodification of nature in pearls for profit. Despite this long poem's reputation for openness and rawness, it poetically kneads its appropriated materials into a larger confection. *Paterson*'s "The Delineaments of the Giants," as indicated by the subtitle, also transnationally mythologizes local geography, allegorizing the city Paterson as a male giant, slumbering side by side with the female giant of the mountain—an anthropomorphic figuration of landscape that goes back to the Norse creation myth of Ymir that Williams cited in manuscript but extirpated from the final text.[103] His collage technique of patching together news and high art recalls cubist paintings such as Picasso's *Still Life with Chair-Caning* (1912) and Braque's *Bottle, Newspaper, Pipe, and Glass* (1913) that paste newspaper cuttings onto canvas or paper alongside other found or designed forms, which, through convergences and contrasts, visual and verbal puns, transform them. It can also be traced to Joyce's *Ulysses*, a news-incorporating prose epic that Williams was reading when he conceived his long poem.[104] In keeping with poetry's deep formal memory, *Paterson* also echoes older intergeneric hybridizations of prose and verse such as the *chante-fable* and prosimetrum, including the medieval French *Aucassin et Nicolette*, introduced to Williams by H.D.[105] In accordance with Williams's homiletic critique of efforts since Alexander Hamilton to capture and commercially exploit the Passaic River's Great Falls, the news story's local geography is absorbed into a moral fable about the greedy destruction of Paterson's natural environment. In sum, in addition to the globalizing forces of market capitalism ("sold to Tiffany") and worldwide communications ("News of this sale") at the level of content, Williams's use of narrative condensation (two stories in one), webs of figuration ("Pearls at her ankles"), personifying myth ("The Delineaments of the Giants"), ethical fable ("ruined"), and imported techniques like collage further translocalize *Paterson*'s local news at the level of form. He creolizes European collage and English verse with American news, news that is already riddled with global movement and conveyed by a form of print journalism earlier transplanted from Europe. "No ideas but in things," he reiterates just after the pearls story, but the local things migrate along multiple axes, and the ideas that inhere in them are neither autochthonous nor immobile (9). Despite Williams's ideological nativism, his poetry reveals the penetration of globality into even the most local news, deconstructing what has been called "the myth of 'the local' in American journalism,"[106] and it further interbraids journalism with artistic and mythical paradigms that move the poem beyond poetry's traditional boundaries, as well as beyond the city's and the nation's.

To interfuse poetry with the news, Williams turned to epic, a commodious and multigeneric form of poetry, but the especially compressed space of lyric may seem unamenable to the incorporation of journalism. Indeed, in recent commentary on "docupoetry" and "documentary poetics," the lyric is often posited as antithesis, a form sealed shut against any merger between the poetic and the journalistic.[107] But American poets concerned with the news have long looked to lyric forms, in occasional poems from Phillis Wheatley's funeral elegies to William Vaughn Moody's "An Ode in Time of Hesitation" and in Walt Whitman's *Drum-Taps* and Herman Melville's *Battle-Pieces*. The polarization of lyric insularity against antilyric reportage risks obscuring the active engagement of many American lyric poets with the news, from colonial times to the present, and overlooking the potentially illuminating frictions between news-informed poetry and the news. Although American lyric poetry's complex relation to the news is inadequately explored, writers as various as the New York school poet Frank O'Hara, the Black Mountain poet Robert Duncan, the human rights poet Carolyn Forché, and the postconfessional poet Jorie Graham cross lyric with the news, even as they question journalism's sometimes naively informational assumptions about representation. Many of these lyric poets work the tension between poetry's deliberate constructivism and the bald positivism of the news, while telling the news by other means.

Drawing on the example of Williams's prose-encompassing epic for lyric poetry, Frank O'Hara's "I do this I do that" poems are in close dialogue with the journalism of his time. In "The Day Lady Died," his elegy for Billie Holiday, O'Hara directly invokes newsprint by reference to "a NEW YORK POST with her face on it," the July 17, 1959, same-day issue of the paper, edited at the time by the lapsed communist James Wechsler. On that day, the headline "BILLIE HOLIDAY DIES" filled up most of the ten-cent paper's cover, sandwiched against a head-and-half-torso shot of the singer in song (see illustration). Page 3 carried reporter William Dufty's

"Billie Holiday Dies," from the front cover of the *New York Post*, July 17, 1959. Author's photograph.

account of Holiday's last days and hours in the hospital, "Billie Holiday Dies after Relapse; First Lady of the Blues Was 44," an article that began with the moment and place of her death: "Billie Holiday died at 3:10 this morning in Metropolitan Hospital as simply and regally as she had lived," before recounting her "46-day stand in Room 6A12."[108]

Whether conservative or liberal, hard or soft, tabloid or serious, broadcast or print, the news is a defining record of public happenings in Eisenhower's 1950s, and O'Hara's lyric takes up and torques the US news media's reporting procedures. In America during the cold war, when, as Edward Brunner and Deborah Nelson have shown, poetry is a form where the boundaries between public and private, state and personal are being negotiated, O'Hara's poem is a kind of mock news story.[109] As in any news account, this (pseudo)reporter details the precise sequence of when and where, except that he dissolves the public-private divide into the flickering data of his own world-immersed experience and eschews the reportorial myth of objectivity. His state of "quandariness" contrasts with the authoritative and unperplexed tone expected in news reporting. Even the poem's title wittily plays on and elegantly refashions the trope of the headline pun, "Day" serving, by syntactic inversion, as both common noun and the stage name of the singer, otherwise unnamed in accordance with elegiac convention.

O'Hara's poem defamiliarizes the news media's core practices of accounting empirically and precisely for time and space. With relentless spatiotemporal specificity, it exaggerates and parodies moment-by-moment news reporting, akin to the live broadcasting in 1950s radio and television news, as well as rapidly produced newsprint. It supplies numerous news-report details about the speaker's location ("in New York," "in Easthampton") and the time ("It is 12:20," "a Friday / three days after Bastille day, yes / it is 1959," "I will get off the 4:19").[110] But even though the speaker assumes a singular reporting location, circling back to Sixth Avenue in New York City, the poem shows this space to be anything but local and unitary, even in its extreme localness: it is instead dispersed and crisscrossed by literary and commodity vectors from multiple countries. Although attracted like Williams to the news for its centripetal localization, O'Hara spins his news-inflected lyrics with centrifugal force. By the time the speaker of "The Day Lady Died" encounters "a NEW YORK POST with her face on it," his words have traveled with tremendous speed from New York City to the Bastille, back to Easthampton, then newly independent Ghana, France again (Verlaine, Bonnard), Greece (Hesiod), Ireland (Brendan Behan), France again (Jean Genet), Italy (Strega), and yet again France (Ziegfeld, Gauloises). This zigzag global movement ends with Holiday's death, instead of beginning there in accordance with the news's inverted pyramidal hierarchy. Closing with an elegiac spiral inward to a memory of a Billie Holiday performance ("and everyone and I stopped breathing"), O'Hara also diverges sharply from the objectifying indices and empirical record of a standard news obituary. He rhymes the present with the past, public news with inner memory. While O'Hara opens lyric poetry to the factual welter of the news, he remakes the journalistic report: he layers it with the meditative inwardness of grief, explodes the myth of the local by uncovering its global flows, satirizes the news's anonymity and objectivity by immersing the subject within these flows, and pushes the news's temporal and spatial specificity so hard that it becomes emblematic of modernity's speed and movement, its penetration and partial dispersal of the subject.

The newspaper headline "LANA TURNER HAS COLLAPSED!" appears twice in a more comic poem O'Hara wrote a few years later, in 1962, setting up an implicit analogy between poem and news report—an analogy the poem plays with and ultimately undoes.[111] Even though the poem begins with a headline, at first in lowercase, it rapidly and satirically switches to a whimsical catalog of the speaker's movements and an oddly dialogic weather report:

> Lana Turner has collapsed!
> I was trotting along and suddenly
> it started raining and snowing
> and you said it was hailing

> but hailing hits you on the head
> hard so it was really snowing and
> raining. . . .

The headline's report on a movie star marks the singularity of the tabloid incident by its finite verb ("has collapsed"). This factual report could hardly be more different from the processual and dialogic texture of the ensuing breathless lines, with their present participles ("raining . . . snowing . . . hailing . . . hailing . . . snowing . . . raining . . . acting"), their paratactic ramble ("and suddenly it started . . . and you said . . . and I was"), their mundanity ("I was trotting along"), their comic alliterations ("hailing / but hailing hits you on the head / hard"), and their humorously retrospective pursuit of a disagreement with a friend over the weather ("you said it was hailing / but"). Although the news report and the poem begin with the same event, they are shown to take dramatically different syntactic, verbal, tonal, and temporal routes. Among the standard qualities of American journalism are said to be timeliness, factuality, an anonymous third-person author, and an "unemotional accounting of events."[112] By contrast with the seeming neutrality of such third-person reporting, O'Hara's poem enacts desire in language, dramatizing it by the rapid-fire tumble of its syntax and thematizing it in the statement "I was in such a hurry / to meet you." Through the impediments of weather, traffic, and physical distance, the poem plunges toward the desired "you," in accordance with the refinement of poetic address in O'Hara's "Personism: A Manifesto": the poem must "address itself to one person . . . thus evoking overtones of love," the "poem squarely between the poet and the person, Lucky Pierre style," in sharp contrast with the generalized addressee of news reports.[113]

But "suddenly I see a headline," a final impediment, and suddenly the poem makes a sharp turn, laying out implied antitheses between the speaker and the celebrity: it rains and snows where he lives, but where she lives there is "no snow" and "no rain in California"; he has been to parties like the ones Lana Turner went to "and acted perfectly disgraceful," but unlike her, he "never actu-

ally collapsed." The speaker was already divided between loca-
tions—between, that is, the place where he was "trotting along"
and his destination, where he hurries "to meet you." But the news
of Turner's collapse translocalizes him all the more dramatically:
now his thoroughly relational self-understanding is splayed across
America, between sunny Hollywood and wintry New York.
Whereas a news report is typically represented as grounded in a
singular location, though globally transmissible, O'Hara's report
on the news report is spatially stretched and fissured. At a time
when traditional privacy is, in Deborah Nelson's words, "eroding
under the . . . market pressures in the form of tabloid journalism,"
O'Hara foregrounds how we sometimes understand our private
lives through their resemblances with, and differences from, the
often evanescent celebrities who crowd our consciousness.[114]

In a final departure from the norms of newswriting, the desire
that had been intently focused on the addressee is in the end
mockingly diverted to the movie icon: "oh Lana Turner we love
you get up." "Conative" language oriented toward the addressee,
in Roman Jakobson's terms, "finds its purest grammatical expression in the vocative and imperative," and "imperative sentences
cardinally differ from declarative sentences: the latter are and the
former are not liable to a truth test."[115] O'Hara plays on lyric poetry's richly conative language, affectively loaded and unverifiable.
"The most important *textual* feature of journalism," writes John
Hartley, "is the fact that it counts as true."[116] Part of the humor
of O'Hara's poem lies in the contrast between the declarative
mode of true-or-false third-person news, as instanced by "LANA
TURNER HAS COLLAPSED!," and the last line's lyrically emotive or
"expressive" statement, "oh Lana Turner we love you," which in
Jakobson's terms is "focused on the ADDRESSER" and "aims a direct
expression of the speaker's attitude toward what he is speaking
about"[117]—a contrast that extends to the final imperative, "get
up." While absorbing and parodying the news's declarative language, O'Hara's poetry twists it around to its lyric opposite: the
conative, the vocative, the expressive, and in this instance even
the imperative, albeit a difference that was being increasingly

weakened by tabloid news, as signaled by the exclamation mark after the headline. The friction between the last line ("oh Lana Turner we love you get up") and the first ("Lana Turner has collapsed"), between affectively charged "personist" address and third-person description, exemplifies Bakhtin's heteroglossia, the literary incorporation of *"another's speech in another's language"* in a *"double-voiced discourse."*[118] Though intertwined with the speed, presentness, impersonality, and bric-a-brac of the news, O'Hara's poetry unsettles these journalistic norms. If Hartley is right that "journalism is *the* textual system of modernity," O'Hara's lyric news energetically takes on a dominant discursive form, greatly complicating any simple notions of unitary location, refusing the subordination of private affect to public reality, rejecting a regulative neutrality, undoing reportorial third-person anonymity, and insisting on desire-charged and dialogic language in which speaker and addressee meet.

The modernist and cold war struggle between American poetry and the news gains renewed intensity in the Vietnam War era, when Americans first began receiving most of their news from television instead of from newspapers or magazines, although the distinction between conventional journalism and other media forms, as Hartley indicates, "should not be overstated, for . . . the technology of journalism is less important than the ideas it communicates and their popular reach."[119] Whereas O'Hara's ironic, knowing, camp pseudonews is written in a discursive register below that of standard news discourse—its "personism" more colloquially familiar—Robert Duncan moves it up several notches in one of the Vietnam era's most powerful poems, applying no less pressure to what Hartley calls the news as "gigantic archive of textuality," whether in imagistic, verbal, or other form.[120] First published in the *Nation* in 1965, his "Up Rising, Passages 25" is a prophetic vision of the Vietnam War. This is not to say that it lacks journalistic content, perhaps surprisingly for a poet of intense mysticism. A couple of years after television networks doubled the length of their news broadcasts but several years before the mass antiwar protests of the late 1960s, Duncan provides a critical chronicle of events: President Johnson is said to have sent planes from Guam over Asia; "the professional military" uses Johnson in its "business of war"; the planes drop napalm on the jungles; the American war enemy is an undifferentiated "communism"; American officials have been elected in part by fraudulent votes; "the closed meeting-rooms of regents of university and sessions of profiteers" have been behind the war; scientists have developed new means of biological warfare, including "new plagues, measles grown enormous, influenzas perfected."[121] But in Duncan's poem, these facts are not dispassionately presented, nor are they fodder for a poetic equivalent to the antiwar editorial: they are metamorphosed into the ingredients of a vatic revisioning of America, written in the style of Blake's prophetic books. If hints of prayer and veneration can be found in Williams's and perhaps even O'Hara's poetic handling of the news (the end of "The Day Lady Died"), Duncan absorbs the news into a more overtly spiritual poetics, his poem straddling these discrepant forms.

How does a poet like Duncan tell "the news" so that, in Pound's words, it "STAYS news"? At the most basic syntactic level, whereas the news report is typically a series of short, discrete declarative sentences, Duncan's poem, in keeping with projectivist principles, is one long sentence that unspools clause after clause. In its Blakean temporality and connectivity, it eschews the news's atomism, which fractures time and space into discrete and unrelated verbal or imagistic snapshots. "Up Rising" syntactically glues together the details of the journalistic present, and it returns these to the deep past that has formed them. The insistence of the past is lexically highlighted by Duncan's use of archaic literary forms of past participles and the past tense: "stirrd," "heapt," "developt," "passt," "workt," "cleard," "feard" (116–18). The war represents, in Duncan's religio-ethical history, the "black bile of old evils arisen anew," in particular the genocide against Amerindian nations on which the US nation was founded: "the pit of the hell of America's unacknowledged crimes," "a holocaust of burning Indians, trees and grasslands, / reduced to his real estate" (118). The white settler is driven by a "deep hatred for the old world" and a disastrously imperial and capitalist approach to "the alien world, the new world about him, that might have been Paradise" (118). Delving back into the country's origins, Duncan recalls the prophetic fear that Adams and Jefferson had of future corruption and despotism. But he displays none of the hatred for the old world that he sees as afflicting the United States. In his transnationalist prophecy, he cites English poets for their pre-scient insight into America, quoting D. H. Lawrence's allegorical figure of overweening pride and materialism in "The American Eagle" and referring to the revolutionary fire-and-blood imagery of Blake's "America." Duncan's vision of America is even darker than theirs, so he quotes Lawrence but substitutes ellipses for Lawrence's vision of the possible emergence of "something splen-did" in America and elides Blake's fervent hopes for the American Revolution.[122] Far from representing his utterance as emanating from a journalist's single location and simple present, Duncan's multilayered poem channels a transatlantic array of voices from different times. He suggests that poetry, by contrast with the self-explanatory and seemingly transparent immediacy of the news, draws on a collective unconscious in its fierce response to the urgencies of the present.

Although Duncan's Johnson is a simplified Urizenic figure of evil, a typological iteration of the lust for fame that drove both Hitler and Stalin, the evil that Duncan envisions in the war ex-tends well beyond any single figure to "small-town bosses and business-men" (117), the "good people in the suburbs" (117), the scientists "we have met at cocktail parties, passt daily and with a happy 'Good Day' on the way to classes or work" (117–18), the "sea of toiling men" (116), and finally, "the all-American boy in the cockpit / loosing his flow of napalm," "drawing now / not with crayons" (117). No one, presumably not even the poet, is exempt from complicity. Indeed, the makers of biological warfare are described as creative in their own way, "dreaming" like the poet, but perverting this creative capacity—"dreaming / of the bodies of mothers and fathers and children and hated rivals / swollen with" diseases (117). In the long, rolling declamations of this sweeping and indeed panoramic vision, Duncan still insists on the particular horrors of the particular moment: "the burning of homes and the torture of mothers and fathers and children, / their hair a-flame, screaming in agony" (117). His framing of the war's atrocities in transnational and even mythical contexts makes their criminality all the more lurid. Unlike the focus on discrete events in news journalism, Duncan's porous and multivoiced poem both formally and diegetically presents America as transected by cross-national and transhistorical realities, even those to which it is willfully oblivious.

Although Williams thought of the news as grounding poetry in America, it has had the reverse function for internationally minded American poets, such as those involved in the Spanish Civil War [123] and a still broader array of poets like Duncan since the Vietnam War. Published near the beginning of the Salvadoran Civil War (1980–92), in which the United States backed the right-wing Salvadoran government in its brutal effort to suppress a leftist insurrection, Carolyn Forché's book of poems about atrocities she witnessed or learned of while working as a human rights advocate in El Salvador, *The Country between Us* (1981), famously incorporates journalistic reportage, but even the prose poetry in this volume can't be confused with a news clipping. Unlike Duncan's long-winding syntax, Forché's short, simple, declarative sentences in her signature prose poem "The Colonel," written in 1978, at first seem to match journalistic discourse: "What you have heard is true. I was in his house. His wife carried a tray of coffee and sugar. His daughter filed her nails, his son went out for the night. There were daily papers, pet dogs, a pistol on the cushion beside him."[124] The flat, clipped syntax and literal descriptiveness hew close to journalistic norms, and the domestic space could hardly be more mundane, except that the detail of the pistol warns of violence and the possessive adjective "his" is imperially stamped on everything and everyone. The next sentence's figurative language clearly marks a departure from a direct transcription of events: "The moon swung bare on its black cord over the house." The ominous metaphor implicitly likens the moon to·

fearful objects and events, such as a hanging, a lynching, a grand-father clock, an interrogation lamp, a dangling telephone, or Edgar Allan Poe's pendulum. In this moment, as when she imagines the wall-embedded broken bottles used to cut a man's "hands to lace," the poem foregrounds its figurative evocation of violence. It twists together horrifying political violence with the mundane particulars of the colonel's home and family life, of the dinner menu and light conversation:

> The colonel returned with a sack used to bring groceries home. He spilled many human ears on the table. They were like dried peach halves. There is no other way to say this. He took one of them in his hands, shook it in our faces, dropping it in a water glass. It came alive there.

The passage oscillates between banality and brutality. The gro-cery sack recalls earlier domestic details, but then the spilling of ears from it jerks the language out of the domestic and into the gothic, before returning again to the domestic in the metaphor of peaches. The reader has been positioned at the dinner table, a participant in this domestic space where public atrocity on a hor-rific scale overwhelms the scene. The metamorphic bursting of the dead body parts into life and the collapse of the homely into the unhomely, of domestic coziness into political killing, disturb distinctions by which news reality is organized. By the end, the poet makes no pretense of reportage. Like the ear in the water glass, other ears are revitalized by poetic language, Forché literal-izing the metaphoric idiom for extreme attentiveness, not unlike the poet's own: "Some of the ears on the floor were pressed to the ground." The colonel is not merely, however, a destructive figure. He has been granted a role as co-creator of this very poem: "Something for your poetry, no? he said," after sweeping the ears to the ground. And indeed, by his dramatic political performance the colonel collaborates in creating the very poem we read. Like O'Hara's blurring of the spaces between speaker and addressee, reader and writer, Forché's poem confounds the static subject positions presupposed by journalism—objective author and subjects of a news report—as well as here and over there, national and international. By her adoption of seemingly plainspoken prose, by her eschewal of lineation and strophe, she nestles the poetic within the journalistic, as if thereby to ward off the ethical dangers of aestheticizing violence, even as her compression, metaphoricity, and self-reflexivity quietly distinguish her language from journalistic norms.

Born like Forché in the spring of 1950, Jorie Graham also grew up in a period of increasing news saturation, and part of her achievement, too, has been to develop inventive strategies for negotiating the relations between poetry and the news, between private experience and global public history. In her poem "Fission" (1991), she returns to one of the epoch-defining events in cultural memory of the 1960s, the 1963 assassination of President John F. Kennedy (incidentally, the first news event I can remember from my childhood, when I was three years old). But unlike a reporter's, her angle of approach to the event is to measure its impact on an autobiographical pubescent "I," then thirteen years old, who learns of it while in Italy watching Stanley Kubrick's 1962 movie *Lolita*.[125] In the interval between modernism and post-confessionalism, between Williams's and Graham's poetry, the visualization, acceleration, and ubiquity of the news media have intensified in the United States, as throughout the developed world. Graham's poem is written out of this experience of ever greater penetration of the news media into human subjectivity and self-understanding. Here the news is apprehended not as objective datum but through the resemblances we construct between ourselves and public figures, our lives and public narratives. The adolescent girl is watching an enormous on-screen Lolita, a character nearly her age, whose image, when the assassination is announced and sunlight floods the movie theater, dissolves into

> vague stutterings of
> light with motion in them, bits of moving zeros
>
> in the infinite virtuality of light,
> some *likeness* in it but not particulate,

> a grave of possible shapes called *likeness*—see it?—some-
>   thing
>   scrawling up there that could be skin or daylight or
>   even . . .[126]

The violent transnational impact of the news is figured in the
sunlight's crashing through the roof of the movie theater, exploding both cinematic and personal illusions. Under the pressure of
the news, the likenesses between the real and the cinematic girl,
between fantasy and history, fray, break apart, and their fissures
are exposed. Usually segregated from one another for movie-
goers, daylight, house lights, and the projector's light collide and
compete in this crisis moment. So too public and private history—normally kept stably separated from one another—criss-
cross traumatically. The movie images seem to lick and play on
the speaker's "small body,"

>   where the long thin arm of day came in from the top
> to touch my head,
>   reaching down along my staring face—
> where they flared up around my body unable to
>
> merge into each other
>   over my likeness,
> slamming down one side of me, unquenchable—here static
>
>   there flaming—[127]

Touching, reaching, slamming down, flaming—the news is experi-
enced neither as spectacle nor as objective datum to be consumed
but as personal and even erotic assault. The curtain between interiority and externality and between subjective experience and
public history has come crashing down. But in Graham's retelling
of the news, an adolescent girl's fall from innocence into experience and her construction and deconstruction of poetic likenesses
between herself and others to make sense of the assassination

are no less a part of the history of November 22, 1963, than what could be seen on TV or read in the next day's newspapers.

One way of understanding twentieth-century American poetry, like twentieth-century Irish, Jamaican, and British poetry, is, in short, in its vexed dialogue with the news. In twentieth-century America, as in these other parts of the globe, you can get the news from poems—tragic child deaths and the despoliation of the natural environment, the loss or fall (literal and figurative) of celebrities, the scientific perversions unleashed in the Vietnam War, US-abetted war crimes in Latin America, JFK's assassination, and so forth. Modern and contemporary public poems rely heavily on journalism to tell the news as they see it. But the news told in poetry isn't conceived the same way as it is in newspapers and other news media, since even newsy poems question journalism's language, procedures, and assumptions. In various poems, as we've seen, the news's localism is translocated, its outward-directed mimeticism is turned around in inwardly recurring ritual, its objectivity is sandwiched between experiential subjects, its present-mindedness is tethered to the deep or mythical past, its denotative language is flushed with metaphoricity, and its transparency is clouded by densely figurative mediation and subjectivity. To the extent that these tropings of the news move it in the direction of long-lived forms and myth, inwardness and ritual recursiveness, they move it—sometimes boldly in the case of Duncan's "Up Rising," often less obviously—in the direction of prayer. Surely we'd never mistake a poem like O'Hara's "The Day Lady Died" or Forché's "The Colonel" for a prayer, and yet even these news poems, in their final moments, sound deeply meditative bass notes that reverberate well beyond the news flash. We could pursue the para-news news history of modern and contemporary American poetry at great length, exploring the many different ways in which poets have told alternative public histories of current events, from the Great Depression and the Spanish Civil War, to the civil rights and women's movement, September 11 and the Iraq War; from Langston Hughes, Carl Sandburg, Muriel Rukeyser, and Denise Levertov to Gwendolyn Brooks, Adrienne Rich,

Fady Joudah, and Juliana Spahr. But to avoid reducing poetry to its historical and mimetic registers, we need to calibrate the generic identity of poetry by considering it in relation to other genres.

•

By characterizing journalism as seen from within poetry, I have been unfair to it. The discourse of the news contains heterogeneous counterdiscourses that partly coincide with poetry's demurrals. From time to time journalism criticizes its own short attention span, fills out broad historical contexts, interrogates norms of objectivity, foregrounds the co-creative role of reporters, inspects its language, calls attention to its metaphors, and even contravenes its own financial interests. Though far from prevailing, these counterdiscourses are wound through the fabric of the news, anticipating poetry's challenges to journalistic norms. Moreover, despite the newspaper's dominance during much of the twentieth century, it may soon elicit from poetry more nostalgia than resistance, given its precariousness as a form. Like Paul Durcan, I confess to buying newspapers every day, and I consume various other radio and Web-based news services. I grew up with a foreign policy expert for a father, his office stacked high with clippings and microfilm reels of the *New York Times*, the *Washington Post*, the Iranian *Kayhan* and *Ettela'at*, and other newspapers, the radio constantly booming headlines and the TV blaring news shows, so my sympathy for poetry's attraction to, and irritation with, the news may have personal roots. Perhaps I was driven into poetry's arms partly because it wasn't the social scientific language of the father, though now, ironically, I find myself exploring poetry's journalistic bearings. Be that as it may, I have tried to extract from poems their implicit self-understanding in relation to the news, and it is a self-understanding often born of ambivalence.

While poetry sometimes plays with and against the secular, mimetic, and empirical imperatives of journalism—contemporary public history "objectively" reported—at other times, as I've been broadly hinting, it moves closer to the recursive and ritualistic norms of prayer. We have heard dialogic overtones of prayer in Heaney's reply to a journalist with rosary beads, Williams's news stories punctuated by "So be it," and Duncan's prophetic mythologizing of the Vietnam War. If poetry responds to current public events when it moves closer to the orbit of the news and assumes ceremonial qualities when drawn to prayer, it often fuses elements of each in a semiritualistic, semi-informational amalgam that exceeds both. Gerard Manley Hopkins's "Wreck of the *Deutschland*" bestrides news report and Catholic prayer; T. S. Eliot's *Waste Land* tells the news of post–World War I civilizational collapse in a language studded with Christian and Sanskrit prayer; and H.D.'s *Trilogy* includes both news of World War II bombings and prayers to a mother goddess. Ingeniously interfusing news and prayer, such poems span the declarative and the conative in linguistics, the constative and the performative in speech act theory.[128] Like the news, they vitally engage the present, at the same time that, like prayer, they address enduring fundamentals of existence. Poetry crosses the informational with the devotional, the present with deep time, mimesis with ritual. As the news that stays news, it bespeaks a "now" ambered in patterned language, the moment preserved and remade in arrangements of style, sound, and image.

3

POETRY AND PRAYER

THE LAST CHAPTER ended with the claim that poetry inhabits what could be schematized as a middle zone between the news and prayer. Given the differences between the news and prayer, the difficulty of straddling such a large discursive divide would seem to be enormous. After all, the news, typically cast in the third person, aims to provide an objective record of contemporary events in the secular world, while prayer, usually in the second person, is addressed to the divine and often secondarily to oneself. Empirical verifiability is the foundation of the news, but beliefs in prayer are seldom factually verifiable. The news transmits information, but when the deity addressed in prayer is omniscient, by definition no knowledge can be transmitted, because, as Kant wryly observes, the being addressed "has no need of any declaration regarding the inner disposition of the wisher," and as Jean-Louis Chrétien elaborates in his phenomenological analysis of prayer, "the function of speech is not in this case to communicate a piece of information or to transmit something we know to our invisible interlocutor."[1] As we saw earlier with poetry's spanning the differences between the novel's granularity and theory's abstractions, poetry's range and elasticity, despite its putative monologic narrowness, enables it to bridge discursive opposites—in this instance, to communicate like the news and transcend the communicative function of language like prayer, to respond to contemporary worldly events and engage the otherworldly, ultimately to cross empirical truth with belief. Although poetry shouldn't be confused with either prayer or the news, we learn something about it by examining how it interacts with, and departs from, the mimetic, presentist, and transmissive norms of the one and the ritualism and spirituality of the other. Poetry co-opts elements of both discursive forms, ultimately assimilating them to its own procedures and imperatives.

Modern and contemporary poetry's conflicted response to the news is intensified, as we've seen, by the media's discursive dominance and massive capitalization; so too, poetry's idiosyncrasy makes for ambivalences toward the institutional weight, religious doctrines, and communal rites and symbols that are often contexts of prayer. Sylvia Plath sounds a characteristically skeptical note of prayerlike antiprayer:

Oh God, I am not like you
In your vacuous black,
Stars stuck all over, bright stupid confetti.
Eternity bores me,
I never wanted it.

Empty, immobile, dull—Plath's God seems the antithesis of this quicksilver verse, fluidly coursing from one imaginative turn to another: "What I love is / The piston in motion."[2] Charles Simic addresses the deity with similar irreverence:

Boss of all bosses of the universe.
Mr. know-it-all, wheeler-dealer, wire-puller,
And whatever else you're good at.

Go ahead, shuffle your zeros tonight.
Dip in ink the comet's tails.
Staple the night with starlight.[3]

But even as they mock the star-maneuvering deity's power and pretensions, accusing him of dull vacuity and manipulative pomposity, these poets find themselves taking up the mode of prayerful address. Although Simic makes fun of worshipers in acts of petition and adoration, "begging you on their knees, / Sputtering endearments, / As if you were an inflatable, life-size doll," even he ends his poem with a self-reflexive glance at the vestiges of prayer in his antiprayer: "As I scribble this note to you in the dark." Both poetry and prayer can be described as scribbling in the dark because of the uncertainty of their audiences and the imponderability of their subject matter. "It's like fishing in the dark," Simic writes in another poem, "The hook left dangling / In the Great 'Nothing.'"[4]

Poetry can easily make use of prayer because of the genres' many interconnections, starting with their rhetorical stance as apostrophic discourses. Paul de Man argued that "the figure of address is recurrent" and perhaps even "paradigmatic" for poetry, and Jonathan Culler identified apostrophe with "lyric itself."[5] This influential body of lyric theory has been generative for poetry studies, but critics deploying it have largely shied away from the similarities between poetic apostrophe and the rhetorical structure of prayer. Analysis of the relationship between poetry and prayer—a surprisingly understudied area in humanities scholarship—needs to begin at this juncture. Kant writes that in prayerful "*address*, a human being assumes that this supreme object is present in person, or at least he poses (even inwardly) as though he were convinced of his presence, reckoning that, suppose this is not so, his posing can at least do no harm but might rather gain him favor."[6] As speech acts directed to an other, yet an other more veiled than a human interlocutor, poetry and prayer function simultaneously as acts of address, albeit partly suspended (hence address modulating into apostrophe), and as forms of meta-address, or images of voicing, because of the decontextualization of address from normal lines of human communication.

Further, in both poetry and prayer, address isn't directed only outward. Both genres frequently take the form of internal dialogue, the speaker self-dividing in two. Although prayer is addressed to the divine, when one prays, as Kant puts it, one speaks "within oneself and in fact *with oneself*, though allegedly all the more comprehensively with God." A person "caught unawares by somebody else," "gesturing in a way which indicates praying," "will fall into confusion or embarrassment," because "a human being found talking to himself immediately gives rise to the suspicion that he is having a slight fit of madness."[7] This last phrase may well bring to mind descriptions of Orphic inspiration, and Kant's surprised petitioner also recalls the artificiality and potential "embarrassment" of poetry's fictive structure of address (as in uses of what Culler calls "the pure *O* of undifferentiated voicing").[8] Like prayer's speech "within oneself and in fact *with oneself*," lyric poetry has often been conceived, at least since the Romantics, as an inwardly or self-directed mode of utterance. Having posed the question "What is Poetry?" John Stuart Mill famously defines it as speech "*over*heard": "Poetry is feeling confessing itself to itself in moments of solitude," "the natural fruit of solitude and meditation."[9] Yeats modifies but extends Mill's antithesis between poetry and the suasive or "heard" speech of "eloquence": "We make out of the quarrel with others, rhetoric, but of the quarrel with ourselves, poetry."[10] Even so, both prayer and poetry have a social dimension as well, so that the circuit of speech is never closed; at the very least, a fissure is opened for the addressed or eavesdropping other. Indeed, despite Mill's and Yeats's antitheses, poetry, especially in forms such as dramatic monologue, incorporates elements of suasive speech, and petitionary prayer has a strongly suasive character. Yet in both poetry and prayer, the rhetoric of persuasion is to some extent bracketed: we inspect the eloquence of Browning's murderers at a remove, and prayers meant to sway God run up against the knowledge of the deity's foreknowledge of any such petition.

The truth status of prayers and poems, moreover, differs from that of most declarative statements: according to Aristotle on prayer and I. A. Richards on poetry's pseudostatements, the utterances in both prayers and poems are neither true nor false.[11] We don't look for empirical evidence to corroborate or invalidate lines such as "Let the lamp affix its beam. / The only emperor is the emperor of ice-cream."[12] Poems often make use of what, as we saw in the last chapter, Roman Jakobson called "conative" language, oriented toward the addressee, such as the vocative and imperative ("Let the lamp affix its beam"), statements that "cardinally differ from declarative sentences" in not being "liable to a truth test."[13] Partly for this reason, from the perspective of scientific epistemology both poetry and prayer seem superfluous and even ridiculous, inassimilable to rational and empirical discourse. Instead, both genres turn partly in on themselves, intensifying rhythm and figuration, manipulating syntax and heightening diction. Their relation to reality is thickly mediated in both cases by generic histories going back thousands of years; they are long memoried and themselves memorable, as dramatized in recitation and performance.

"Absolutely unmixed attention is prayer," said Simone Weil,[14] and magnified awareness—to language, the world, feelings—has often been seen as part and parcel of poetry. Little wonder that W. H. Auden, whose "Horae Canonicae" sequence and other poems are patterned on Christian prayers, should write: "To pray is to pay attention or, shall we say, to 'listen' to someone or something other than oneself. Whenever a man so concentrates his attention—be it on a landscape, or a poem or a geometrical problem or an idol or the True God—that he completely forgets his own ego and desires in listening to what the other has to say to him, he is praying."[15] This concept of prayer as openness to the other, as intense listening, as making of oneself a vessel for the other's speech, recalls many descriptions not only of prayer but also of the poet's relation to the muse. Both the worshiper seized by prayer and the writer possessed by poetic inspiration lose their everyday selves and potentially rediscover themselves anew in the grips of nonnormative, semicommunicative utterance. While there are many inadequacies in, and exceptions to, these and other generalizations about prayer and poetry, from Kant to Auden, they can at least help tease out some of the shared expectations that are often brought to bear on both genres.

Even so, important differences between these discursive cousins will also emerge over the course of this chapter and can be outlined here, forestalling any simple assimilation of one genre to the other. First, poetry and prayer often differ in degrees of sociality. Although they both have deep histories, the long-evolving communal and institutional contexts of prayer, as I've indicated, diverge from the idiosyncratic individualism of lyric poetry, even when rooted in literary coterie or school or movement, or responsive to real or anticipated audiences. Writing of the eighteenth-century English hymn, or sung prayer of worship, Helen Gardner states, with implications for prayer more generally: "It should not be too individual, too original, in its images and phrasing. Its symbols should be stock symbols, from the Bible and the liturgy. . . . People . . . do not want fresh insights from hymns, but a sense of their unity with their fellow-believers, with their fathers and forefathers, and with those who will come after them."[16] By contrast, readers of poetry have long prized originality, freshness, and peculiarity of language and insight. When A. R. Ammons titles a poem "Hymn," he activates familiar associations of ritually sung worship and communal coalescence, even as his conditionals ("if I find you"), indeterminacies ("you"), ambivalences ("if I find you I will have to leave the earth" or "to stay with the earth"), and luxuriant diction (from "noctilucent clouds" to "microvilli sporangia") decisively mark this work and the four "hymns" that follow as soi-disant hymns better suited to a book of poems than to a hymnal.[17] In Christianity, as in other faiths, there are, of course, many different forms of prayer: private or communally codified, scriptural or made up, memorized and spontaneous, sung or spoken, silent or spoken or uttered silently with movement of the lips, mental or accompanied with physical enactment (genuflection, seated, standing, etc.), brief or lasting multiple days, and so forth.[18] But even if silent, mental, and spontaneous, a private prayer that seemed to revel too much in its verbal and formal ingenuity might seem to strain against prayerful norms.

Second, poetry and prayer differ in their relative fictiveness. As A. D. Nuttall writes of George Herbert, what seem to be "prayers in poetic form are really poems which imitate or represent prayer," "dramatic fictions, with . . . a fictional addressee within the poem—God—and a real addressee outside the poem—the reader." They are "pictures of the way a man might pray,"[19] or in Bakhtin's terms, images of the language of prayer: as cited above, they are able "to sound simultaneously both outside it and within it, to talk about it and at the same time to talk in and with it."[20] In comparison with prayer, poetry often has additional layers of fictionality, additional devices of distanciation and framing. Embedded in Leslie Marmon Silko's "Prayer to the Pacific" is an obeisant apostrophe to the Ocean that closely resembles prayer ("I return to you   turquoise   the red coral you sent us, / sister spirit of Earth"), but a surrounding frame situates this speech act in a personal narrative ("I traveled to the ocean") and a mythological prehistory ("Thirty thousand years ago / Indians came riding across the ocean / carried by giant sea turtles").[21] We overhear Silko's speaker dramatically enacting a prayer to the spirit of the Pacific. The apostrophe within a poem is self-fictionalizing, unlike the address to the divine in prayer. "To read apostrophe as sign of a fiction which knows its own fictive nature," writes Culler of lyric poetry, "is to stress its optative character, its impossible imperatives: commands which in their explicit impossibility figure events in and of fiction."[22] The imperatives in both prayers and poems are often optative, but in prayers, unlike in poems, they are not necessarily believed to be "impossible." Petitionary prayers, for example, are "performative utterances," in J. L. Austin's terms: they are verbal actions that do not merely describe or report but do something, change something.[23] Although they may lack the visibly world-changing character of performatives such as marriage vows or contractual statements, their utterance, though optative, still has illocutionary force. Poems incorporate the performativity of prayer but stand outside and inspect it; they give voice to prayer but fictionalize it. Although poetry is sometimes loosely described as "performative" in Austin's sense of the term, it is more properly understood as performative utterance aesthetically held in suspended animation. It is a ritual-like act that has been self-consciously aestheticized.

Third, they differ in their degrees of self-consciousness. Self-reflexivity has long been believed a feature of lyric poems, whereas prayer has often been characterized in terms of self-forgetfulness: successful prayer may be seen as extinguishing itself in approaching the divine, often in silence. While relying heavily on the rhetorical structure of prayer, Geoffrey Hill's prayerlike poems, for example, often bristle with self-ironizing verbal paradoxes and self-materializing verbal knots. In his poem "A Prayer to the Sun," three crosslike concrete stanzas descend down the page, the last of which calls out:

> Blind Sun
> o u r r a v a g e r
> bless us
> so that
> we sleep.[24]

While echoing traditional prayers for protection at nightfall, Hill builds on the verbal tension in Milton's catachresis "Blind mouths!" and ironically addresses not the divine and all-seeing "Son" but the destructive, unseeing, and night-dispersing sun as guardian over sleep. Together with the graphic visualization of the cross on the page (formed by a typographically distended horizontal word beam), the stanza's paradoxes and verbal materiality call attention to its poeticity. The verbal action of poetry is often inscribed with a "meta-" layer, speaking both within and outside itself, whereas prayer typically immerses itself in the divine object of its contemplation, worship, or petition. Building on rabbinic hermeneutics, Kinereth Meyer and Rachel Salmon Deshen comment: "Resisting absorption in paraphrase, poetic words retain their materiality and keep our attention riveted upon the 'untranslatable' remainder that is always left after their referentiality has been explored.

Even poetry that talks about ultimate Unity and the absorption of the many in the One seems to be self-reflexively aware of itself as a non-transcendent human language."[25]

Fourth, as this quotation suggests, they differ in their weighting of signifier and signified. Although language and form are intensified in both poetry and prayer, their function is more vehicular in prayer. In prayer, language and form are scaffolding that may help bring the worshiper into the presence of the divine; in poetry, they are paramount. To a greater extent than in prayer, the medium of poetry is its message. As William T. Noon, S.J., summarizes, "[I]n poetry the image is a sign which as a rule arrests our attention to its own proper validity precisely as a sign. In prayer the image is usually unarresting save insofar as it serves to remind one of an inscrutable other reality, which no sign, however affirmative, can ever fully signify or reveal."[26] Eliot writes in "Little Gidding":

> And prayer is more
> Than an order of words, the conscious occupation
> Of the praying mind, or the sound of the voice praying.[27]

By contrast, even this prayer-defining and prayer-enriched poem demonstrates that in poetry, the syntax ("order of words"), the self-scrutiny of verbal artifice ("conscious occupation"), the sonorities and resonances, chimes and rhymes and rhythms ("the sound of the voice"), are of paramount significance.

Because of poetry's dalliance with the sign, its preoccupation with aesthetics, its nonconformism, materiality, and often ludic propensities, the lyric muse has periodically come under suspicion in stricter varieties of Christianity, Islam, Hinduism, Judaism, and various other religious cultures. Conversely, as we see below, prayer has sometimes come under suspicion even in poems that seek to appropriate its practices and attitudes. Poems that adapt prayer often guard themselves against allowing the religious intergenre to overwhelm poetry's restless creativity, aesthetic prerogatives, and formal contrivances. Samuel Johnson provides, in Helen Gardner's words, "the fullest and most carefully reasoned expression of the view that there is an incompatibility between worship and prayer, that is religious activity, and poetry."[28] Encapsulating the difference between poetry and prayer, in his life of Edmund Waller he articulated what he saw as the problem of devotional poetry: "The essence of poetry is invention; such invention as, by producing something unexpected, surprises and delights. The topicks of devotion are few, and being few are universally known; but, few as they are, they can be made no more; they can receive no grace from novelty of sentiment, and very little from novelty of expression."[29] If Johnson were strictly right, the prayer-poem would be a contradiction in terms; but he powerfully illuminates a tension inherent within prayer-poetry, an ambivalence that we will trace through a variety of modern and contemporary examples. Addressing the "claim that devotion is incompatible with invention," Kevin Hart counters that there are "many strong poems that are also prayers," even as he concedes the tension: "The metaphor required to express the transcendence of God can distract writer and reader from the truth of the faith."[30] In a prayerful poem, the aesthetic risks leaping out ahead of the devotional.

Despite the long enmeshment between the liturgical and the literary, as indicated by the close interrelations among hymns, psalms, and odes, or more broadly between poetry and charms, chants, magic, and runes, the resistance to conventional forms in much modern and contemporary poetry has amplified poetry's sometimes latent ambivalence toward prayer, even when imbued with it. In general, modern and contemporary poetry is less obviously akin to prayer than were, say, sixteenth-century lyrics by Herbert, Donne, Crashaw, and Vaughan, or seventeenth-, eighteenth-, and nineteenth-century lyrics by Bradstreet, Wheatley, and Dickinson, let alone the *Vedas*, the *Kanteletar*, the Psalms, ancient Greek hymns to the gods, Rumi's *Masnavi*, bhakti poetry, Christian chants and hymns such as the "Dies Irae," and so forth.[31] Not as many distinctly modern and contemporary poems overtly resemble psalms, hymns, litanies, or rosaries as in earlier eras, when the secular and religious were less sharply divided. Works that court these resemblances may sometimes hem themselves in. Even after Eliot had written poems infused with Anglo-Catholic prayer, he credited the view "that when you qualify poetry as 'religious' you are indicating very clear limitations. For the great majority of people who love poetry, '*religious* poetry' is a variety of *minor* poetry."[32] If we were to focus the exploration of prayer and poetry on twentieth-century "religious" or "spiritual poets" such as Thomas Merton and Kahlil Gibran, we might not get very far in understanding the broader intertwining of prayer with distinctively modern and contemporary poems. Yet one strand of this chapter's argument is that some of the fundamental characteristics of prayer survive, albeit often twisted or disguised, in many poems that turn divine homage on its head, or that seem resolutely secular, or that flaunt artifice over devotion. Conversely, I also argue that modern and contemporary prayer-poems often make visible long-standing, if often buried, frictions between prayer and poetry. To get at the intricate tensions and continuities between them, I focus on a handful of examples, both Western and postcolonial, reluctantly setting aside an abundance of other poets whose work could be explored through this lens, from Robert Frost, Hart Crane, and Stevie Smith to Derek Walcott, Allen Ginsberg, and Anne Carson.[33] My hope is that some of the chapter's intergeneric strategies of reading will have implications for poems and poets beyond the few I'm able to take up.

POETRY AND PRAYER, FROM GERARD MANLEY HOPKINS TO CHARLES WRIGHT

Having begun with poems such as Plath's and Simic's, which thumb their noses at prayer, let us turn to some major modern and contemporary poems that represent themselves as drawing sustenance and inspiration from it. Gerard Manley Hopkins, a Jesuit priest and one of the great progenitors of twentieth-century verse, is perhaps the most obvious example of a "modern" poet who fuses poetry and prayer (though writing in the last decades of the nineteenth century, and so also a Victorian poet, he was largely unpublished before Robert Bridges's 1918 collection). His poems are now frequently reproduced in collections of Jesuit prayer and on religious websites. His translation of the seventeenth-century prayer "O Deus, ego amo te" circulates widely, a prayer that begins with an emphatic address and adoration, "O God, I love thee, I love thee—," and chronicles Jesus's suffering "nails and lance, / Mocked and marred countenance, / Sorrows passing number."[34] Similarly, a refrain in Hopkins's "Rosa Mystica" runs as follows: *"In the gardens of God, in the daylight divine, / Find me a place by thee, mother of mine"* (107). Many of Hopkins's poems resemble traditional prayers in a number of ways. The aforementioned commonalities between poetry and prayer can all be found, including address, internalized dialogue, speech overheard, untestable belief, extrarational inspiration, memorability, heightened diction, intimacy, and magnified attention. Specifically in Roman Catholic theology, according to a canonical account, prayer or *oratio*, "meaning petition, request, pleading," is "in the strict sense, the filial expression of one's desires for self and others to the heavenly Father from whom come all good things, natural or supernatural," and "in the widest sense, it is speaking with God."[35] Many of Hopkins's poems can be seen as petitions or pleas, expressions of filial gratitude, or colloquies with God. The ends of prayer are "adoration, thanksgiving, propitiation, and petition," the last of which is an "obligation," "a necessary means of salvation,"[36] and such speech acts are recognizable in Hopkins's poems beginning with his first fully achieved work, "The Wreck of the *Deutschland*" ("Be adored among men, / God"; "I admire thee, master of the tides") (121, 127). Finally, prayer is characterized as being "devout," meaning "humble and submissive," "attentive," "full of confidence in God," and "persevering"—descriptors often applicable to Hopkins's poems.[37] His poems draw nourishment and energy from the orthodox ingredients of Catholic prayer.

Take a late sonnet that begins, like "O Deus, ego amo te," by addressing its praise to God: "Thou art indeed just, Lord" (201). At least in the poem's beginning, elements of prayer in general and of traditional Catholic prayer in particular vividly structure the rhetoric. In the first assertion ("Thou art indeed just, Lord"), the "devout" speaker, both "humble and submissive," speaks to God in the mode of adoration and seems "full of confidence in God." The sonnet evidences the intimacy ("Thou") and magnified attention (especially to the speaker's inner world) that we associate with both poetry and prayer. As often in prayer, and more explicitly than in most of Hopkins's poems, this poem draws language directly from the Bible, specifically Jeremiah 12:1, as cited in the Latin epigraph that begins *"Justus quidem tu es, Domine."* Other points of intersection between poetry and prayer are in evidence through the poem. Addressed to the divine being, this utterance also comes to have the quality of internal dialogue, or even self-divided wrangling. The speaker's praise, blame, and claims to misery aren't verifiable in the same way that a news report would be. In many ways, the poem evidences the hyphen in the term "prayer-poem."

But it also reveals the strains and striations that traverse that hyphen. By the end of the first line, as emphasized by the enjambed verb, "if I contend / With thee," the speaker's tone is no longer either humble or submissive, and by the next line Hopkins has wrenched the word "just" from the divine addressee and fitted it to this ardent complaint: "so what I plead is just." Frustrated, dispirited, smoldering with anger, the speaker enunciates a twofold grievance: that sinners, though stupefied and imprisoned by their passions, are allowed to prosper ("the sots and thralls of lust / . . . thrive"); and that he, though devoting his life to God, fails at everything. "Wert thou my enemy, O thou my friend," he asks, "How wouldst thou worse, I wonder, than thou dost / Defeat, thwart me?" Complaint is, of course, a long-lived feature of prayer, and Hopkins tempers his remonstrance by addressing God as an intimate "friend" and more formal "Sir," as well as by couching his accusations in the biblically authorized rhetoric of Jeremiah and the "scriptural tradition of *interrogatio.*"[38] But neither the conditional protasis ("Wert thou") nor the affectionate appellation ("friend") fully blunts the force of "enemy," an epithet often reserved in a Christian context for Satan; in a sermon, for example, Hopkins refers to those in sin as "GOD'S ENEMY," "under Satan's standard and enlisted there."[39] And Hopkins gives Jeremiah's protest a more personal edge in the not merely hypothetical charge that God does indeed "Defeat, thwart" him. As William Empson said of Hopkins's "The Windhover," the speaker holds opposite views "with agony in his mind."[40] The tone of "Thou art indeed just, Lord" twists between would-be intimacy and strained formality, humble concession and self-assertive accusation, resignation and resentment.

Having been ensnared in conflicted reflections on divine (in)justice that have delayed the Petrarchan *volta* to the middle of the sonnet's ninth line, the verse suddenly quickens in describing the generative natural life from which the poet feels shut out: "See, banks and brakes / Now, leavèd how thick! lacèd they are again / With fretty chervil, look, and fresh wind shakes // Them." Hopkins unleashes the poetry of his poetry when the focus is no longer God or the petitioner's merits but the overbrimming life that he ostensibly scorns. Turning from the octave's abstract complaint to the sestet's vivid description, the poem also shifts from questions to imperatives ("See," "Look"), from a suspended, iterative time to the immediate present ("Now"), from verse with little internal sonic patterning to the alliterative rush of *banks/brakes*, *leavèd/lacèd, fretty/fresh, chervil/shakes*—the last two pairs interlacing like the chervil they evoke, an herb apparently from the Greek "rejoicing leaf."[41] Poetically instancing the generative lushness that taunts and confounds him, the poet sets sounds to breeding other sounds. The "poetry" of the poetry and the "prayer" of the poetry turn in different directions.

Finally, the poem impedes this sonic, rhetorical, and imagistic rush with choppy syntax, a series of negations (*not, no, not*), and a painful contrast hinged on bilabial stops: "birds build—but not I build; no, but strain, / Time's eunuch, and not breed one work that wakes." Still, "one work that wakes" from this personal wasteland is the very work we read, the fulfillment of the poem's final petition: "Mine, O thou lord of life, send my roots rain." The fulfillment recorded by the poem may be less spiritual than literary, less like the fruition of prayer than of invocation, since at poem's end the dramatic speaker still languishes in despair. In his poetic if not devotional success, Hopkins has generated fresh aesthetic life out of grievance, anger, and desolation, has revitalized the Petrarchan sonnet (his betraying lover not a coy mistress but God), and has revivified Jeremiah's biblical imagery ("Thou hast planted [the wicked], and they have taken root; they prosper and bring forth fruit" [Jeremiah 12:1–2, Douay-Rheims Bible]). In the story the poem tells, a "fresh wind" helps other life forms thrive, though not the poet (who will in fact die a few months later); even so, the sonnet's figurative, tonal, and formal inventiveness evidences the infusion of this very poem with imaginative afflatus.

The fracturing within Hopkins's prayer-poetry of what we might crudely label the spiritual and the poetic makes visible a split latent within poems that may share close family resemblances with prayer. This is not to say, with Blake on Milton, that the reason Hopkins "wrote in fetters when he wrote of Angels & God, and at liberty when of Devils & Hell, is because he was a true Poet and of the Devils party without knowing it," but that perhaps he was more of poetry's party than the arguments of his prayerlike poems acknowledge.[42] Compared with the stock imagery and phrasing that characterize his "Rosa Mystica," and indeed many standard Catholic prayers, his poetry takes flight in rich aesthetic play—figuration, sound patterning, tonal oscillation, psychic drama, and generic remaking—that overspills the traditional boundaries of prayer. In Dr. Johnson's terms, invention outstrips devotion. "All strong poets," in Harold Bloom's insightful overstatement, "must ruin the sacred truths to fable and old song, precisely because the essential condition for poetic strength is that the new song, one's own, always must be a song of one's self."[43] If Bloom and Johnson are even partly right, then the tension between poetry and "the sacred truths" should be detectable much earlier. In his first "Jordan" poem, Herbert had tried to affiliate himself not with poetry's "fictions only and false hair" but with the plainness of devotion, resorting by poem's end to the starkest prayer: *My God, My King.* But, as Nuttall writes, this "poetry is crucified by inconsistency. It is, necessarily, poetically parasitic upon the devices it so austerely renounces . . . because that which is renounced is finally poetry, *simpliciter,*" and "*My God, My King*" may be all he feels he needs to say, but "*that* is not a poem."[44] Hopkins isn't afflicted by the Puritan anxieties about art that beset

Herbert, but even his poetry, though somewhat sheltered from these issues by the Catholic doctrine of the incarnation, is productively strained by the push and pull between aesthetics and piety, creative self-assertion and ascetic self-immolation.

The use of "Thou art indeed just, Lord," a poem sometimes numbered among Hopkins's sonnets of desolation,[45] to gauge the relation in his work between poetry and prayer may well seem to skew the results, given the severe bleakness of these late poems. "Pied Beauty," a poem of exultant thanksgiving, often read as a hymn to creation akin to Psalm 148, is a different kind of poem that may well seem to coincide more fully with expectations of prayer (144). Even though it isn't in the second-person mode of colloquy with God but of third-person exclamation, beginning "Glory be to God for dappled things," it meets many other traditional prerequisites for Catholic prayer, including "filial expression of one's desires for self and others to the heavenly Father from whom come all good things, natural or supernatural"; adoration, as indicated by its opening rendition of the Jesuit motto attributed to St. Ignatius of Loyola, *Ad majorem Dei gloriam*; and thanksgiving, as an expression of gratitude for God's multifarious excellence. "Every prayer," Catholic scholarship explains, "is an act of homage in which man bows before God, recognizing that all good things come from him."[46] "Pied Beauty" has been seen as so imbued with Duns Scotus's theology of *haecceitas*, the "thisness" of everything as unique and a total image of its Creator, that it has been called "Hopkins's Scotist manifesto."[47] At the simplest level, the poem's listing of different items for which the speaker expresses gratitude structurally resembles prayers of thanksgiving. Its use of well-worn devotional phrases, bookending the content of the poem between the theological exclamation "Glory be to God" and the injunction "Praise him," helps contain the intervening idiosyncratic language and sprawling content within the more codified language of prayer. The ringing repetitions of "all" also serve to encompass heterogeneity within a unifying devotional framework. The four elements further structurally undergird the first stanza: after the initial ejaculation, the succeeding descriptive lines are organized around air ("skies"), water ("trout that swim"), fire ("Fresh-firecoal chestnut-falls"), and earth ("Landscape"), though also crossing the lines between them. The poet's manipulation of sound also suggests an underlying unity, alliteratively yoking together opposites such as "swift, slow; sweet, sour; adazzle, dim."

But even in this joyously reverent poem, something of Dr. Johnson's tension between devotion and invention is perceptible. When we compare the densely packed figurative, imagistic, and sonic texture of Hopkins's "Pied Beauty" with the inherited phrases and images in a prayer such as his rendering of "O Deus, ego amo te," the divergence between a poem's inevitably stronger orientation toward the aesthetic and prayer's toward devotion becomes apparent. Unlike the transparent prayer, Hopkins's poem is extraordinarily compressed, to the extent that parts of it demand considerable interpretive labor. This compression is evident both at the macrocosmic structural level—a "curtal" (curtailed or abbreviated) sonnet scrunched down to a perfectly proportioned six-line octave and four-and-a-half-line sestet—and at the microcosmic level of poetic language: we must linger over the compounded compound of "Fresh-firecoal chestnut-falls" to unpack the proportional metaphor of nuts within burrs compared with fiery insides of burning coals.

Attention to connotations of key words further reveals the fruitful jostling between poetry and prayer within this prayer-poem. The title's participial adjective, "Pied," has Catholic resonances, having originally applied to the black-and-white coloring of a friar's habit; but a rarer meaning of this synonym for dappled, "Variable, inconstant; flawed," suggests a crosscurrent that may also flow beneath the poem's surface, the question whether its aesthetically overcharged celebration of multiplicity may risk straying from the proper object of devotion.[48] In a poem alert to the embedding of "all" in "falls" and "fallow," of "pie" in "pied" and "pieced," the word "appled" can also be seen tucked inside "dappled" (like the French *pommelé*, a past participle that historically preceded the finite verb), recalling the primal abundance and straying in the Garden of Eden.[49] In the abbreviated sestet, Hopkins dares to celebrate "Whatever is fickle," a word that connotes not only changeability and inconstancy and unreliability, of the sort that poets regularly decry, as "Fortune . . . fickle" (Shakespeare) or "fickle Chance" (Milton), but also, as indicated by its cognate, "deceit," in *fickle*'s older meaning, "False, deceitful, treacherous."[50] Hopkins again reins in such meanings with his penultimate assertion that God's "beauty is past change." But this unifying net may not be enough to contain the poem's figurative and imagistic leaps, its "shocks" and "ecstatically instressing" perceptions, in Helen Vendler's words.[51] After all, this verbal artifact's showily changeable and varied texture is the poem's most immediate example of "All things counter, original, spare, strange." Indeed, in its first two figures the poem knowingly winks at acts of inscription. To see the cloud-speckled sky as being spotted, streaked, or even branded ("brinded") like a cow's hide; to attribute to trout engravings ("all in stipple") that resemble miniature flowers ("rose-moles"); to see in things that change from swift to slow, sweet to sour, bright to dim the variegations of freckles—"freckled (who knows how?) / With" such opposites: by these and other imaginative somersaults, invention may surpass devotion, even within an all-encompassing Scotian framework that would enfold the one within the other and a theology that would see all creation, including the poet's, as imitating and honoring God's. There are many reasons for the tensions and distortions of Hopkins's poetry, but among them is the underlying friction between the overlapping but divergent imperatives of *oratio* and *poesis*, imperatives his poems forcefully yoke together while exhibiting their magnetic pull toward different compass points. Hence his example will be generative for later poets raised in other religious traditions, such as Charles Wright and Agha Shahid Ali, particularly in their attempts to straddle these interlocking but not always harmonizing genres.

Another modern Christian poet who frequently interleaved poetry and prayer might have been expected to relish Hopkins's verse, but T. S. Eliot said of Hopkins's seemingly settled Christianity: "[I]n the matter of devotional poetry a good deal more is at issue than just the purity and strength of the author's devotional passion. To be a 'devotional poet' is a limitation: a saint limits himself by writing poetry, and a poet who confines himself to even this subject matter is limiting himself too."[52] Notwithstanding Eliot's reading, skeptical countercurrents course beneath the "purity" of the "devotional" surface of Hopkins's poetry, as we've seen, and both poets can be thought of as realizing what Eliot declared, in his valediction to Valéry, the highest stage possible for civilized people: "to unite the profoundest scepticism with the deepest faith."[53] If, indeed, as Eliot also claimed, "doubt and uncertainty are merely a variety of belief," then the fusion of skepticism with faith is part of faith itself.[54] But more important for Eliot than the attempted articulation of faith in poetry was poetry's close relationship with ritual, since he thought, as he put it, in a twist on Pater's famous claim *"All art constantly aspires to the condition of music," "all* art emulates the condition of ritual. That is what it comes from and to that it must always return for nourishment."[55] Hence the ritual performance of prayer plays a strong role in Eliot's poetry, though it is a verbal rite that his poetry often fragments, decontextualizes, and suspends. As early as Josiah Royce's seminar, Eliot was alert to the irreconcilable differences between the perspectives of a believing performer and an outside observer of a ritual, between religious feelings, purposes, and intentions and the "external order in ritual and creed," and yet it is these differences that his prayer-infused poems straddle.[56] They are one of the most fruitful outcomes of the seemingly impossible commingling of skepticism with ritualism.

The kinship between prayer and much of Eliot's late poetry fits neatly into the narrative of his 1927 conversion to Anglo-Catholicism, but even in his preconversion poetry, prayer plays a significant role amid the jumble of multitudinous discourses. The early poetry often draws on the ritual energies of prayer while immobilizing them in an icy reserve—a distancing that persists, as we will also see, even in the later, more obviously prayerful poetry. Quoting a passage from Dante's *Purgatorio* (a passage also cited in *The Waste Land*, "Ash-Wednesday," and elsewhere), Eliot chose as the title for an early volume of poems the phrase "Now I pray you," or *Ara Vus [Vos] Prec*, uttered in Dante's Purgatory by the Occitan troubadour Arnaut Daniel, who is imagined as doing penance for lust.[57] Daniel's word for "pray," *prec*, calls attention to Eliot's speakers' clamorous performances of precatory longing and their precariousness as suffering purgatorial subjects. In ventriloquizing Dante ventriloquizing Daniel, Eliot's title tropes poetry as multiply framed purgatorial prayer and so associates poetry with prayer while inserting an ironic distance. Poetry is like prayer in the urgency of its utterance, but it encases such speech acts in the de- and recontextualizing, language-foregrounding medium of poetry.

Some of Eliot's most ambitious preconversion poems move toward climax and closure with structurally embedded prayer—one of many genres, including drama, song, opera, philosophy, and poetry itself, that this bricoleur poet plucks out of context and inserts into the body of his work, where it protrudes, not wholly digested. At the pivotal end of "The Fire Sermon" section of *The Waste Land*, Eliot quotes from Augustine's grateful praise of God in *The Confessions*: "And I, though I speak and see this, entangle my steps with these outward beauties; but Thou pluckest me out, O Lord, Thou pluckest me out; *because Thy loving-kindness is before my eyes.* For I am taken miserably, and Thou pluckest me out mercifully."[58] In Eliot's poem, as in his appropriation of Daniel's *"ara vos prec,"* Augustine's prayer of thanksgiving turns into a desperate plea for salvation from the fires of lust, an utterance of longing to transcend the debasement of desire in sexual encounters such as those between the typist and the clerk, between Elizabeth and Leicester. Intensifying the speech act of prayer as address to God, Eliot introduces the quote with an extra vocative, "O Lord." But in a strategy Eliot repeats elsewhere, one version of the repeated line is truncated, as if to leave the prayer suspended: "O Lord Thou pluckest me out / O Lord Thou pluckest."[59] The struggle between entanglement in "outward beauties" and prayerful abjection, between aesthetics and asceticism, drives the poem. Surrounding Augustine's prayer with lines about the "burning" of desire and emotion in the Buddha's Fire Sermon, Eliot rhymes two religious discourses uttered by representative figures of vastly different cultures. As he puts it in a note: "The collocation of these two representatives of eastern and western asceticism, as the culmination of this part of the poem, is not an accident" (note to line 309). Whereas prayer typically issues from a single religious context, Eliot's transcultural straddling unmoors Augustine's prayer and changes it from a purposive speech act into a would-be prayer, a figure for the yearnings of, and for, prayer. For Eliot and other modern subjects, whose comparative awareness of various religious cultures opens a fissure in their relation to a single inherited or chosen religion, prayer becomes, as emphasized by *The Waste Land*, a dialogized discourse that can be understood and practiced only as one among the many.

Just as the poem's climactic third section comes to a close with prayer, so too the entire poem closes with a Sanskrit prayer, the *shanti* mantra that wills peace by performing it verbally and mentally: "Shantih   shantih   shantih" (line 433). Far from being incidental, the concluding prayer reframes the entire poem: all the preceding violent discordance is suddenly seen from the outside. Adapting a phrase from Philippians, Eliot attempted in a note to translate the mantra into Christian terms, even as, with characteristic alertness to the impossibility of dissolving the differences between Eastern and Western philosophies traversed by his poetry, he mocked himself for thinking there could be a cross-cultural equivalent: "'The Peace which passeth understanding' is a feeble translation of the content of this word." After unleashing a cacophony of twisted and bitten-off utterances, Eliot reasserts in the concluding line poetry's connection with ritual, which "it comes from" and to which "it must always return for nourishment." But by casting the ritual speech act in a language unknown to most of his English-reading audience, by snipping off the *om* that would usually precede the concluding prayer, and by leaving open the graphic space (a blank line in the original manuscript and printing) and the metaphysical gap between the final Sanskrit willing-of-peace and the verbal, psychic, and cultural turmoil that has come before, Eliot also displaces the ritual prayer from any context in which it could possess full performative efficacy.[60] At least in its modern guise, the prayer in poetry is uncanny, unhoused from religious doctrine, defamiliarized and deinstrumentalized.

Like *The Waste Land*, "The Hollow Men" is a five-part poem in which the final section turns to prayer and in which the disjunction between the first four parts and the conclusion is marked. This time the quoted prayer isn't in Sanskrit but in English, from the central prayer of Christendom, the Lord's Prayer or Our Father. Eliot unusually justifies the repeated line *"For Thine is the Kingdom"* along the right-hand margin, setting it off from the rest of the poetic text.[61] Like the *shanti* mantra, the doxology, or short verse praising God ("For Thine is the kingdom, The power, and the glory, For ever and ever. Amen"), is both part of the religious discourse that precedes it and yet outside it: sometimes the Book of Common Prayer doesn't print it, as if extrinsic to the Lord's Prayer, and sometimes it includes it, as if integral to the prayer.[62] Returning to the doxology after an intervening right-justified quotation from Joseph Conrad's *An Outcast of the Islands*, *"Life is very long"* (85), Eliot produces a graphically and audibly fractured version:

> For Thine is
> Life is
> For Thine is the (86)

Whether stripped of its subject ("kingdom") or of its adjectival predicative ("long"), the devotional act stalls. Repeating "For Thine is" and merely adding the article "the," the poem underscores the prayer's inability to advance. Prayer devolves from a ritual speech act, which would join the speaker with God, into a stutter, an utterance unable to will even itself into completion. As Robert Crawford observes, Eliot's "blasphemous" version of the prayer is "an anti–Lord's Prayer": "Shockingly juxtaposed with an apparently childish survival of a primitive chant, the Lord's Prayer grows increasingly fragmented."[63] The solemn repetitions of prayer are joined with manic repetitions of a nursery rhyme, Eliot's version of "Here We Go round the Mulberry Bush." He replaces the rhyme's deciduous flora with a cactus, the prickly pear, suited to the hollow men's desiccated world, and he returns to this childlike rhythm in a bleak twist on "This is the way we clap our hands" in "This is the way the world ends" (86). The dynamic discourses of prayer and nursery rhyme are played against a series of abstract dichotomies that demarcate a paralytic, Prufrockian no-man's-land ("Between the idea / And the reality / Between the motion / And the act," etc. [85]). The performative language of prayer and of children's ritual shifts the emphasis of the poem's preceding dryly descriptive sections, as if to propel the speaker out of passivity and stasis, but the collaging of sampled prayer with twisted nursery rhyme and philosophical abstraction saps the potency of the devotional language. Here, as elsewhere in his preconversion poetry, Eliot summons and makes use of the ritual energies of prayer, but his skepticism, dialogism, and multiperspectivism take the speaker outside the ritual act of attempted communion with the divine. Poetry is broken prayer, stuttered adoration, would-be thanksgiving. It is the echo of a half-enacted ritual, with multiple reverberations. It is too caught up in shifting discourses and stammering signifiers to transcend itself in fusion with God.

Unlike the skeptical fracturing and collaging of prayer in Eliot's early poetry, his postconversion poetry may well be presumed to deliver full-throated devotional speech and to return poetry to genuine prayer as part of the ritualism that he thought nourished all art. After all, this is the Eliot who, according to Barry Spurr, availed himself of the seven sacraments of Anglo-Catholicism and the Catholic Church ("baptism and confirmation, eucharist, holy orders, matrimony, penance and extreme unction"), except for the seeking of orders.[64] This is the Eliot who praised Bishop Lancelot Andrewes's prayers as illustrating "devotion to private prayers (Andrewes is said to have passed nearly five hours a day in prayer) and to public ritual."[65] This is the Eliot who was absorbed in the purgative mysticism of St. John of the Cross's dark night of the soul. And this is the Eliot who, as Ronald Schuchard has shown, gradually developed into an admirer of Ignatius's *Spiritual Exercises* and especially of Herbert's prayer-infused sequence *The Temple*.[66] Parts of inherited prayers are heard in Eliot's later poems: "Ash-Wednesday," for example, quotes the close of the Hail Mary: "Pray for us sinners now and at the hour of our death / Pray for us now and at the hour of our death."[67] As Gardner notes, this poem's spiritual aspiration "is expressed mainly in phrases taken from the classic prayers of Western Christianity, and hardly at all in the poet's own words."[68] Drawing on the Catholic litany to the Virgin Mary, the poem addresses her, "Lady of silences" (91); it cries out humbly, "Lord, I am not worthy / Lord, I am not worthy / but speak the word only" (93); it beseeches, "Will the veiled sister pray / For children at the gate / Who will not go away and cannot pray" (96). In his choruses to *The Rock*, the speaker petitions: "O Lord, deliver me from the man of excellent intention and impure heart" and "Preserve me from the enemy who has something to gain: and from the friend who has something to lose," while also offering thanks: "O Father we welcome your words," and "O Light Invisible, we give Thee thanks for Thy great glory!"[69] Examples of quoted prayers, half-quoted prayers, and made-up prayers could be multiplied at length. There can be no doubt that prayer is one of the most prominent discourses energizing Eliot's late poetry.

Let us single out a significant example to help us consider more precisely some complexities in Eliot's use of prayer in the late poetry. In *Four Quartets*, the fourth part of "The Dry Salvages," which "uses boldly the language of Christian prayer," has been called "a prayer to Our Lady, addressed . . . as Queen of Heaven," "a prayer to the Virgin of the one Annunciation," and "a prayer, to the Lady who conceived the Word, to pray for all who are in the sea's power."[70] It begins:

> Lady, whose shrine stands on the promontory,
> Pray for all those who are in ships, those
> Whose business has to do with fish, and
> Those concerned with every lawful traffic
> And those who conduct them.[71]

This lyric in "The Dry Salvages" seems indistinguishable from petitionary prayer, a speech act willing Mary's protection for sea-voyagers and those they leave behind. Mimicking a prayer for the precarious, Eliot sets up a self-returning devotional circuit: the speaker beseeches Mary to "pray," to perform a "prayer," his intercession preparing the way for the intercessor's wished-for intercession. Yet as a poem, the supplication is not only an oral speech act. Drawing attention to its arrangement in lines (four in pentameter and one in dimeter), the lyric includes line endings that are strangely off kilter. Instead of marrying lineation to syntax and thus dissolving graphic text into devotional utterance, the poem obtrusively enjambs words such as "those" and "and" just after a syntactic period, and in the opening lines of the succeeding stanzas, it continues to enjamb seemingly insignificant words, "of" and "and" (189). In a standard printed prayer or hymn, in which the petitionary meaning of such utterances is paramount, the text would hardly be expected to open up, as does this work, a slightly jarring separation of the semantic and syntactic from the lineal. Coming close to but eschewing common meter's quatrains and alternating rhymed tetrameter and trimeter, while distantly recalling Herbert's heavily rhymed quintain poems, Eliot's lyric might almost look at home in a hymnal or book of prayers, but not quite.

Like these lines at the micro level, the entire lyric is disjunctively enjambed at the macro level with both the preceding and the succeeding sections of the quartet. Although surface coherence is much greater here than it is in *The Waste Land*, the theological and tonal fissures are nonetheless significant. Directly preceding this Christian prayer is an address to travelers inspired by the Heraclitean idea of fluvial transience, the Buddhist renunciation of the world of flux, and the Hindu rejection of teleological thought. According to Eliot's paraphrase of Krishna in the *Bhavagad Gita*, one should "not think of the fruit of action" but the action or voyage in and of itself (188). Drawing on Heraclitus, the Buddha, and Krishna, Eliot apostrophizes:

> Fare forward, travellers! not escaping from the past
> Into different lives, or into any future;
> You are not the same people who left that station
> Or who will arrive at any terminus . . . (188)

The shift from the third to the fourth section of "The Dry Salvages," as indicated by the discrepancies between the Eastern and Western theological contexts, is sharply discontinuous. If the travelers are not the same people as those who embarked, as the third section asserts, then there would seem little justification for importuning Mary:

> Repeat a prayer also on behalf of
> Women who have seen their sons or husbands
> Setting forth, and not returning . . . (189)

According to the third section, such maternal grief and attachment would be incoherent, because the sons and husbands who left would not be the same as those imperiled on the voyage: "You are not the same people who left," and "You are not those who saw the harbor / Receding" (188). Some readings of *Four Quartets* tend to downplay the significance of such transtheological juxtapositions. ("Insofar as any 'beliefs' are explored there," insists one critic, "they are Christian ones," while another claims that "the poet's juxtaposition of contrary spiritual figures is not as radical as it at first appears to be.")[72] But this lyric, if akin to a Marian hymn like the "Salve Regina," is inserted in a poem that, unlike a prayer or a Mass, gives voice to a variety of theologies, some of which conflict. The privilege of poetry, unlike more doctrinal and devotional forms, is to utter sometimes contending viewpoints and beliefs. "The Dry Salvages" enacts Christian ritualism but at the same time slightly decenters it.

Moreover, despite the fourth part's use of diction that is normative for prayer, the metaphors in the final stanza begin to tip the balance of the scales slightly away from communal ritual and toward imaginative idiosyncrasy:

> Also pray for those who were in ships, and
> Ended their voyage on the sand, in the sea's lips
> Or in the dark throat which will not reject them . . . (189)

The "dark throat" metaphor is often read as an allusion to the biblical story of Jonah and the whale, without full acknowledgment of Eliot's upending of it: here the voyagers never find their way out of the whale's belly. The surreal metaphor of the "sea's lips" stresses the poet's figurative reimagining of the sea.

To recast prayer as poetry is, in short, to build on a discursive kinship that nevertheless transforms it into something else. Eliot himself warns that a poet's "private belief becomes a different thing in becoming poetry."[73] He responded angrily to a "damned fool of a Cambridge paper" that referred to "Ash-Wednesday" "as devotional poetry, which rather misses the point."[74] When we casually refer to his late poems as prayers, we honor the extent to which they are rhetorically suffused with, and propelled by, a ritualistic sister genre. But we also need to remember that the theological, tonal, and metaphoric disjunctures between prayerful and other discourses, the self-fictionalizing use of prayerful address, and the deinstrumentalization of prayerlike petition complicate an effort to read his late poems as prayers tout court. Otherwise it would be impossible, as Eliot indicates, for non-Anglo-Catholic readers to take pleasure in these poems as poems: "*If* there is 'literature,' *if* there is 'poetry,' then it must be possible to have full literary or poetic appreciation without sharing the beliefs of the poet."[75] Even as Eliot draws heavily on prayer, his collage and fragmentation, his decontextualization and idiosyncrasy, his metaphoric reach and imaginative flourishes suspend his poetic almost-prayers between ritual speech act and self-conscious fiction.

If it is unsurprising that devoutly Christian poets such as Hopkins and the late Eliot should make abundant use of prayer, we might not expect poets Eliot condemned as examples of modern heresy and unorthodoxy to write poems knit with prayer, but then again, we've already seen that prayer—albeit often violently distorted—enriches Eliot's own early "blasphemous" poems.[76] For W. B. Yeats, though no less lapsed in his Protestantism than late Eliot is ardent in his Anglo-Catholicism and Hopkins in his Roman Catholicism, prayer is also a serious intergeneric context, most obviously in poems that announce those affiliations in their titles: "A Prayer on Going into My House," "A Prayer for My Daughter," "A Prayer for My Son," and "A Prayer for Old Age." A range of other poems court the conventions of prayer, such as in Soul's spiritual exercises for approaching a heavenly state in "A Dialogue of Self and Soul." But even as this poem and others play on prayer, in Yeats, more explicitly than in Hopkins and Eliot, devotion is regarded as a potential danger to poetry, because of the risk of its short-circuiting verbal invention: "But when I think of that my tongue's a stone."[777] Hence in "Vacillation" the Heart disavows the Soul's urgings toward salvation—"Struck dumb in the simplicity of fire!"—and affirms the pagan progenitor of poets: "Homer is my example and his unchristened heart" (502, 503). Muteness is, paradoxically, the fullest expression of devotion, a humble self-silencing before the divine that seems incompatible with the eloquence and effulgence of poetry. For all his misgivings about religious discourse, gyrelike turnings between spiritual transcendence and pagan earthliness, the sacred and profane, "prayer" and "poetry," animate these and other of Yeats's dialogue poems.

In some of his other poems, Yeats still more directly scorns prayer on different grounds, casting it as poetry's opposite, a form of boringly predictable and mechanical speech. In the first stanza of "September 1913," he twice couples prayer with grubbing after money: to "add the halfpence to the pence / And prayer to shivering prayer," "to pray and save" (289). He represents Ireland's new Catholic middle class—resistant to his hopes for a new art gallery in Dublin—as favoring cautious piety and prudence over boldness, debasing the promise of Ireland's rebel leaders who risked all: O'Leary, Fitzgerald, Emmet, Tone. Institutionally sanctioned prayer seems to him an index of rote predictability, hardly a friend to poetry.

But for all his wariness toward prayer as either silencing or deadening poetic speech, Yeats absorbs, preserves, and extends the rhetorical strategies of prayer, partly by secularizing them. Hence his poems often direct prayerful address elsewhere than to God. In a refrain of "Meditations in Time of Civil War," the speaker, trapped in his home, prays not to a vast, singular Creator but to minute and multitudinous honeybees, beseeching them to lead the way in rebuilding a world shattered by internecine strife and bloodshed: "O honey-bees, / Come build in the empty house of the stare" (425). Prayer is the speech act on which Yeats builds this variation. Another of his best-known poems labels itself a prayer, but to whom is "A Prayer for My Daughter" addressed? A father's expression of wishes for his daughter's future protection and well-being, the poem patterns itself on appeals for divine intercession while holding these at a distance. In keeping with petitionary prayer, as well as poetic apostrophe, Yeats repeatedly deploys the exclamatory verb "may" in the optative mood, with the traditional inversion of verb and subject ("May she be granted," "May she become," "O may she live," "And may her bridegroom bring") (403–5). As Aristotle claimed, in the classic association of poetry with potentiality, "it is not the function of the poet to relate what has happened, but what may happen."[78] At the beginning of this poem, the father represents himself as having "walked and prayed" and "walked and prayed for this young child an hour," and Yeats's poem broadly follows the traditional pattern of meditative exercises and prayers, beginning with a scene-setting in the present (*memory*), then analyzing the world into which she has been born, with glimpses into past and future (*understanding*), and finally proposing wishes for her future (*will*): "And may her bridegroom bring her to a house / Where all's accustomed, ceremonious" (405).[79] The ritual and collective virtues for which he prays ("all's accustomed, ceremonious") are also those of prayer. But the ultimate ideal held out by the poem isn't a form of holiness or sanctity but a state akin to art's autotelism, or "self-delighting" self-sufficiency: to have "no business but dispensing round / Their magnanimities of sound" describes nothing so well as poems (405, 404). The divine appears in the poem only as a trope for this self-sufficiency, when the soul casts off hatred and turns within, learning "that its own sweet will is Heaven's will" (403). The result of the father's earnest praying is a poem as metaprayer, more image of prayer than prayer, more artfully shaped lyric in ten stanzas of adaptive ottava rima than humble petition to God. It demonstrates the virtues of secular "custom" and "ceremony" by redeploying inherited poetic stanzas, myths, and tropes, not religious liturgy. Even so, the poem's measured and gracious form may function magically, as an apotropaic warding off of extremes, particularly those that in this anxiously protective father's view may afflict a young woman. Even when Yeats's poems petition God or saints or ghosts, these quasi-prayers also tend to subordinate spirituality to aesthetics. The third stanza of "Sailing to Byzantium" seems to take the form of full-throated prayer. "O sages standing in God's holy fire," it begins, beckoning them with commands, "Come" and "perne" and "be" and "Consume," but ultimately the plea is to translate the speaker into an artifact like the one that we read: "gather me / Into the artifice of eternity" (408). Toward the end of "Man and the Echo," which secularizes the *ars moriendi*, Man addresses Echo with ultimate questions about his final fate: "O rocky voice / Shall we in that great night rejoice?" (632 [var. title], 633). But metaphor, in the form of the speaker's implied resemblance to a rabbit struck by a hawk or owl, breaks off theological speculation ("I have lost the theme"): the animal's death cry "distracts" his thought, plunging him back into life's vulnerabilities and uncertainties, artifice remaining this poet's access to reflection on final things (633).

Two of Yeats's titular prayer-poems directly beseech God's help. "A Prayer for Old Age" begins, "God guard me from those thoughts men think / In the mind alone; / He that sings a lasting song / Thinks in a marrow-bone," recalling but inverting the language of "September 1913," where prayer had helped dry "the marrow from the bone"; here, instead, the poet prays for a song that expresses all aspects of his being (553, 289). This poem tropes prayer as a self-repeating and long-continuing discourse akin to verse: "I pray—for fashion's word is out / And prayer comes round again—" (553). Prayer's appeal lies especially in its longevity and its physicality as a speech act, in which meaning is inseparable from performance. As conceded by William T. Noon, S.J., however, the poem, "whether an actual or an imaginary prayer, or both, does not ask God for any of those graces that most men and women have felt the need to ask for when they have said last prayers: forgiveness for their sins, a change of heart, or, most of all, an enlargement of their love in adoration paid to a sovereign

Lord."[80] In effect this prayer-poem functions more as an invocation than as a traditional last prayer: it entreats a muselike deity to help guard against dryly intellectual poems and induce instead works such as this one that fuse body and mind. Another poem that petitions the Almighty, "A Prayer on Going into My House," begins: "God grant a blessing on this tower and cottage / And on my heirs, if all remain unspoiled" (371). But the conditional "if" sets the tone for the rest of the poem, which twists a prayerful supplication for blessings into a bitter malediction: if someone should spoil the view by cutting down a tree or building a government-planned house, "shorten his life, / Manacle his soul upon the Red Sea bottom." The magical speech act of blessing, invoking protection and preservation, flips into the cognate but opposite speech act of cursing in the poem's grim final lines, which violently bestow death and suffering. A curse can serve as a speech act that relies less on divine (or malign) cooperation than on the poet's verbal resourcefulness and vigor, the linguistic enactment of the destruction it wills. Despite Yeats's use of "prayer" in his titles, the related speech genres of curses and blessings are more congenial models, since in them poetic agency seems more important in effecting change than divine will, poetic invention than pious devotion. When he longs for a heavenly state, or expresses wishes for his or his family's future, or meditates on final things, he draws on elements of prayer as a powerful, ritualistic, and long-lived discourse; but, often transmuting prayer into invocation, he enrolls prayerlike ingredients in the service of art above all else, checking its encroachment upon poetry's *sprezzatura*.

For all of Yeats's anxieties that piety ultimately results in muteness, most prayer is, with the exception of silent or "mental" prayer, orally performative. Later poets from Irish and other strongly oral cultures instance the continuing significance of prayer as shadowgenre, including Seamus Heaney, who patterns his sequence "Station Island" on pilgrimages to Station Island in Donegal, which involve "walking barefoot and praying around" stone circles. But by the sequence's end, art has superseded prayer, when James Joyce's ghost bids the pilgrim to leave off "the common rite," "the sackcloth and the ashes," cultivating instead his singular music:

"Let go, let fly, forget. / . . . Now strike your note."[81] Like Yeats, Patrick Kavanagh also collapses prayer into poetic invocation when in "Canal Bank Walk" he apostrophizes, "O unworn world enrapture me, encapture me," beseeching it to give him "ad lib / To pray unselfconsciously with overflowing speech," words spoken in search of more words, the spontaneous overflow of poetic inspiration.[82]

Early in the twentieth century, the Irish example radiated outward to other communities of writers. "What the colored poet in the United States needs to do is something like what Synge did for the Irish," declared James Weldon Johnson, calling for African American writers to develop an oral poetics in parallel with writers of the Irish Literary Renaissance.[83] Like other poets of the Harlem Renaissance, including Langston Hughes and Sterling Brown, Johnson absorbed prayer among other African American oral speech genres into literary verse, a vitalizing intergenre as well for later poets such as Robert Hayden, Amiri Baraka, and Thylias Moss.

Though an agnostic, Johnson began his landmark 1927 sequence of poems that adapts African American sermons and other religious speech acts, *God's Trombones*, with "Listen Lord: A Prayer," a poem that sets down as literary verse the oral performativity, creative exuberance, incantatory rhythms, and energy of an African American prayer-sermon.[84] Since the poem is spoken by a preacher as intercessor for the congregation, as if a public prayer, or what Kant calls an "*address* formally directed to God through the mouth of the clergyman in the name of the whole congregation,"[85] it assumes the doubly overheard structure of prayer as dramatic monologue, in which, as the speaker ostensibly addresses God, the congregation overhears the prayer, and the reader overhears the overheard prayer. This double nesting of the prayer foregrounds its performative and aesthetic strategies. After its conventional address to the divine being, the poem immediately turns to expressions of humility:

O Lord, we come this morning
Knee-bowed and body-bent

Before thy throne of grace.
O Lord—this morning—
Bow our hearts beneath our knees,
And our knees in some lonesome valley.[86]

Each of the hyphenated compounds enacts humility, immediately humbling "knee" and "body" with a participle ("-bowed," "-bent"). God is magisterially seated on a throne, and the bowing and bending suggest subjects groveling before a king. As if this self-humiliation weren't enough, the hearts are figured hyperbolically as bowing beneath knees—and just in case the body hasn't sunk far enough, those knees are lowered in the landscape by reference to a spiritual, "Jesus Walked This Lonesome Valley."

Ironically, however, the more humble the state described, the more imaginatively extravagant the poetic figuration used to evoke it. Much of the sermon's language is conventional and accords with expected rhetorical formulas and inheritances. But Johnson's imaginative stretching of these images, his aesthetic flourishes and surprises, suggests that even a poem such as this one, which, like Hopkins's verse and Eliot's late poetry, seems largely to accord with religious precepts, is subtly divided by conflicting impulsions toward devotion and invention, as indicated by an earlier poet-critic named Johnson. The preacher petitions the Lord to use his cleansing powers on the "man of God": "Wash him with hyssop inside and out, / Hang him up and drain him dry of sin" (14)—an injunction that echoes the verse of a biblical prayer but deletes from it language that, in early twentieth-century America, would have been racially problematic: "Purge me with hyssop, and I shall be clean: wash me, and I shall be whiter than snow" (Psalm 51:7). Remaking for modern African American verse the language of what Johnson called "the greatest book in the world," the King James Bible, the prayerful poet must strike a delicate balance between humble self-subordination and revisionary and imaginative self-assertion.[87] "Lord, turpentine his imagination," he writes, but this novel metaphor for God's cleansing powers instances an imagination that has hardly been wiped clean (14).

Though writing largely in Standard English, Johnson uses throughout the poem the kind of "constant iteration and repetition" he ascribes to African American spirituals,[88] such as the phrase repeated every few lines, "this morning" (13–14), or the so-called worrying or varying in lines such as the imperative to God to "ride, ride by old hell, / Ride by the dingy gates of hell" (14). In accordance with African American church rhetoric, he employs hyperbole and homely figures of speech, such as the intercessory prompting to God to "open up a window of heaven, / And lean out" (13), as well as the orality of repetitions and insistent rhythms. Despite Johnson's misgivings about the use of dialect in poetry, by poem's end, having moved from the first section's propitiation ("no merits of our own" [13]) to the middle section's intercessory prayer on behalf of both sinners and good people, and finally to petition on the speaker's behalf ("Lower me to my dusty grave in peace" [15]), the language more overtly incorporates African American vernacular in the final section's second line, "When I've done drunk my last cup of sorrow" (14), and its last, "To wait for that great gittin' up morning—Amen" (15). While playing prayer's protestations of humble self-abnegation against poetry's imagistic and verbal inventiveness, Johnson brings the figurative, rhetorical, rhythmic, and lexical properties of African American speech into a prayer written as literary verse, creolizing the normative language of poem-prayers in English.

Agnosticism might seem an infertile ground for prayer-based poems: is there or isn't there a divine being to address? Because another self-described agnostic across the Atlantic figures religion as "That vast moth-eaten musical brocade / Created to pretend we never die," the last rhetorical model we might expect to find in his poetry is prayer.[89] Taking Philip Larkin's skepticism a step further, Christopher Hitchens canonizes him as essential reading for the nonbeliever in *The Portable Atheist*.[90] Yet many of Larkin's poems, like Johnson's, have affinities with prayer. Amusingly imagining himself as a kind of religion consultant, perhaps in a postreligious world, Larkin suggests in "Water" that a poet's specialization in imagery might be useful:

> If I were called in
> To construct a religion
> I should make use of water. (56)

Of course this consultant's idea is hardly original, given the significance of water in a variety of world religions. More novel, if not unprecedented, is his artful crafting of a poetic tone that, in poems like this and "Church Going," blends skepticism with awe, irreverence toward institutional religion and hankering after spiritual fulfillment, bored knowingness with "A hunger in himself to be more serious" (37). "Water" ends with the poet performing an imaginative blessing or consecration, a pseudo-Eucharist that adapts conventional religious vocabulary—"raise," "east," "glass," "water," "light," "congregate," "endlessly"—for a newly invented rite:

> And I should raise in the east
> A glass of water
> Where any-angled light
> Would congregate endlessly. (93)

The multifarious radiance of the divine is sublimated in a fusion of traditional images of light, water, and chalice. But unlike the social congregation of an institutional order, it's merely in the poet's raised glass, a token in part for this very poem, that anything is imagined to "congregate."

In "Faith Healing," Larkin ironizes an American preacher's "prayer / Directing God about this eye, that knee" (53). And in "Compline," named after the final church service, or "office," of the day, Larkin mocks a variation on the Lord's Prayer as "hurried talk to God" intended only to ward off death:

> *Thy Kingdom come, Thy will be done,*
> *Produce our lives beyond this night,*
> *Open our eyes again to the sun.* (270)

Yet "Solar," a dramatically open-eyed paean to the sun, is cast in a rhetorical posture and language that resemble prayer. Written like "Water" in compact trimeters, the poem apostrophizes the (unnamed) sun:

> Suspended lion face
> Spilling at the centre
> Of an unfurnished sky
> How still you stand,
> And how unaided
> Single stalkless flower
> You pour unrecompensed. (89)

Like godhead, the sun is radiant, central, self-sufficient, still, singular, and "unrecompensed." Like a prayer, the poem expresses wonder before this radiant presence, as close as Larkin can come to a prayerful act of adoration such as Hopkins's "Glory be to God" or Eliot's choruses in *The Rock*. The sun is like a lion, a flower head, and a gold coin—the latter isolated in a one-word line that accentuates the but-for-one-letter nearness of "Gold" to "God" (90).[91] As in "Water," an overtly religious vocabulary floods the end of the poem:

> Our needs hourly
> Climb and return like angels.
> Unclosing like a hand,
> You give for ever. (90)

Needs are imagined, in the language of Genesis 28, as being like "angels of God . . . ascending and descending" in Jacob's dream, except that they arrive not to the Lord in heaven but at the sun.[92] Like God's hand extended to Adam in Michelangelo's Sistine Chapel fresco, this hand ignites the world with the gift of its energy. The figuration of the go(1)d sun as an open hand grants it the intimacy of the bodily part that plays a crucial role both in prayer and in poetic writing. Despite its atheism or agnosticism, Larkin's work presses together the poet's hand in writing and the supplicant's hand in secular prayer.

Because Larkin and other twentieth-century poets including

Hopkins, Eliot, Yeats, and Johnson remake inherited poetic forms, they might well be presumed to draw occasionally, if ambivalently, on prayer, as well as other religious discursive forms. We may be less inclined to look to poets such as the objectivists for continuities with prayer, because of their putative emphasis on what Louis Zukofsky called "the detail, not mirage, of seeing, of thinking with things as they exist."[93] But the awe of poems such as Charles Reznikoff's "Te Deum" (named after the Latin hymn of praise to God) and Lorine Niedecker's *New Goose* poems should alert us to the connections. Witness the interdiscursive vibrations between poetry and prayer in one of the most celebrated objectivist poems, "Psalm," a title that raises the question whether and in what sense George Oppen's poem is indeed a psalm—a prayer, a sacred song used in worship, like the biblical hymns in the book of Psalms. Even though "psalm" comes from a Greek word literally meaning the twanging or twitching of harp strings, Oppen's poem is an exercise in asceticism, in contrast to the figurative extravagance and musical resonance of Johnson's "Prayer," Yeats's "A Prayer for Old Age," and Hopkins's "Pied Beauty." Maeera Shreiber notes the sometimes "contentious" relationship between poetry and prayer in Judaism, Maimonides even identifying prayer-poems as "a significant source of distraction" and "'the major cause of the lack of devotion.'"[94] In Judaism, prayer has sometimes run into trouble because of its anthropomorphization of Godhead; poetry's "unbridled penchant for metaphor" puts it in conflict with "Judaism's central commitment to a disembodied deity," even more so than the friction we found lurking in Hopkins's, Eliot's, and Johnson's poems.[95] Oppen's epigraph from Aquinas, "*Veritas sequitur,*" or "Truth follows," brings Christian language into play, but the elision of "*esse rerum*" (the being of things) circumscribes its implications.[96] Oppen's declaration of existence is nontheological: "That they are there!" he exclaims of the wild deer.

Even so, in a poem called "Psalm," the deer recall the first psalm in the so-called Exodus section of the Psalms: "As the hart panteth after the water brooks, so panteth my soul after thee, O God" (Psalm 42). Oppen secularizes the trope, since his deer, instead of allegorizing human incompleteness in longing for the divine, are emblematic only of themselves and of existence, or Heideggerian being there:[97]

> Their eyes
> Effortless, the soft lips
> Nuzzle and the alien small teeth
> Tear at the grass
>
> The roots of it
> Dangle from their mouths
> Scattering earth in the strange woods.
> They who are there.

The "Effortless" eyes of the deer exemplify the state of mind to which the poet aspires, a noncoercive consciousness that lets existence emerge, lets it appear as mere being. The sentence fragment "They who are there" seems utterly simple, unadorned, in keeping with Oppen's objectivist poetics. But, as with the trope of the deer, there is more to it: the refrainlike repetition and variation create a muted ritualism, and the poem's final line, repeating the phrase "wild deer," also resonates with the *r*-colored vowel sounds in "they . . . *are* there": "S*ta*rtle, and st*are* out." This echo of "are" in "Startle" and "there" in "stare," not to mention the embedded eye-rhyme of "are" with "stare," subtly accords with the musical and liturgical implications of the poem's title.

Though restrained and intently focused on the encounter with deer, Oppen's "Psalm" is at the same time enriched by its echoes of a high Romantic poet and a Romantic modernist poet, each of whose work frequently intersects with prayer. As is often the case with poetry, this lyric's response to existence is mediated through echoes of earlier poems. Despite the view that "Oppen's poems are written out of the faith that things can be seen with clarity, and that words can refer to and name an extant reality without trying to mediate it with transcendental or symbolic overlays," his poetry is hardly devoid of symbolic, religious, and literary "overlays."[98] Perhaps surprisingly, "Psalm" recalls an extravagant

Romantic celebration of being, Shelley's "Ode to the West Wind," in which the poet, striving with the wind "in prayer," beckons it to drive his "dead thoughts over the universe / Like withered leaves":

> Scatter, as from an unextinguished hearth
> Ashes and sparks, my words among mankind!
> Be through my lips to unawakened Earth . . .[99]

Echoing the word cluster *scatter-earth-leaves*, Oppen's severely economical poem tries to steer clear of anything like Shelley's voluptuous prophecy; yet it, too, begins by extolling the being of nature and ends up meditating on "words," or in Oppen's phrase "small nouns," as the home of being. Those words or nouns include, of course, the poet's own, his "leaves" of "grass" torn from the language, including—however discretely—the language of previous poems and psalms. The leaves in Oppen's poem "Hang in the distances / Of sun," recalling Wallace Stevens's late poetic thought experiment in trying to conceive of being without human projections, appropriately titled "Of Mere Being," initially published with the phrase "bronze distance" in the 1957 *Opus Posthumous*: "In the bronze distance, // A gold-feathered bird / Sings in the palm, without human meaning, / Without human feeling, a foreign song."[100] Like Oppen's deer "bedding down," Stevens's bird is emblematic of being, and its feathers "dangle down."[101] Though they may seem innocently "natural images" in the tradition of Pound's imagism, Oppen's deer also recall, along with the hart of the Psalms, the deer at the end of Stevens's "Sunday Morning," and the participle "Crying" is also key to Stevensian vocabulary in poems such as "Waving Adieu, Adieu, Adieu." Akin to the bird in Stevens's "Of Mere Being" that sings "a foreign song," Oppen's deer have "alien" teeth and live in "strange woods," the diction of alienation emphasizing their existence beyond anthropomorphism. Despite Stevens's more extravagant artifice, Oppen resembles him in summoning but craftily muting the anthropomorphism central to prayer in many religious cultures. The word "small" repeats through Oppen's poem ("small beauty," "small teeth," "small nouns"), bridging the potential gap between non-verbal and verbal being and underscoring Oppen's effort at radical simplicity and restraint. Cultivating poetic smallness, or as he says in a letter of December 21, 1962, writing "carefully, lucidly, accurately, resisting the temptation to inflate,"[102] Oppen puts his restrained figurative language, barely audible music, unadorned diction, and preference for nouns over finite verbs in the service of a negative poetic theology, whereby being reveals itself through the space cleared by the writer's verbal and artistic austerity.

An admirer of Oppen's "clean, austere, dynamic poetry" of "silence" who shares his distanced affiliation with Jewishness,[103] Louise Glück published a poetic sequence, *The Wild Iris* (1992), that abounds in prayer-poems, many of them titled "Matins" and "Vespers," in a startling trialogue among gardener-poet, flowers, and God. Some of the initial critical response suggested astonishment at an acclaimed contemporary American poet's assimilation of religious discourse.[104] She adapts the apparatus of prayer, including address to God, apology, petition, pleading, thanksgiving, complaint, and lament, but repeatedly questions the structures she is mobilizing. Tonally evident in what Shreiber describes as the sequence's "quarrelsome" and "confrontational, highly critical relation to the divine,"[105] this questioning can also be located in these prayer-poems' probing of figuration—a version of the tension between prayer and the aesthetic already seen in Hopkins, Eliot, Yeats, Johnson, and Oppen: if God is unembodied, how can he be addressed without being figuratively likened to embodied beings, such as humans and flowers?

The third of the prayer-poems titled "Matins" begins conventionally enough as an apology, "Forgive me if I say I love you," but then immediately seems partly to retract the apology as a deliberate feint of the sort "the weak" make to "the powerful," who are "always lied to."[106] This is troubled love, at best. "I cannot love / what I can't conceive, and you disclose / virtually nothing," complains the speaker. God is secretive, withdrawn behind a veil of "silence." As the nothing that both is and is not there, God defies poetic comprehension in part because he is beyond figuration. The poet asks, "are you like the hawthorn tree," with its constancy, "or are you more the foxglove, inconsistent"? And in the next poem titled "Matins," she pursues these comparisons with the vegetable world: "I see it is with you as with the birches: / I am not to speak to you / in the personal way."[107] The question of what God can be compared to is in part a theological question about the abstract and disembodied spirit that can never be fully known, but it is also a crucially poetic question about vehicle and tenor, metaphoricity, and resemblance. It is impossible to understand God without comparing him to something, in this case trees and flowers, but at the same time that she does so, Glück skeptically interrogates her inevitably inadequate efforts at poeticizing God. As if addressing an aloof lover, she accuses him of an "absence / of all feeling, of the least / concern for me," and then concludes, "I might as well go on / addressing the birches." Closely related to the question of God's evasion of figurative likeness is that of his nonhumanity. Glück uses prayer's structure of address but deconstructs it. Having called into question how she is "to speak to you," she raises the specter of the absence of anything to be addressed: "Or / was it always only / on the one side?" It may be, she suggests, that her prayers are self-returning speech acts, hall-of-mirrors reflections without opening to, or reciprocity with, any genuine other.

Oppen and Glück turn away from models such as Hopkins's richly loaded, if agonized, prayer-poems, exalting being-in-itself in a poetics that eschews metaphor and verbal splendor, and questioning the very act of address through which their works give utterance to the divine. Among postwar American poets, Charles Wright, by contrast, pays homage to the priest-poet he calls "God-gulped and heaven-hidden," adapting his predecessor's alliterative compounds and apostrophizing him in the Englishman's diction, "Father Candescence" and "Father Fire."[108] If Oppen and Glück poeticize prayer under the sign of litotes, or understatement, Wright does so, like Hopkins, with rhetorical opulence; if their poems restrain trope and anthropomorphism, his abound with extravagant, almost baroque figurations of landscape, affect, and an absent God; if theirs approximate silent or mental prayer, ascetically subduing verbal music, his are written in strongly cadenced lines rich with sonic patterning. Some of these differences can be traced to sensibilities shaped by distinctive regional and religious inheritances, Wright's Episcopalianism and exposure to southern evangelicalism by contrast with a northeastern Jewish heritage. But Wright's affiliation with Hopkins, despite the broad dissimilarities between an American Protestant background and an Englishman's Catholicism, demonstrates even prayer-inspired poetry's transnational and intercultural reach.

Not that Wright is a "religious" poet in the same way as his priestly Roman Catholic predecessor, let alone the pastor-poets of the Renaissance, and neither is Oppen nor Glück. Like a range of postwar poets, including Oppen and Glück, Wright simultaneously deploys and dismantles prayer, earnestly embraces and skeptically interrogates it. Self-described as a "God-fearing agnostic,"[109] he abandoned long ago the Christianity of his teenage years but still has often written poetry on Sunday mornings, has installed God as a powerfully absent presence in haunted landscapes, and has referred to his poems as "little prayer wheels" and "little wafers," "hymns" and "notes toward sacred texts."[110] From early in his career to late, prayer has persisted as an animating interdiscursive force in his poetry, though a force that the poems frequently question and impede.

If Wright's crisscrossing of poetry with prayer deserves further exploration, it has not passed unnoticed. "The urge to pray," as David Lehman observes, "outlasts the conviction that God will hear the prayer," citing Wright's comment "Each line should be a station of the cross."[111] In Edward Hirsch's view, Wright has "an essentially religious sensibility," "a nonbeliever with a tremendous longing for belief," who refigures "a Christian terminology into a secular epiphanic aesthetic. . . . The concepts of penance, grace, and redemption occur often, though . . . the beads of the rosary are broken and the religious hymns have fallen. Faith is elusive, redemption thwarted."[112] In the poem in which he tags himself a "God-fearing agnostic," Wright both elicits God and cancels him out; he addresses the divine, comments on address to the divine, and ridicules such address: "Are you there, Lord, I whisper, / knowing he's not around, / Mumble *kyrie eleison*, mumble

O three-in-none."[113] From one phrase or line to the next, prayer and antiprayer jostle, intertwine, and clash. In Bonnie Costello's words, Wright applies "the ancient practice of the *via negativa* to a modern skepticism about language and myth."[114] As indicated by the negatives that open up like quicksand under his invocations of the divine, Wright composes as-if prayers and metaprayers, discursive embodiments of a modernized negative, or apophatic, theology.

Like many of Wright's poems, "Stone Canyon Nocturne" inter-mixes prayer with melancholy over prayer's inefficacy, exaltation with lament, awe with scorn. It begins with a biblical epithet for God, "Ancient of Days," as well as an intimate appellation, "old friend," the poem nestling in the ecclesiastical language of song, praise, and worship.[115] A nineteenth-century Episcopal hymn had also begun with the epithet:

Ancient of Days, who sittest throned in glory,
To Thee all knees are bent, all voices pray;
Thy love has blessed the wide world's wondrous story
With light and life since Eden's dawning day.

O Holy Father, who hast led Thy children
In all the ages, with the fire and cloud,
Through seas dry shod, through weary wastes bewild'ring;
To Thee in rev'rent love our hearts are bowed.[116]

Although Wright launches his poem with the same words as the hymn, the grandiloquent affirmation of prayerful address is immediately turned on its head by the rest of his first line, which banishes what the speaker had just summoned: "no one believes you'll come back." God's ancientness is attributable not to his durability but to his pastness. The line doubles back on itself, short-circuiting address to the divine as impossible, a rhetorical structure that has outlived its communicative function, if ever it had one. Instead of the hymn's glorious "light and life since Eden's dawning day," Wright's poem is a nocturne, and its description of the night setting gives but more evidence of the deity's withdrawal

from the world: "The moon, like a dead heart, cold and unstartable, hangs by a thread / At the earth's edge." The speaker gazes
on a corpse, from which the once infusing spirit has departed.
But Wright hardly seems content with the God-abandoned material world he is left with. The remarkable simile of the moon as
a "dead heart, cold and unstartable," evokes a longing to restart
that most vital of vital organs, as if vivid figuration could shock
it back into life. The simile of moon as heart is overlaid with the
metaphor of moon as a life hanging by a thread, though this divine heart is dead even without benefit of Atropos's shears. The
hymn "Ancient of Days" had also incorporated cosmic images,
but those traditional verses' fire, cloud, seas, and wastes remain
comfortably within a familiar biblical framework, unlike Wright's
jarringly cardiac-arrested moon. "Pray we that Thou wilt hear
us, still imploring / Thy love and favor kept to us always," ends
the Christian hymn. Wright's poem, holding out scant hope that
"Thou wilt hear us," turns away from the beginning's apostrophic
"you": "Like a bead of clear oil the Healer revolves through the
night wind, / Part eye, part tear, unwilling to recognize us." God
reappears at poem's end, in the guise of Emerson's transparent
eyeball, slightly blurred by pity ("Part eye, part tear"), but instead
of being wide open and all-penetrating, he seems reluctant to share
his healing powers with humanity and only revolves in the circuit of himself. Having begun with a religious vocabulary—"Ancient of Days," "friend," "believes"—the poem returns at the end
to religiously charged words and phrases such as "bead of clear
oil," "Healer," and "tear," a vocabulary that in Wright's *via negativa*
summons a divine presence under erasure. With all the yearning
but none of the conviction of an Episcopal hymn, Wright's poem
both reanimates prayer and mourns its demise.

Any number of Wright's poems instance the whirligig of religious and counterreligious utterance that generates the poignancy
of his work. Toward the beginning of "Apologia Pro Vita Sua,"
a title borrowed from Cardinal Newman's classic defense of his
religion, we are invited to walk along "Spring's via Dolorosa,"
to hear "Church bells like monk's mouths tonguing the hymn,"
to conceive of journal and landscape as "breath and blood," to

contemplate the "meat of the sacrament," and so forth, but with each of these transcendent abstractions, we're quickly drawn back to earth by down-home, deadpan, folksy phrases such as the droll "They've gone and done it again," interjections such as the dismissive "All that," and the wisecracking "I'll say."[117] Titles such as "The Gospel According to Yours Truly" archly combine biblical diction and a deflating everydayness, a poem that asks, "Tell me again, Lord, how easy it all is, / renounce this, / Renounce that, and all is a shining—."[118] "Little Prayer" addresses a God not of grand sublimities and eschatological eventualities but, in its first lines, "Lord of the ugly chair and broken sofa, / Lord / Of mouse piss and pack rat shit."[119] This isn't to suggest that Wright's poems are works of easy or dismissive secularism. A strophe in "Clear Night" bespeaks a yearning to be overwhelmed by a no-longer-available transcendence:

> I want to be bruised by God.
> I want to be strung up in a strong light and singled out.
> I want to be stretched, like music wrung from a dropped
>   seed.
> I want to be entered and picked clean.[120]

To these ritualistically anaphoric and dramatically end-stopped wishes, however, the wind and the castor beans skeptically ask, "What?" "And the stars start out on their cold slide through the dark. / And the gears notch and the engines wheel." Far from a force of Love that will penetrate the speaker—in Wright's erotically charged tropes for divine revelation—what the poet is left with is a frighteningly indifferent, mechanical, and empty universe. But in his work, neither the skeptical nor the religious, the sacred nor the profane is allowed to dominate, and the power of the poetry lies in his rich language's seemingly endless twists and turns between these poles. At one and the same time, Wright blurs the lines between poetry and prayer, and between prayer and antiprayer.

A protomodernist Jesuit, an Anglo-Catholic modernist, a lapsed Protestant Anglo-Irish modernist, a Harlem Renaissance agnostic, an Anglican agnostic, two nonreligious Jews (an objectivist and a postconfessionalist), and a post-Episcopal American southerner—these poets represent various strands of modern and contemporary poetry, as of belief and disbelief, yet they have in common a blurring of the lines between poetry and prayer, a rubbing of these discursive forms up against one another that reveals both likenesses and differences. To put it simply, we have seen that many of the more overtly religious poems, from Hopkins and late Eliot to Glück and Wright, subtly betray prayer in prayer-poems that grant primacy to the aesthetic, and many of the seemingly nonreligious poems, from Yeats, early Eliot, and Larkin to Oppen and Plath, reanimate prayer despite skeptical misgivings. By incorporating prayer and many of its conventions—intimate address, intercession, adoration, awed colloquy, ritual incantation, solemn petition, anthropomorphism, musical repetition, the language of the Bible, and so forth—poets from Hopkins and Eliot to Glück and Wright reinfuse poetry with sacramental and ritualistic qualities. At the same time, often in the same work, they play on tensions between poetry and prayer, between invention and devotion—tensions they reveal as inherent within prayer itself. They ritualistically redeploy prayer and skeptically reframe it. They spin out startling figurations that both enhance prayer and ultimately exceed its conventions. How, their work invites us to ask, can poets speak to and pay homage to the divine without at the same time accruing power to their imaginative work? If God is beyond the human, how can she or he be addressed without humanizing and self-delighting figurative language? If, as some of these poets suggest, God has withdrawn from the world, then what is prayer but self-address detoured through an elusive other? Prayer's absorption within poetry reveals the survival of long-lived religious and poetic traditions, even within modern and contemporary poems that seem to negate or refuse, to mourn or austerely surrender God. But by virtue of its deliberate and self-conscious artifice, poetry also exposes the metaphoricity, rhetoricity, and anthropomorphism that structure human engagements with the divine. Even as modern and contemporary poetry enriches and entangles itself with prayer, it often subtly distinguishes itself from its sacred other. In our time, some prayer-poetry seems as if it is—to recur to Simic's poem, not accidentally dedicated to Charles Wright—"The hook left dangling / In the Great 'Nothing.'"

POSTCOLONIAL POETRY AND PRAYER

Although I have focused thus far primarily on elements of Catholic, Protestant, and Jewish prayer in Western poetry written in English, poetry and prayer have long nourished one another in many other religious cultures, as already noted of the South Asian *Vedas* and bhakti poetry, and the West Asian Rumi's *Masnavi*. In modern-day poetry rooted in the Caribbean, Africa, South Asia, and Oceania, poets bring prayer's energies of oral performance and sacral engagement into literary works even as they often hold religion's truth claims at a measured distance. Because missionary Christianity marched across the world frequently hand in glove with the economic and military forces of European colonialism, postcolonial poets often betray a vexed if intimate relation to Christian prayer. Sometimes they more warmly embrace non-Western devotional forms, though even then the religiously inspired works they write—belief as mediated through the distancing medium of poetic self-reflexivity and artifice—are often as-if prayers, pseudoprayers, or metaprayers.

Christopher Okigbo, the grandson of the priest of the river goddess Idoto, invokes this ancestral Igbo god in his most famous lyric and leans on her totemic tree, but at the same time, as the son of Catholics, he echoes Christian parables and Catholic prayers to the Virgin Mary:

> Before you, mother Idoto
>   naked I stand;
> before your watery presence,
>   a prodigal
>
> leaning on an oilbean,
> lost in your legend.[121]

By virtue of his language's inextricability from Catholic prayer and the Psalms, the poet acknowledges that his nativist return to precolonial religious sources cannot escape cultural syncretism. Layered with lyric self-consciousness, the poem's liturgical hybridity reflects the discrepant religious systems it mobilizes and melds in the idiosyncrasies of an improvised literary rite.

The Barbadian poet Kamau Brathwaite also invokes the language of a Christian prayer, namely the thirteenth-century hymn "Dies Irae," or Day of Wrath, paradoxically appropriating its propulsive rhythms, repetitions, and rhetoric to indict European peoples for atrocities at My Lai, Sharpeville, Wounded Knee, and elsewhere, despite Christianity's complicity in colonization. His poem "Irae" ends with this prayer:

> mighty & majestic god
> head savior of the broken herd
> heal me nanny cuffee cudjoe
> grant me mercy at thy word
>
> day of fire dreadful day
> day for which all sufferers pray
> grant me patience with thy plenty
> grant me vengeance with thy sword[122]

The poet summons leaders of the Maroons, ex-slave rebel warriors, as prototypes for the kind of fierce resistance he attempts to reenact in language; a syntactical ambiguity seems to put them in a relation of apposition to the apostrophized deity. The emphatic twinning of "word" and "sword" at the end of the last two stanzas enlists them both in anticolonial destruction, a word placement Brathwaite switched in a later version of the poem.[123] The God in whose name Europeans subjugated and killed Caribbean, African, and other non-European peoples is invoked here as the agent for unleashing the "righteous rage" of the oppressed.

Whereas poets such as Okigbo and Brathwaite repossess Christian prayer for native returns or anticolonial judgments, other poets reject and fiercely satirize it as a colonial tool. Ugandan poet Okot p'Bitek's *Song of Lawino* often quotes Christian prayers, but his defamiliarizing translations make these prayers seem ridiculous. Deploring her cravenly westernized husband's zealous Christianization, Lawino exclaims:

> Ocol laughs at me
> Because I cannot
> Cross myself properly

> *In the name of the Father*
> *And of the Son*
> *And the Clean Ghost*[124]

But Okot's estrangingly literal translation of Holy Ghost as "Clean Ghost" makes the prayer momentarily seem absurd to readers versed in Christianity, as it is to this African village woman. Similarly, when she attends a Catholic class, everyone seems to her to be

> shouting
> Meaninglessly in the evenings
> Like parrots
> Like the crow birds

> *Maria the Clean Woman*
> *Mother of the Hunchback*
> *Pray for us*
> *Who spoil things*
> *Full of graciya.* (75)

Elsewhere, Okot p'Bitek explains the miscommunication with Italian missionaries that led to the mistranslation of the Christian God and Jesus as "Hunchback" in Acholi (*Rubanga*), the Acholi having assimilated God/Jesus to the spirit who molds people—namely, by causing the tuberculosis of the spine.[125] "Hunchback," "Clean Woman," and Okot's other literal translations of mongrelized Acholi semitranslations have the effect of making the Christian prayers seem nonsensical.

By contrast, when Okot incorporates indigenous prayers into his long poem, they are made to seem entirely comprehensible. If there are troubles such as infertility and famine, Lawino explains, it is because the "ancestors are angry, / Because they are hungry, / Thirsty, / Neglected" (101). So the elders gather at the clan shrine, make offerings to the ancestors, and then lead prayers to the dead to cleanse the homestead:

The troubles in the homestead
Let the setting sun
Go down with them! (101)

The assembled villagers repeat these prayers. The metaphoric coupling of the setting sun with the departure of the homestead's troubles has the effect of naturalizing the prayer, in contrast to the abstract and gratingly unfamiliar Christian prayers.

Non-Christian prayer also plays an important role in the work of poets of South Asian origin, such as A. K. Ramanujan and Agha Shahid Ali. A Kashmiri Shia Muslim by origin, Ali laces much of his poetry with prayers and references to calls to prayer. According to an Islamic proverb, to pray and to be Muslim are synonymous, and the Qur'an is sometimes regarded as a book of prayers. In everyday Urdu speech, prayers of Arabic and Persian origin are part of the fabric of greetings, partings, thanks, and other such speech acts. When the Arabic phrase *ar-Rahim* from the beginning of the Qur'an finds its way into one of Ali's many ghazals, it is explained in a footnote: "'The Merciful'—one of God's ninety-nine names in Arabic. The traditional Muslim prayer begins: 'Begin in the Name of God, the Beneficent, the Merciful'" (*Bismillah al-rahmaan al-raheem*), a prayer that performatively prefaces many daily tasks.[126] To bring Muslim prayer into English-language poetry is to attune a literary language long saturated with Christianity to the discursive experience of the Islamic world.

Even so, Ali could hardly be said to be an orthodox Muslim,

and neither are his poems orthodox prayers. He sees prayer not as a means to connect with the one and all-merciful God but as a performative rite that survives nonbelief, a vivid husk that outlives what it once contained. He asks in one ghazal, "When even God is dead, what is life but prayer?" ("In" 66), and asserts in another:

> I believe in prayer and the need to believe—
> even the great Nothing signifying God. ("God," 75)

The title poem of *Rooms Are Never Finished* asks, "Now that God / is news, what's left but prayer?," belief voided in part by violent conflict on behalf of a Muslim God in Chechnya, Kashmir, and elsewhere.[127] In these and other instances, the rituals and language of prayer are emptied out of the divine but retain the devotional posture and rhetorical forms of prayer, the aesthetic patterning and self-reflexivity of poetry.

Prayer and disbelief tumultuously intertwine in Ali's elegy for his mother, "Lenox Hill," in which the poet, frantic for connection, vertiginously addresses his dead mother, a personified Kashmir, elephants, saints, and a negative deity. He recounts his mother's dream:

> She was, with dia-
> monds, being stoned to death. I prayed: If she must die,
> let it only be some dream. But there were times, Mother,
> while you slept, that I prayed, "Saints, let her die." (17)

By dint of sonic and imagistic repetition, death is changed into diamonds and vice versa, in part by word-splitting enjambment; so too, fate is transformed into an object of longing, the poet praying for the death he cannot prevent. Contemplating the return of his mother's body to Kashmir, he beseeches an inversely defined deity: "O Destroyer, let her return there, if just to die" (18). Recalling his earlier play on "die" and "diamonds," he prays, near the poem's end, not for his mother's but for her destroyer's death:

Mother,
I see a hand. *Tell me it's not God's.* Let it die.
I see it. It's filling with diamonds. Please let it die. (18–19)

To stay the divine hand that will record a death, the poet paradoxically turns intercessory prayer inside out as prayer against the
divine—here, a nightmarish figure who would stone (or diamond)
his mother to death, though the poet, too, seeks by wordplay to
locate the radiant permanence of diamonding within irreparable
loss.

Despite Ali's resistances to Islamic orthodoxy, Shia prayers and
rituals resonate through a long elegiac sequence he also wrote for
his mother, "From Amherst to Kashmir." The first section of the
sequence, "Karbala: A History of the 'House of Sorrow,'" nar-
rates in prose the defining trauma of Shia Islam, the martyrdom
of Hussain, grandson of the prophet Muhammad, whose memo-
rialization on "the tenth of Muharram (*Ashura*) is *the* rite of Shi'a
Islam—so central that at funerals those events are woven into
elegies, every death framed by that 'Calvary'" (23).[128] The same
could be said of Ali's elegiac sequence for his mother, which interweaves the lamentations of Zainab, Hussain's sister, with Agha
Shahid Ali's mourning for his mother. The identification is curi-
ously doubled, since Ali writes that his mother, ever since girl-
hood, "had felt Zainab's grief as her own" (26): both Ali and his
mother occupy the dual roles of martyr and mourner, Hussain
and Zainab. In a dramatic monologue, Zainab cries out, praying to multiple addressees to join her in mourning, her prayerful voicing accentuated by virtue of its being unhitched from any
single potential auditor: "Paradise, hear me—," "Let the rooms of
Heaven be deafened, Angels, / with my unheard cry," "*Syria hear
me,*" "*World, weep for Hussain*" ("Zainab's Lament in Damascus,"
28). The sequence of poems, enacting geographic movement from
Amherst to Delhi to Srinagar, recalls the Ashura processions in
which Ali had witnessed mourners crying, praying, even wound-
ing themselves in grief.

But just when the reader might begin to think Ali has fully

rejoined his Shia Muslim roots, the sequence repeats a prayer to a different kind of deity: *"(Dark blue god don't cast me into oblivion, // in the temples, all your worshippers are asleep)"* ("Summers of Translation," 29). Ali is recalling a *bhajan*, or Hindu devotional song, and even as he quotes prayers from the Qur'an, such as *"There is no god but God"* (*la ilaha illallah*, the *shahadah*, or Islamic creed) ("Srinagar Airport," 42), he also makes room in his elegiac sequence for prayers to Krishna, including an entire poem that recreates a "Film *Bhajan* Found on a 78 RPM," melding *bhajan* with the blues:

> Dark god shine on me you're all I have left
> nothing else blue god you are all I have
> I won't let go I'll cling on to your robe (40)

While cross-gendering himself as Zainab, wailing for her beheaded brother in the central Shia story, Ali also adopts the voice of Radha, Krishna's primary consort, swearing her devotion and beseeching the blue god Krishna not to abandon her. The poem's interweaving of Shiism with Hinduism allows Ali to place his grief within meaning-giving narratives that nevertheless, in combination, undo the priority of either religion. In a syncretic strategy he derived in part from T. S. Eliot, about whom he wrote his dissertation, Ali's modernist juxtaposition of prayers turns them into the poetic afterimages of prayers. "'In the Name of the Merciful,'" begins a poem titled simply "God," translating part of a basic Muslim prayer; but by poem's end, the mourner meditating on his mother's death turns this prayer on its head: "In no one's name but hers I let night begin" (44). Ali's poetry is imbued with Shia Muslim prayer, but his humanistic insistence on his mother's priority in the naming ritual of verse also differentiates his transreligious poetics from monotheistic prayer.

Another Indian-born poet, not of Muslim but of Hindu heritage, activates a different set of religious contexts in his prayer-studded poems. A. K. Ramanujan's eleven-part sequence "Prayers to Lord Murugan" was inspired by "Guide to Lord Murugan," a sixth-century Tamil poem, "the first long devotional or *bhakti* poem to appear in any Indian language, the first religious text to appear in any native tongue" other than Sanskrit.[129] A major god of the ancient Tamils, Murugan, whose worship continues in South India, probably originated as a fertility god and has six faces, twelve eyes, and twelve hands.[130] According to Ramanujan, his sixth-century predecessor spiritualized an older secular tradition of poems about the relation between poet and patron, shifting its subject to the relation between devotee and god (190). If so, Ramanujan's poem inverts this literary historical process through resecularization, inserting twinges of self-reflexive irony in what he called his "antiprayers" (192). The sixth-century precursor poem was, he said, "a poem of faith and strength; mine is one of lack and self-doubt" (192). Ramanujan Indianizes the modernist dicta that the poet should "make it new" (Pound) and that the "past [is] altered by the present as much as the present is directed by the past" (Eliot):[131] his metaprayers "use an old poem in a well-known genre to make a new poem to say new things. The past works through the present as the present reworks the past" (192).

In his prayers to the six-faced god, Ramanujan honors Murugan and yet mildly ironizes the deity for his defining peculiarities, the poet himself for his doubts, and the contemporary world for its fallenness into abstraction. An initial hint of the poetic sequence's distance from devotional mimicry and its inability to close the gap with the object of its attention is its length: Murugan has twelve eyes and twelve hands, but the sequence has only eleven parts. Indeed, the sequence sharply interrupts itself, after praying to end prayers "at once," its abrupt end highlighting the difference between the sequence's eleven limbs and the god's twelve:

Lord of lost travellers,
find us. Hunt us
down.

Lord of answers,
cure us at once
of prayers.[132]

The prayer begins seemingly in earnest, the hunt metaphor recalling Murugan's iconography with an arrow in one hand and bow in another. But the paradoxes of being found by the lord of the lost, of a "Lord of answers" addressed by a poet of questions, lead into the more pointedly ironic suggestion that prayers are like an illness or disease in need of a "cure." In a final irony, this is the one prayer that definitely seems to achieve its aim, since the moment it is pronounced ("cure us at once / of prayers"), the sequence of prayers shuts down, a circuit between the human and the divine that short-circuits in its final plea.

Like the ending of the sequence, line breaks throughout serve an ironic purpose by virtue of their abruptness. Ramanujan plays the graphic poetic text on the page against the oral performance of prayer, in which such ironies would disappear. In the third poem, for example, strong poetic enjambments humorously multiply meanings:

> Lord of green
> growing things, give us
> a hand
>
> in our fight
> with the fruit fly. (114)

The image of a twelve-handed god swatting fruit flies and the supplication of a god for such banal purposes seem overtly comic, but ironic twinges are also subtly embedded in the line turnings: is he a "Lord of green" or a "Lord of green / growing things"? And is that to be understood as "Lord of green-growing things" or as "Lord of green, growing things"? The enjambment of "give us" suggests a weighty supplication for something momentous, but Ramanujan completes this predicate with a cliché, "give us / a hand," which jangles when applied to a god with twelve hands. Sonically amplifying these ironies are the triple alliterations of "green," "growing," and "give," followed by "fight," "fruit," and "fly."

Some of the sequence's other ironies cluster around the god's multiple hands and faces. Murugan is said to have "six unforeseen / faces," a phrase that "bristles with paradox" since a god is expected to be "prescient," as R. Parthasarathy remarks in an essay that observes how Ramanujan's "clinical" and "cold, glass-like" English seems to "turn language into an artifact."[133] His clinically ironic inspection of religious discourse turns the language of prayer into an artifact in these embalmed prayers, or what Bruce King calls "these imitation-antique poems."[134] The supplicant's metadevotional tone keeps expressing itself in humorously colloquial phrases split up by enjambments, such as "found work / for" and "made // eyes at":

> Unlike other gods
> you found work
> for every face,
> and made
>
> eyes at only one
> woman. (113–14)

"Unlike other gods" seems ready to open out into fulsome praise for the god's distinctiveness, but shrinks in the next line to a compliment for not being on the dole, "you found work," and for being monogamous.

But Ramanujan's hand-and-face irony is directed not only at the god but also at himself and his faithless contemporaries:

> Lord of the twelve right hands
> why are we your mirror men
> with the two left hands
>
> capable only of casting
> reflections? Lord
> of faces,
>
> find us the face
> we lost early
> this morning. (116)

Ramanujan and other moderns are but diminished reflections of the god's magnificent multiplicity. With his many faces and hands, Murugan seems like someone seen in mirrors reflecting on other mirrors, but it is modern humans who, though praying to him, are inverted, empty images of his multitudinous fullness. And indeed these poems instance the mirroring of mirrors, since they show the speaker to be capable of prayers that are but reflections of, and on, prayers. For all their divinity-deflating ironies, Ramanujan's "antiprayers" turn out to instance prayerful humility after all. If Murugan seems a diminished thing for the poet under modernity, he is a marker at the same time of human diminishment in the absence of the divine. Even with his many faces, this god is unlikely to help the faithless poet who "prays" to him to recover lost face—another dead metaphor humorously revivified by his dead faith.

African, Caribbean, and South Asian poems in English are, in short, interlaced with prayer, both Christian and indigenous, but irreducible to it. Like other kinds of modern and contemporary poetry, even when they seem close to prayer in their use of address and in their intensity, they nevertheless put devotional speech acts under inspection, interrupt them with poetic devices such as enjambment, or dialogically juxtapose discrepant religious systems. Still, as we've seen over the course of this chapter, lyric poetry—by virtue of its apostrophic stance, figurative richness, self-reflexivity, and other features—is especially well suited to incorporating, pluralizing, playing on, reexamining, and mimicking prayer. I have artificially separated so-called postcolonial poetry from the "Western" poetry examined in the chapter's first part to avoid eliding its distinctive preoccupations, partly with tensions between colonially imposed and indigenous religions, partly with religious traditions that until recently have had only a modest presence in the West. But under global modernity, as we've seen, there are many commonalities across this divide, most obviously straddled by poets born in the global South who migrate north, from Claude McKay to Lorna Goodison, Agha Shahid Ali, and A. K. Ramanujan, and by "Western" poets who incorporate non-European forms of prayer, such as Native American poets Leslie

Marmon Silko and Joy Harjo, as well as others of European descent, such as Gary Snyder and Les Murray.

Despite the often secularizing impact of modernity, poets across the globe have renewed the age-old congress between poetry and prayer. No doubt ours isn't an age comparable to that which produced Herbert's and Donne's prayer-poems, but even so, modern and contemporary poets from Hopkins and Eliot to Glück, Wright, Ali, and Ramanujan have written poems enriched with prayer, drumming new sounds and meanings out of devotional forms. They have reanimated the ancient dialogue between poetry and prayer not by subordinating *poesis* to *oratio*. Instead, they have twisted prayer's conventions in different religious traditions, have sometimes suspended the religious content of devotional speech acts, or have subsumed prayer under the imaginative prerogatives of poetry. "The relation of art to life," according to Wallace Stevens, "is of the first importance especially in a skeptical age since, in the absence of a belief in God, the mind turns to its own creations and examines them, not alone from the aesthetic point of view, but for what they reveal, for what they validate and invalidate, for the support that they give."[135] Whether or not an individual poet is a believer, the secular cast of modernity has made prayer one of the creations that the modern literary mind turns to and examines, poetically encasing the devotional sister genre in highly wrought verbal chambers that both illuminate and distort it. Modern and contemporary poets have embraced but bracketed prayer, echoed but inverted it, in poems that may be less prayers than metaprayers, less addresses to the divine than images of such address, less petitions of the supernatural than self-scrutinizing commentaries on the figurative, rhetorical, and theological underpinnings of such petition. Even as modern and contemporary poetry has been strengthened by its intercourse with prayer, as also with the news, the law, theory, and the novel, it has jealously defended its distinctive freedoms, its varied forms of playfulness, its self-reflexive scrutiny, its wayward imaginings and linguistic exuberance.

4

POETRY AND SONG

FOR ALL THE interconnections between poetry and prayer, between poetry and the news, and between poetry and the novel, theory, and the law, song has long been conceived as poetry's closest generic kin. Turning from the news, a powerful but younger and more distant cousin, to prayer, an older, closer relative with many resemblances, and now to song, poetry's closest "sister" genre, we have been exploring poetry in proximity to ever closer family relations. Even so, the question of poetry's kinship with song may seem an unlikely framework within which to explore modern and contemporary poems. The primal unity between song and lyric poetry (the Greek *lyrikos* meaning "singing to the lyre") is often said to have been fractured long ago by written texts and then exploded by print culture. In Giorgio Agamben's history of European lyric, "the poetic text's definitive break with song (that is, with the element Dante called *melos*)" came around the twelfth century, when a poem became "essentially graphic."[1]

Emphasizing English texts, James William Johnson dates this "crucial metamorphosis" later, in the fifteenth and sixteenth centuries, when "the poet ceased to 'compose' his or her poem for musical presentation but instead 'wrote' it for a collection of readers"; now suited "to a visual as well as an auditory medium," the lyric "found itself bereft of the very element which had been the foundation of its lyricism—music."[2] The divide is said to have occurred still later in postcolonial African and Caribbean societies, which had rich traditions of oral poetry but took up literary verse to a significant degree only in the twentieth century. Whether the "story of the separation between song and speech" is set in the Middle Ages, the Renaissance, or modernity, it is haunted by the possibility of a split even at the point of origin, according to Jacques Derrida: "Degeneration as separation, severing of voice and song, has always already begun."[3]

Some modernist writers in the West—of European, African, and mixed ancestry—were intent on healing this fundamental breach, even though they often betrayed an ambivalence toward song that persists in contemporary poetry. Drawing on Homeric and Irish bardic examples, Yeats sought to return a musical orality to poetry and reverse the modern tyranny of the eye over the ear. He proposed a method of words spoken to delicate accompaniment on the psaltery. Yet he was emphatic that it must not stray into singing, which obscured sense behind sound and marred poetry's internal music. Song and print were a Scylla and Charybdis that the living poem must navigate: "I have always known that there was something I disliked about singing," begins his essay "Speaking to the Psaltery," "and I naturally dislike print and paper."[4] Yeats explained that "when I heard anything sung I did not hear the words, or if I did their natural pronunciation was altered and their natural music was altered, or it was drowned in another music which I did not understand. What was the good of writing a love-song if the singer pronounced love 'lo-o-o-o-o-ve,' or even if he said 'love,' but did not give it its exact place and weight in the rhythm?" (14). When he and Florence Farr tried to combine music and poetry, they "got to hate the two competing tunes and rhythms that were so often at discord with one another, the tune and rhythm of the verse and the tune and rhythm of the music" (16). Yeats's friend Ezra Pound thought that poetry was at its best (as in ancient Greece and medieval Provence) "when the arts of verse and music were most closely knit together, when each thing done by the poet had some definite musical urge or necessity bound up within it," and so claimed of poets, "We all of us compose verse to some sort of a tune."[5] Yet for all his nostalgia for the synthesis of music and verse in preprint *melopoeia*, Pound was no less critical than Yeats when it came to actual musical settings of poems: the resulting "distortion may horrify the poet who, having built his words into a perfect rhythm and speech-melody, hears them sung with regard to neither and with outrage to one or both."[6] Despite their longings for poetry to be reunited with performed music, both Pound and Yeats scorned the actual results of such fusion in music's distortions of the internal music and meaning of poetry. Another author of what is often thought of as highly "musical" poetry, Gerard Manley Hopkins also wanted to bring musical performance and poetry back together, but the notation systems available to him for melody and rhythm proved insufficiently elastic to accommodate his far-reaching poetic innovations. He was frustrated that he could not write songs successfully in quarter-tones and break the boundary of the musical bar.[7] Although Yeats, Pound, and Hopkins struggled in different ways to rejoin what print had sundered, all three of them acknowledged deep-seated genre differences that thwarted the union of these spheres of endeavor if the poetry of their poetry was to be maintained.

During the modernist era, writers of the Harlem Renaissance also famously tried to achieve such a synthesis: they wanted to reinvigorate and African-Americanize print poetry by infusing it with musical and song traditions, including jazz, ballads, spirituals, and the blues. Langston Hughes called on African American artists to open their work to the "colorful, distinctive material" of black music, including "the blare of Negro jazz bands and the bellowing voice of Bessie Smith."[8] Signature poems of the movement self-consciously creolize the scribal with the oral, combine literary verse with musical works. Hughes's "The Weary Blues" incorporates lyrics from an eight-bar blues and a twelve-bar blues, and its lines are inflected by blues syncopations ("Droning a drowsy syncopated tune"), interjections ("O Blues!"), vernacular ("sad raggy tune"), and call and response. But by anchoring the poem's speaker in rhyming iambic pentameter lines that aurally and visually contrast with the blues quotations, and by setting the speaker's lines apart as a written record of his reflective response to an overheard blues song ("I heard a Negro play," "I heard that Negro sing"), Hughes also marks the social and medial distance the poem straddles between literary speaker and blues singer.[9] As Hughes said, he wrote his early poems "after the manner of the Negro folk-songs known as Blues," a prepositional phrase that inscribes both likeness and ineradicable difference.[10]

So, too, do the song-based poems of Jean Toomer's *Cane.* "Song of the Son" begins:

Pour O pour that parting soul in song,
O pour it in the sawdust glow of night,
Into the velvet pine-smoke air to-night,
And let the valley carry it along.
And let the valley carry it along.[11]

This poem deliberately incorporates features of African American spirituals—apostrophe, repeated lines, melancholy tonality, and antiphony (e.g., the alternating refrain in the last stanza)—and fuses them with a self-understanding as a songlike poem grown from the "seed" of slave songs and spirituals. But as a modern poem written by a descendant or "son," it represents itself as self-consciously belated ("I have returned to thee," "late" though "not too late yet"), singular rather than collective ("saved for me"), and high literary rather than vernacular ("So scant of grass, so profligate of pines, / Now just before an epoch's sun declines").[12] Even more persistently than their white contemporaries, poets of the Harlem Renaissance labored to rejoin poetry and song, but their song-poems also acknowledge their literary difference.

In the aftermath of modernisms black and white, the gap between poetry and song, understood as verse vocally performed to music, has arguably yawned ever wider. At the most basic level, contemporary poetry's largely free-verse techniques have relegated most song forms to the margins, while most songs have clung to regular forms. But if poetry and song have irrevocably parted ways, why do many modern and contemporary poets, like Toomer, designate their poems "songs" in titles and texts, including prominent "American" poets from T. S. Eliot and H.D. to Adrienne Rich and W. S. Merwin, and "postcolonial" poets from Derek Walcott and Okot p'Bitek to A. K. Ramanujan and Jean Binta Breeze?[13] How do we explain poetry's abundant quotations of song lyrics from rock, pop, blues, jazz, folk, and opera, as also from funeral dirges, praise songs, abusive songs, reggae, and rap? Why have song lyrics continued to play a crucial role in poetry since modernism, from the wartime pop and Wagnerian opera in Eliot's *Waste Land* to the radio-blared blues "Love, O careless Love" overheard by the isolated speaker of Robert Lowell's confessional "Skunk Hour," to the more than eight hundred goofily distorted song lyrics that make up Kenneth Goldsmith's conceptualist *Head Citations* (2002), beginning with "This is the dawning of the age of malaria"?[14] How do we understand the survival of at least some song structures in modern and contemporary poems? What is the influence on poetry of the rise of technologies for the mass distribution and circulation of recorded song, most recently in digital form? Though we might think of the intergeneric and intermedial crossing between poetry and song as more relevant to medieval carols, Renaissance madrigals, and Romantic ballads, we understand modern and contemporary poetry more deeply by teasing out its self-understanding in relation to song, both its interfusions with it and its implicit self-definitions by contrast.

As we've seen in poetry's spirited engagements with the novel, theory, the law, the news, and prayer, although the widely embraced dissolution narrative of modern literary history postulates ever-more-blurred generic lines, it needs to be supplemented with a countervailing narrative: even as poetry appropriates and mimics song, among other genres, becoming ever more porous, it also asserts its specificity. To the extent that song is poetry's closest "sister" genre, the stakes for poetry may in this case be especially high. Characteristically chiastic and overstated, Jacques Roubaud's aphorism is nonetheless suggestive: "It's an insult to poetry to call it song. It's an insult to song to call it poetry."[15] Even as it celebrates its likeness to song, modern and contemporary poetry is alert to differences between musical singing and poetic inscription, between melodically vocalized verses and printed text.

If we consider the complex relation in song between music and text, reasons behind poetry's sometimes fractious engagements with its musical kin begin to emerge. Although song's musical elements are usually thought to be in a relation of mutual enhancement with its verbal elements, they are in tension more often than we typically acknowledge. Instead of adopting the conventional view that music supports and elaborates the poetry in song, the musicologist Lawrence Kramer argues that song's "dissociative" quality, "the disintegrative effect of music" on words, is such that vocal styles—whether the crooning in American pop or the explosive sounds of rock, the rhythmic exaggerations of nursery songs or the language-bending stylizations of lieder—variously "attack the text."[16] In his words, "the relationship between poetry and music in song is implicitly agonic"; the "music appropriates the poem by contending with it, phonetically, dramatically, and semantically."[17] Kramer conceptualizes as "songfulness" song's relative independence of "verbal content,"[18] its "manifestation of the singing voice, just the voice," its Lacanian retrieval of the mother's "enveloping voice."[19] From a less theoretical vantage point, that of a practicing composer, Martin Boykan comes to similar conclusions about what he calls "the disjunction between music and text" in song, noting that "music obliterates so many of the effects poetry relies on," including the complexities of verbal sounds and rhythms.[20] Musical accents are often at odds with poetic rhythms and enjambments, and the music forces the poetry to follow a different tempo, typically slowing it down and even obscuring the text's intricate semantic networks—hence the commonplaces that "the best texts for music are the simplest" and that composers should "avoid poetry with complicated syntax or involved intellectual frameworks."[21] Needless to say, such a prohibition would rule out a great deal of poetry after modernism, with its syntactic dislocations and conceptual complexities, even if composers, in settings of poems by Yeats, Rilke, Pound, Stein, W. S. Merwin, and many others, have ignored this advice. Paradoxically, even as poetry has cannibalized numerous song texts, the poetics of difficulty in modernism and its aftermath has driven the formal logic of poetry and song farther apart.

Although literary critics have yet to consider adequately the bearing of this heightened music-text friction on modern and contemporary poetry, scholars who elaborate the critical tradition that regards music and literature as sister arts have been aware of "episodes of jealousy, ironic misunderstandings," and efforts at control between them.[22] Citing Paul Valéry's comparison of hearing a good poem set to music with seeing a painting through a stained-glass window, John Hollander may take issue with it, but even so, he concedes "the deep rift in English verse between literary lyric and song text" and acknowledges what he calls the "incompatibility of major lyric poetry in the English language with the traditions of musical setting available to it."[23] In *The Experience of Songs*, Mark W. Booth also invokes Valéry's aphorism, noting the paradox that verse "highly patterned with musical sound of its own may clash with the music of its tune": in the music-text interplay, "there is a constant tug against the resolution of the words to carry out their own business."[24] Although sound repetition is central to poetic language, Booth points up its greater prominence in song:

> Given the relationship of redundancy to information, a songwriter should not have anything really new to say, at least if he expects to say it with words of the song alone. A poet on paper has much greater freedom to test the patience and ingenuity of the reader and to stretch his comprehension. He can aspire to enlarge the reader's world of experience and ideas. But a song, hedged by the demands of unity and clarity, must say things that are simplifications, and generally familiar simplifications.[25]

Similarly, Charles O. Hartman attributes to "practical necessity" the many forms of repetition in song, such as refrain, rhetorical pattern and formula, and duplicated lines, as well as the genre's being less dense in imagery and meaning than poetry tends to be, since "a song is its performance; and this means that it exists for its audience at a pace which is set, not by the person experiencing the song, but by the performer."[26]

These genre differences are, of course, shifting and unstable, and neither literary verse nor song is an essential or determinate, transhistorical or transcultural entity. Exceptions are often made to distinctions between poetry and song, including the poetic work of songwriters Bob Dylan, Van Morrison, Chuck Berry, Patti Smith, Cole Porter, and, as we will see, Lord Kitchener, or whole genres, such as lied, hip-hop, avant-garde art song, crooning, country, and calypso, but they are exceptions that are telling by their exceptionality. Songs in a number of different kinds of music typically subordinate the semantic, rhythmic, and imagistic dimensions of words to music and voice. Booth avers that in "classical singing and in jazz singing, notably, the voice may often be more a musical instrument than a medium of language."[27] In the poem "Syrinx," Amy Clampitt conjures a diva whose singing, "all soaring / pectoral breathwork, / . . . rises / past saying anything."[28] In rock singing, too, the young Mick Jagger was hardly alone in deliberately obscuring lyrics in performance; as one critic summarizes, "lyrics—the literary component of rock songs—are secondary to other, more meaningful elements," including performativity, sonic excess, communal event, and star personalities.[29] The words of a songwriter-poet such as Bob Dylan are, as even Christopher Ricks concedes, "one element only, one medium, of his art. Songs are different from poems, and not only in that a song combines three media: words, music, voice."[30]

Let's return to half of Roubaud's aphorism: why is it "an insult to poetry to call it song"? If we treat poetry as song, we obscure capacities it possesses and song lacks. The comparison to sung verse also makes literary verse seem deficient in melody and harmony, the physicality of the embodied voice, and the thick social and performative contexts. Even poetry in performance cannot compete on these terms. What Roland Barthes conceptualizes as "the grain" in a singer's voice—"the materiality of the body," heard in "the lungs, . . . the glottis, the teeth, the mucous membranes, the nose," "the body in the voice as it sings"—disappears from the printed poem and is of lesser significance in poetry recitations and readings than in song.[31] As Robert Pinsky writes in his poem "The Uncreation," we hear in songs "sentences turned and tinted by the body."[32] The materiality and bodiliness of the Barthesian "grain" can be powerful elements of song, more so than the critical fictions of voice constructed around literary verse. Sound poetry is, like other kinds of performance poetry, an obvious counterexample, but as we will see, it diverges from song in yet other ways.

Alive to the differences between performed song and inscribed verse, contemporary poets often pay homage to aspects of song that are beyond the powers of literary texts. In one of a number of elegiac poems for her mother in *Mercy* (2004), "last words," Lucille Clifton prays for the return of her mother in her thirties, particularly the grain of her singing voice, but she concedes its irrecuperability in a poem: "I can barely recall her song," she writes, and it is the physical embodiment of her mother's voice in song that she longs for, "my mother's calling, / her young voice humming my name."[33] Song seems to realize a fullness of vocal presence and interpersonal melding that are beyond the scope of the written poem—belated, estranged, fractured by elegiac yearning. In Tim Nolan's "At the Choral Concert," song affords a moment of cross-generational communion, when parents are surprised to find themselves joining "at exactly the right moment," "in one voice with our beautiful / children," singing the Hallelujah Chorus of Handel's *Messiah*.[34] Similarly, in Sebastian Matthews's "Barbershop Quartet, East Village Grille," father and son experience through song an oceanic fusion with each other, the singers, and the music itself: "we dive into the song. Or maybe it pours / into us, and we're the ones brimming with it."[35] Lyric poetry may aspire to this Dionysian dissolution of boundaries between self and other, as in Nietzsche's *Birth of Tragedy*,[36] but by its desire for that state, the written text marks itself as more beholden to the Apollonian *principium individuationis.* In the title work of C. K. Williams's *The Singing* (2003), the poet overhears a young man "making his song up," "obviously full of himself hence his lyrical flowing over," including improvised references to the poet's height.[37] But when the poet thinks of singing back in kind, he "couldn't come up with a tune" and is left instead in writerly alienation, inscribed in long, emphatically unsingable lines, clause awkwardly tumbling over clause, his syntax eschewing songlike fluency.[38]

Conversely, says Roubaud, "It's an insult to song to call it poetry." If we treat song as poetry, we effectively overvalue textual elements, which may be secondary, if not peripheral. Deracinated from their musical, vocal, and social contexts, song lyrics often seem skeletal, diminished, caricatured by expectations of semantic, graphic, syntactic, imagistic, allusive, psychological complexity and imaginative reach. Although contemporary poems thrill at the affective force of the voice in song, they point up the difference in poetry's layers of self-scrutiny. In "The Boleros," about these traditional songs sung in Spanish by Pedro Vargas, Lola Beltrán, and others, Alberto Ríos admires their emotional power and immediacy, like a screw, "each repetition another whole turn // Full of feeling, forced into you. / The words, and a half-sob as well // In the voice of the singer."[39] But the poem, self-reflexively aware that it lacks sobs, vocal grain, and instrumental music, pulls away from song's almost violent intrusion ("forced into you"), critically interposing itself in the affective relay between voice and audience: "It's easy to feel / Sympathy for the singer."[40] In "callas lover," D. A. Powell conjures the great soprano's rendition of an aria, "Un bel di" or "One Beautiful Day," in Puccini's *Madame Butterfly*, "her voice a sashed kimono," "such a pitch of tenderness in the voice," but this poem, too, draws back, dryly observing that "the emotion is, after all, an artfully conjured gesture."[41] Powell calls attention to the mechanics of digital mediation ("this is the track I've had on REPEAT all afternoon," "[shuffle play]"), and the distance of the technological simulacrum from the living singer corresponds in turn to the poem's remove from the voice it textualizes and tropes.[42]

Poetry's relation to digital technologies of recorded song is a subject to which I return in the second half of this chapter, which extends the book's purview to song-crossed American poems written in the twenty-first century. But the first archive I've selected for exploration is one in which the traffic between poetry and song has been especially heavy: postcolonial poems from Africa, the Caribbean, and black Britain. If even such song-enriched poetry reflects on its divergence from the songs it absorbs, then like novelized, theorized, and legalized poetry, like poetry that tells the news and poetry that prays, poetry that sings illuminates both poetry's dialogic engagements with its others and its awareness of its peculiarities as poetry.

CARIBBEAN, AFRICAN, AND BLACK BRITISH POETRY AND SONG

Although this chapter looks at song as seen from within contemporary poetry, as it both affiliates itself with and distinguishes itself from song, I want to acknowledge from the outset that, despite the just-cited statements to the contrary by Yeats, Pound, and other poets, Kramer, Booth, and other theorists, a song's intonation, melody, and instrumentation can sometimes enhance rather than diminish a poetic text. There are indeed examples of lieder, arias, raps, jazz songs, blues, folksongs, dirges, praise songs, calypsos, and rock tunes that successfully fuse music and poetry without relegating the poetry to secondary or tertiary importance. Like at least some novels, theories, legal texts, news reports, and prayers, some songs exceed the generic typologies that poetry and poetry criticism such as mine strategically attribute to them when incorporating and "othering" them.

So let's begin with a real song—vocally performed verses set to music—that deftly melds text, music, and voice. In the context of a discussion of postcolonial poetry and song, one fitting example is calypso. Setting witty, clearly articulated, topical verses to a musical, sambalike duple meter, calypso often works well as both musical performance and "poetic" text, conveying at its best, even if anesthetized on the page, some of its verbal, formal, and imaginative artistry. Kamau Brathwaite argues that calypso, rooted in slavery in Trinidad, marked "the first major change in consciousness" for Caribbean artists, as a "folk" poetry that rejected British colonial norms.[43] Lord Kitchener, one of the most accomplished calypsonians, had been a passenger on the *Empire Windrush* when it took the first large group of West Indian migrants to Britain in 1948, and many of the songs he wrote before his return to Trinidad in 1962 offer trenchant verses on colonialism, immigration, and race relations.

To take one example, Kitchener's "If You're Not White You're Black" works at three different levels simultaneously, levels that commingle ironically in recorded performance: as verse, its clever and pointed second-person address effectively deploys rhyme, wordplay, and syntactic parallelism; as music, it makes tongue-in-cheek use of a commercial big band sound, while evidencing a complex intercultural amalgamation that surpasses it; and as social critique, it pokes fun at the pretensions and delusions of an internalized colonial mentality. Recorded in Britain in 1953, several years before decolonization swept through Africa and the Caribbean, the song is cast as a mock-serious address to a mimic who thinks he can hide his blackness, his relation to "Africa, / The land of your great grandfather."[44] If the semantic and poetic content of song is often less significant than its other features, it is integral to this singer's chiding of a wannabe who wishes always to be among whites and to have nothing to do with his African cultural heritage. "After having been the slave of the white man," writes Frantz Fanon of this kind of self-alienation, "he enslaves himself."[45] The unknowing victim of the sense of racial inferiority foisted on him by colonialism, the mimic is constantly trying to "run away" from and "annihilate his own presence": "Subjectively, intellectually, the Antillean conducts himself like a white man. But he is a Negro."[46] In his own intergeneric synthesis, Fanon had blended psychoanalytic social theory with poetry in *Black Skin, White Masks* (published in French a year before Kitchener's song). Like Freud, Fanon knew that the poets were there before him: he cites long passages revaluing Africanness by Aimé Césaire,

Léopold Senghor, David Diop, Jacques Roumain, and other poets of negritude. Kitchener similarly merges social analysis with poetry, but unlike Fanon, with an emphasis on wit:

> Your skin may be a little pink,
> And that's the reason why you think
> That the complexion of your face
> Can hide you from the Negro race.
>
> No, you can never get away from the fact:
> If you not white, you consider black.

The refrain's use of "consider" marks a subtle difference from essentialism, indicating that British society constructs such a person's racial identity ineluctably "black," despite more complex affiliations—the "fact" of his racialization amusingly accentuated by the creolized rhyme's elision of the *t* sound. The lyrics represent this man as a racial hybrid ("Your father is an African; / Your mother may be Norwegian"), though he is trying to suppress all African traces from his identity. Wishing he were "really white," he shakes "his waist like Fred Astaire." Indeed, the song's suave musical orchestration is ironically suggestive of Astaire-like movie music, transformed by distinctly West Indian syncopations that enunciate calypso's African and Latin roots.

As we will see, poets often represent song as an especially powerful bearer of cultural memory, and here song musically, thematically, and rhetorically reminds the would-be Brit of his African cultural and racial origins, which he ignores at his peril. The mimic, refusing to acknowledge the black speaker-singer, passes him by at a distance and puts on "superior" airs, all to no avail, given the dividing line between black and white in 1950s Britain:

> Your negro hair is obvious;
> You make it more conspicuous:
> You use all sorts of Vaseline
> To make out you a European.

You speak with exaggeration
To make the greatest impression
That you were taught apparently
At Cambridge University.

No you can never get away from the fact
If you not white, you consider black.

In Lord Kitchener's comic portrait, as in Fanon's more somber
analysis, the postcolonial subject's desire to show "mastery" of
the standard European language is unmasked as the desire to become "whiter" and so "closer to being a real human being."[47] The
song's clever linguistic creolization, merging Standard English of
elevated diction ("conspicuous") with West Indian verb forms
("you consider black"), syncopations (*"No*, you can ne*ver* get
a*way* from the *fact"*), and pronunciations ("European" as three syllables), shows a mastery of both the standard and vernacular, and
in so doing takes apart notions of European linguistic superiority
by playing supplely with and between these registers. The wick-
edly funny rhyme of "Vaseline" with "European," though riffing
on signifiers of whiteness, itself demonstrates—as does the syncopated Astaire-like music—the very creolization denied by the
white-masked black man. The song explodes the wannabe's Euro-
pretensions by its inventive use of a black-entwined language and
music that display a dazzling intercultural dexterity, a dexterity
that can be contained along neither Afrocentric nor Eurocentric
lines. During the period when Kitchener composed and recorded
the song, the African presence in Caribbean culture, Stuart Hall
indicates, still remained largely unacknowledged in day-to-day
discourse;[48] through music, poetry, and voice, calypso tells a different story.

Although songs such as Kitchener's calypso skillfully incorporate poetry, as do songs in a variety of other forms, the rest of this
chapter reverses the genre lens, exploring contemporary poetry's
various ways of incorporating song: once more I look at a closely
related genre as refracted from within the poetry that internalizes

it. How is poetry invigorated by its intergeneric mingling with song, and yet how does it mark its difference? In the postcolonial world, many oral traditions including song forms have strongly shaped poetry, notably in Africa and the African diaspora in the Caribbean, Britain, and elsewhere. The cross-genre continuities are stronger, the friction less, than in the contemporary American poems we turn to later.

Indeed, some written African verse seems nearly indistinguishable from song, in the sense of text scripted for musical performance. The Ghanaian Kofi Awoonor, for example, transcribes musically accompanied song lyrics into verse forms for the page. His "Songs of Sorrow" sequence recasts Ewe dirges as literary verse, including lines that lament estrangement and loss:

> My people, I have been somewhere
> If I turn here, the rain beats me
> If I turn there, the sun burns me[49]

The semantic contrasts yoked to syntactic parallelism between and across such lines suggest in part Awoonor's effort to mimic something of the rhythmic patterning of Ewe lyrics sung to drumming; but, as Robert Fraser notes, the poet working in a strictly literary medium is bereft of the resources of communal responses and musical accompaniment.[50] In transmogrifying American blues songs into blues poems, Langston Hughes, Sterling Brown, and other African American poets met with similar challenges—the difficulties of removing song from its communal, performative, and musical contexts to the isolation of the printed page.

As in West Africa at the time of Awoonor's efforts, East African poets were also trying to capture aspects of song in literary verse. In *Song of Lawino*, Okot p'Bitek registers in the very title of his work its intimate relation to Acholi song, and within the work, the Ugandan village woman Lawino names specific song forms, many of which are partly digested into this long dramatic monologue:

> Provocative songs,
> Insulting and abusive songs

Songs of praise
Sad songs of broken loves
Songs about shortage of cattle.[51]

She also refers along the way to satirical beer-party songs, dance songs, war songs, and funeral dirges. Upbraiding her West-intoxicated husband Ocol, Lawino recalls songs in her reliance on second-person address ("Listen Ocol, you are the son of a Chief"), verbal and syntactic repetition and parallelism ("Stop despising . . . / Stop treating"), and Acholi proverbs ("Who has ever uprooted the Pumpkin?").[52] But as Okot remarked, his "long, long, long songs" were generically "a new thing altogether" in their difference from the "tradition I grew up in"—"love songs, funeral songs and so on and so forth to be danced, to celebrate particular important occasions, birth and circumcision and so on and so forth."[53] He was forcefully alerted to the difference between his songlike literary poem and indigenous song when he tried to read the first draft of *Song of Lawino* to his mother, herself a composer of songs, in one of the funniest accounts of the disjunction between poetry and song:

> I took it to her with great pride and said, "I've got a song for you." And she completely surprised me by asking me to sing it! Of course, I couldn't, and my balloon just collapsed. She went on and asked, "Is it a love song?" I couldn't answer that. "Is it a war song? Is it . . . What kind of song is it?" So I said, "You shut up. Let me read it to you." She shut up and I read it aloud. She was very pleased but kept on saying, "I wish there was some tune to it." You see, it was not really like an Acholi song.[54]

Okot had transformed Acholi songs by tying them together and encompassing them in a metasong, writing them down and so abstracting them from specific occasions, and fusing them with Western models, such as the novel, Longfellow's long poem *Song of Hiawatha*, Victorian dramatic monologue, and anthropological discourse.[55] Even at its most oral and indigenous, postcolonial

African poetry is, in short, inspired by song but should not be mistaken for it.

That said, there is a spectrum between such poems, songlike by virtue of their strong rhythmic or syntactic or sonic patterning, and more strictly textual poems. Some African poems present themselves even more obviously as written artifacts to be read, with little relation to song. Take Wole Soyinka's knotty, dense, elliptical early verse in *Idanre and Other Poems* and *A Shuttle in the Crypt*:

Hanging day. A hollow earth
Echoes footsteps of the grave procession
Walls in sunspots
Lean to shadows of the shortening morn[56]

Syntactically complex, imagistically contorted, this lugubrious prison meditation by a punning postcolonial Hamlet is far from a script for musical performance. Like Okot and Awoonor, later Nigerian poets such as Niyi Osundare hew more closely to song, orality, and performativity than does Soyinka in his early high literary verse.

African Caribbean and black British "dub" or performance poetry also exemplifies the close interrelations between poetry and song. Reggae is a particularly strong influence, finding poetic expression in the work of dub poets such as Jamaican-born black British poet Linton Kwesi Johnson, who has often performed his lyrics backed by a reggae band, and Jean Binta Breeze, another poet of Jamaican origin, who has lived mostly in Britain since 1985. Whereas Johnson's often songlike and strongly rhymed poetry sometimes approaches reggae's socially prophetic lyrics and the music's heavy four-beat rhythms, Breeze intercuts her free verse with actual song lyrics. In her performances, she sings these verses but not the free verse, noticeably shifting from "poem" to rhythm- and rhyme-rich "song" and back again. Consequently her performances both interweave poetry and song and differentiate the "songs" in the body of the poems from the written verse. The effusions of song elaborate and emphasize the poetry's performative dimensions—since "song" in most modern cultures is more of a performance art than "poetry"—at the same time that they draw attention to the poetic verse as spoken, not sung. In Breeze's best-known poem, "riddym ravings (the mad woman's poem)," the speaker, displaced by poverty from the countryside to a degrading and alienating Kingston, believes a radio inserted in her head plays the song that functions as her monologue's refrain:

Eh, Eh,
no feel no way
town is a place dat ah really kean stay
dem kudda—ribbit mi han
eh—ribbit mi toe
mi waan go a country go look mango[57]

Within the poem's first-person narrative, Breeze marks off the song lyrics typographically by italics, sonically by paired rhymes (*way/stay, toe/mango*), and rhythmically by four-stress measures. Although Breeze chops up the lines to look like ragged free verse, making them seem graphically continuous with the rest of the poem, they are, in fact, aurally structured like a tightly metered and rhymed quatrain in couplets. The phonic text of the song leaps out of the poem, while the graphic text reassimilates it. Repeated four times in the poem, the song-as-refrain plays against the forward momentum of a story-in-verse of a countrywoman's abject decline in the city. The insertion of the song in the body of the poem corresponds with the insertion of the radio in the madwoman's body. Forced by poverty and dislocation to scavenge for food in back lots, to eat banana peels, to wear coarse scraps for clothing ("crocus bag"), to wash herself by a standpipe drain, she nearly loses her one source of emotional sustenance in an operation. She believes the doctor and landlord surgically remove the radio from her head, but when they, thinking she is unconscious, leave, she reinserts it:

mi tek de radio
an mi push i up eena mi belly
fi keep de baby company
fah even if mi nuh mek i
me waan my baby know dis yah riddym yah
fram before she bawn (60)

A trickster who, like the female speakers of Louise Bennett's poems, confronts and cunningly subverts the powerful, this madwoman clings to her song-encoded memories of an alternative life, as distinct from the horrors of the alienating city street and madhouse (Bellevue). Whereas an earlier Jamaican poet, Claude McKay, is overwhelmed by nostalgia when he gazes on tropical fruits—"tangerines and mangoes and grape fruit"—in a New York City shop window,[58] Breeze's madwoman is transported into the countryside not by visual images but by song's mnemonic properties of rhythm and rhyme. When she pushes the radio up inside her belly, she specifically wants the baby to feel "dis yah riddym yah / fram before she bawn." Song's rhythmic pulse reconnects the displaced urban mother and child with an otherwise inaccessible past. The poem represents the musical verse's regular rhythms and rhymes as an umbilical link with maternal and pastoral origins, implicitly coding song as a primordial genre that devolves into the less musical discourse of poetry. Poetry is understood as an interstitial art, with one foot (so to speak) in the rural past, another in the urban present, one in oral and musical memory, another in socially alert commentary and narrative.

In a poem that Breeze wrote to commemorate the fiftieth anniversary of the arrival of West Indian migrants (such as Lord Kitchener) on the *Empire Windrush*, "The Arrival of Brighteye," one of the songs intercut with the prose poetry is explicitly linked to the preservation of memory. In this case, a young girl whose mother has had to go to England for financial reasons—

My mommy gone over de ocean
My mommy gone over de sea

she gawn dere to work for some money
an den she gawn sen back for me

—sings in hope of remembering her mother after more than five
years of separation:

granny seh it don't matter
but supposin I forget her
Blinky Blinky, one two tree
Blinky Blinky, remember me[59]

When the daughter arrives in the mother country, she at first mis-
takes for her natal mother a "white white woman . . . wid white
white hair," though "is nat mi madda at all" (just as this turns
out not to be a welcoming mother country)—a mistake so up-
setting that she urinates on herself, liquid that she hopes might
rejoin her with her grandmother across the seas in Jamaica (55).
Hers is again a crisis in part of memory amid dislocation: "An
me, what ah going to do, ah don't belong here, but ah don't belong dere eider, ah don't remember nobody, an all who would
remember me, dead or gawn" (56). By intermixing the especially
recursive structures of song with often unrhymed and unmetered
poetry, Breeze both acknowledges the longing for return and
suggests its impossibility—the strandedness of the postcolonial
subject in language that cannot fully rhyme the present with the
pre-postcolonial, preurban, preglobalized past. Even this song-
incorporating and -invigorated poetry both blends with and diverges from "song."

Patience Agbabi, a black British poet influenced by Breeze,
Johnson, and other "dub" poets but London-born of Nigerian par-
entage, writes and performs poems inspired by yet another African diasporic musical genre, as she puts it in "R.A.W.":

rap is my delivery   raw
more bitter than sweet
more twisted than bitter

> no throw away words
> cos I never drop litter[60]

Rap's insistent and rapid-fire end and internal rhymes are the most obvious techniques Abgabi lifts ("Poetry is theft"), as well as quick syncopated rhythms and self-reflexive wordplay (49). But whereas, in Tim Brennan's words, "the central aesthetic of rap is excess,"[61] Agbabi merges rap techniques with the modernist insistence on poetic economy, her humorous rhyme on "bitter" and "litter" updating Pound's dictum "To use absolutely no word that does not contribute to the presentation."[62] Like many rappers, she credits other African diasporic song forms, such as gospel, blues, soul, and "belowthebeltjellyrocknrolljazzfunk," believing they all help "articulate the pain / of our ancestors' ball 'n' chain," with rap as the quintessence of "taking our languages back / using our own black words" (50). As Brennan puts it, "rap tries to be (in an Afro-conscious gesture peculiar to the present conjuncture) both the encyclopedia and the built-in commentary on all the African cultural production that existed before it."[63] As poetry, Agbabi's verse harnesses the energies of the retrospective drive, although, as in the case of Breeze's intercutting of songs with poetry, it also maintains a reflective aesthetic distance from the musical form it draws on, tethering it to the page, separating it from techno-musical accompaniment, and fusing it with high literary aesthetics.

Agbabi's manifesto poem, titled initially "Word" and then "Prologue," is a rap-poetic tour de force. Agbabi draws on both the rapper's boastful account of authorial prowess and the ars poetica tradition, seamlessly melding the two. "Give me a word," begins the poem, enjoining attention to her oral poetics:

> Open your lips
> say it loud
> let each syllable vibrate
> like a transistor.
> Say it again again again again again
> till it's a tongue twister

till its meaning is in tatters
till its meaning equals sound[64]

As Roman Jakobson observes, the "reiterative 'figure of sound,' which Hopkins saw as the constitutive principle of verse," and which is even more pronounced in song, results from the emphasis on the medium as message,[65] until sometimes the meaning is nearly eclipsed by sound ("its meaning is in tatters"). A cross between Horatian instruction manual and rap boast, Agbabi's poem indicates how poetic self-reflexivity can highlight not only the oral but also the graphic dimension of language ("now write it down")—something that her literary rap can trade in but rap per se cannot—as when she frames a "word picture" in each of the epanaleptic lines "letter by letter" and "loop the loops," and in the rhymed lines beginning "till" that sandwich a third line:

now write it down,
letter by letter
loop the loops
till you form a structure.
Do it again again again again again
till it's a word picture.
Does this inspire?
Is your consciousness on fire?
Then let me take you higher. (9)

Riffing on the lyrics of a 1969 song by Sly & the Family Stone ("I Want to Take You Higher"), Agbabi represents her address as inspired by poetry's embrace of the materiality of language, foregrounded by phonetic and graphic repetitions that refuse subordination to the referential function. Rap poetry retrieves childhood play with words as material objects, as in Freud's jokes and Julia Kristeva's semiotic chora: "let me take you back / to when you learnt to walk, talk," words such as "mama / dada," the second word the name of an artistic movement that foregrounded an artist's materials.

> If you rub two words together you get friction
> cut them in half, you get a fraction.
> If you join two words you get multiplication. (9)

Near rhyme is a frequent feature of rap, and Agbabi's deft use of Wilfred Owen–like pararhyme, or double consonance in end rhyme (*friction/fraction*, or earlier, *motion/mission*), instances the rubbing together of word sounds that she commends to her audience as generative.

Rhyme, onomatopoeia, syntax, metaphor—Agbabi not only uses the resources of literary verse, she also plays on this classical vocabulary of poetic form:

> I got more skills than I got melanin
> I'm fired by adrenaline
> if you wanna know what rhyme it is
> it's feminine. (10)

She humorously calibrates poetics in relation to race. Drawing on rap's savvy interpolation of contemporary technological references, as well as its wordplay and boastful self-descriptions, Agbabi wittily fuses rap with Christian myth, ars poetica, and soul lyric:

> Cos I'm Eve on an Apple Mac
> this is a rap attack
> so rich in onomatopoeia
> I'll take you higher than the ozone layer. (10)

Not to show favoritism toward one computer platform over another or neglect the World Wide Web, her playful rap continues:

> So give me Word for Windows
> give me 'W' times three (10)

Wordplay proliferates as Agbabi punningly shows how words can spawn other words: "I'm living in syntax," she says (a joke emphasized in performance by her pausing between the syllables in "syn-tax"), only to tumble into another pun, on "iamb":

> You only need two words to form a sentence.
> I am I am I am I am I am
> bicultural and sometimes clinical,
> my mother fed me rhymes through the umbilical,
> I was born waxing lyrical.
> I was raised on Watch with Mother
> The Rime of the Ancient Mariner
> and Fight the Power. (10)

Not accidentally multiplying "I am" by five in a line of *I-am*-bic pentameter, Agbabi repossesses the basic metrical unit of English verse to sound out a cross-cultural declaration of identity. BBC children's television, Romantic verse, and Public Enemy's political rap are all cited as wellsprings of the very poem we are reading or hearing, which has indeed fused rap with childlike verbal playfulness and high-art poetic self-nomination. Both Agbabi and Breeze show poetry to be ineluctably intercultural and, pace Bakhtin, intergeneric, playing off its generic others in the negotiation among heterogeneous cultural and formal ingredients. Agbabi's poem is saturated with rap's rhythms, rhymes, and exuberant wordplay, even as her heteroglot mélange of the high and low, classical and vernacular, and her insistence on language's visual materiality on the page also separate her poetry from musical performance.

Rap has many different roots, among them spoken-word poetry of the 1960s and 1970s, and so for a spoken-word (if also literary) poet to turn to rap as a poetic resource is in some sense to return the form to one of its sources. Early in his career, the Soweto-born poet Lesego Rampolokeng also took cues from rap artists, as well as from the African American Last Poets and Gil-Scott Heron, and from reggae poets of Jamaican origin, Linton Kwesi Johnson and Mutabaruka. He has titled many of his poems "raps," including a fifty-rap sequence in *Horns for Hondo*, and has recorded raps backed by music. His apartheid-era poetry furiously denounces racial killings and economic inequities, and his postapartheid poetry is no less skeptical about the new South Africa: "nation-birth tumult amber survivals born   crippled amid fires / rooted in dread the race-thread holds in jesus bread moulds."[66] Compressed by asyndeton, his poetry of blood, feces, semen, and vomit trades in rap's insistent internal rhymes, vertiginous wordplay, and political rage. As he puts it in "rap 31" in *Horns for Hondo*:

> . . . I'm a rap-surgeon come to operate
> my tongue has no speed limit
> in the intensive care unit[67]

Rap's intensely rhymed and rhythmically uttered lines—often dense with wit, wordplay, syllabic echoes—make use of formal resources that are the poet's stock in trade.[68] Rap is a song-related form, even if its music-word fusion is less melodically performed than in most song forms, and an oral poetry, formally patterned with mnemonic devices and heavily borrowing from the past. Postcolonial poetry, as we've seen in Kofi Awoonor's and Okot p'Bitek's song-inflected verse, has frequently attempted to bend European literary traditions in the direction of a precolonial orality. Still, like such poets as Okot and Breeze in relation to other song forms, Agbabi and Rampolokeng concede by their formal hybridization of literary verse with the orality of rap—a diasporic form shaped by African American and African Caribbean sources—that postcolonial poetry in English is far from being some preliterate African oral essence. It draws on song but makes something new, formally interstitial, and specifically literary from it, when, like Awoonor's poetry, it transfers the syntactic and rhythmic patterns of oral dirges to the page but without the vocal and communal and musical contexts, or when, like Okot's poetry, it invokes the orature of abusive songs, dance songs, and praise songs but subsumes them in a hybrid dramatic monologue, or when, like Breeze's poetry, it intercuts its free verse and prose poetry with the distinctively regular rhymes and the framed rhythms of ballads and other songs, or when, like Agbabi's poetry, it dances between writerly texts and rap orality, high-art reflexivity and hip-hop exuberance. Some varieties of postcolonial poetry are among the most songlike contemporary verse in English, but even so, they often tease into view their poetic difference from the song forms they ride.

TWENTY-FIRST-CENTURY AMERICAN POETRY AND SONG

If "song" in the titles of postcolonial poems sometimes harks back to precolonial and preliterary funeral dirges, war songs, love songs, and so forth, a contemporary American poem that calls itself a "song" often signifies something less ritualistic and communal, something more like "poem suggestive of the sound, spontaneity, and simplicity of song." It evokes the sibling genre's affective and performative properties, its sound features (e.g., repetition, refrain, and rhyme), or its venerable kinship with poetry, as inscribed in a long Western tradition of poetic self-troping as song, from Homer's "Sing, goddess" and Virgil's "Of arms and the man I sing" to Walt Whitman's "I sing the body electric" and Emily Dickinson's "I shall keep singing!"[69] No wonder Michael Palmer felt so overwhelmed by the interconnections between the genres that, when given the seminar assignment as a student to speak on "Verlaine and Song," he remembers "literally being taken sick": "Not that I couldn't think of what to say, but that there seemed so much to say—the topic of song seemed endless—that I couldn't decide what to put in and what to leave out."[70] Yet the use of "song" in contemporary American poems, as in African, Caribbean, and black British poems, never entirely eclipses the figurative leap from one kind to another. Like his early poem titled "Song" in *Field Guide* (1973), Robert Hass's "Three Dawn Songs in Summer" in *Time and Materials* (2007), though lacking the formal properties typical of song, elicits song's frequent associations with emotion, brevity, and impulse. In the second of the "dawn songs," summer light is described as "very young and wholly unsupervised. / No one has made it sit down to breakfast. / It's the

first one up, the first one out"—a personification that partly justifies the title by linking the light's delightful irrepressibility and
irresponsibility to song.[71]

In contemporary American poetry's intermapping of itself with
various kinds of song, the genre's musical other occupies the imaginative space of both long-lost origin in the distant past and admired contemporary art form in the present. Song is poetry's *arche*
and its *telos*, what it was and what it might aspire to be. The influence of rock and roll is, according to Jim Elledge in his anthology of
American poems about the music, "integral, often all-consuming":
"the poets heard rock and roll lyrics more often than they read
poetry, and so learned many of the basics of poetry writing from
it."[72] In a representative prose statement collected from poets in the
anthology, David Wojahn celebrates this tutelage: "Rock and roll
music played a great role in my life" and even "started the process
which made me become a poet."[73] Updating and refining this affinity model, Stephen Burt argues that whereas baby-boomer poets
"used rock to invoke youth, rawness, energy, spontaneity, sex"
(qualities felt to be less immediately available in poetry), younger
American poets have found in indie or underground rock's mar-
ginality and "quasi-conspiratorial collaboration" a model for poetry.[74] At a more general level, this affiliative nexus can be traced to
other kinds of song as well—contemporary poems that evoke the
physical vocality and overwhelming pathos of arias, that incorporate downhearted motifs and repetition from the blues, and that,
as seen in Agbabi and Rampolokeng, model their braggadocio and
insistent rhyme on rap. By the twenty-first century, poetry's age-
old interplay with song had become a facet of the contemporary
genre's broadly dialogic engagements with other discourses and
media, at a time when interdiscursive collage is no less central to
poetry of many different kinds than unity and irony were to mid-
twentieth-century formalism. Within this context of heightened
dialogism, some American poets are especially drawn to poetry's
musical other, including a number of contemporary writers seldom
thought of as having much in common with one another. In recognition of the variousness of contemporary poetry's assimilations of
its text-music-and-voice other, I consider popular song in the Lan-

guage poetry of Rae Armantrout and Michael Palmer, the sound poetry of Tracie Morris, and the postconfessional poetry of Frank Bidart and Jorie Graham; hybridizations of poetry with the blues, reggae, hip-hop, and other forms in song-inspired poems by Kevin Young, Patricia Smith, Harryette Mullen, and Terrance Hayes; and poetry's awareness of its song inheritances in the intercultural poetry of Cathy Park Hong and Paul Muldoon.

But despite poetry's long-lived attraction to song, a closer look at contemporary American poetry's entanglement with its sister genre reveals not only attention but also tension, not only cross-genre longing and idealization but also rivalry and friction. Contemporary American poetry often represents song not only as its lost beloved origin or vital intergeneric twin or ego ideal but also as an antagonist. A poem from the 1990s that stages the conflicted relation between poetry and song may help lay the groundwork for a discussion of American poetry's dialogue with song in the new millennium. In his witty but self-elegiac "Self-Portrait in Tyvek[(TM)] Windbreaker," James Merrill describes himself listening to the great Neapolitan singer Roberto Murolo on a "yellow plastic Walkman."[75] Murolo, who continued to record albums in old age, just as Merrill composed this poem while facing death from AIDS,[76] is the poet's double, a latter-day Orpheus who "Modulates effortlessly" and "bears the old songs" into a postformalist era (670, 669). Murolo is also, more subtly, the poet's rival. Perhaps revealing something about poetry's relative imaginative freedom, Merrill not only transmits but also shatters inherited forms—or in the poem's own trope for its revisionism, unzips them, most dramatically in the final octave, which becomes a word picture for the unzipping of a windbreaker, of a traditional form, and ultimately of the poet's life. Ironically, this last stanza is said to be sung by Murolo, a conceit that emphasizes all the more its difference from song.

Don't ask, Roberto. Sing our final air:

Love, grief etc. * * * * for good reason.
Now only * * * * * * * STOP signs.

> Meanwhile * * * * * if you or I've ex-
> ceeded our [¿] * * * ~~more than time~~ was needed
> To fit a text airless and * * as Tyvek
> With breathing spaces and between the lines
> Days brilliantly recurring, as once *we* did,
> To keep the blue wave dancing in its prison. (673)

Replacing phrases with asterisks, striking out words, splitting a participle across an enjambment, inserting a silent and unsoundable bracketed question mark, capitalizing the word "STOP"—the text's extravagantly graphic and typographic features highlight poetry's visuality and their unavailability in song. As Johanna Drucker notes, poetry's "visual codes" have semantic force, which shouldn't be obscured by "nostalgic attachment to the idea of an 'origin' of poetry in song."[77] Merrill's poem names its "text airless" by punning contrast with Murolo's "air." For all the singer's skill, moreover, he can only recycle tired, if worthy, subjects ("Nannetta's fickleness, or chocolate, / Snow on a flower, the moon, the seasons' round") (670), whereas Merrill, reflecting on himself in the planetary context of late-capitalist environmental degradation, takes in everything from Blaise Pascal's philosophy and eco-friendly recordings of "whalesong and rain-forest whistles" to "Oprah" and "Pay-phone sex" (669, 670, 671). At the same time that the self-portrait's pentameters affectionately mimic the fluency, regularity, and spontaneity of song, "the blue wave dancing in its prison," the poem dramatizes proclivities by which poems sometimes distinguish themselves as poems—in their verbal and imaginative inventiveness, substantive and stylistic range, graphic significations as typographic art, and capacity to cannibalize song among other art forms.

Although poetry's affectionate rivalry with song is to some extent structural and perennial, it has arguably intensified in recent years as technologies of recording and transmission have made song all the more pervasive. The cassette Walkman sported by Merrill was no longer produced in Japan after 2010, but as noted above, Powell's "callas lover" refers to digital technologies that, even more than analogue portable music players, enabled song in the new millennium to permeate public spaces and private interiors. Along with other compact digital music players, the iPod, first sold in 2001 and promoted as putting "1,000 songs in your pocket," ensured the ubiquity, portability, and paradoxical isolation-in-communion of song experience.[78] Already near the beginning of the twentieth century, as T. Austin Graham observes, new sound technologies meant that Americans found themselves more surrounded by music than ever, immersed like the protagonist of Eliot's *Waste Land* "in an increasingly musical and mechanical culture" that makes of him "a walking collection of pop, something of a record himself."[79] Walter Benjamin intimates the dramatic effects of the "technical reproduction of sound," transporting music from its site of performance to countless other spaces, both private and public, and reorganizing sense perception.[80] Since 1900, entertainment industries and recording technologies have expanded at a fierce pace. As Graham shows, they have taken advantage of a well-known catchy song's exceptional ability to invade, cling to, and possess the imagination.[81] In such a context, the Nietzschean concept of music as "the art of collapsing distances" takes on new meaning.[82] The likelihood of one's being surrounded, penetrated, even possessed by recorded songs had reached a new height by 2007, when Apple sold its one-hundred-millionth iPod.[83] If poetry shares with music the impetus to efface boundaries, it is nevertheless an art of reflective distances that defamiliarize language, emotion, and perception; it is an art, too, of sharpened edges that finely discriminate the sounds, images, and discourses yoked together. At the same time that song has, thanks to commercial technologies, increasingly permeated everyday lives, literary verse's social marginalization since the early twentieth century has deepened its self-reflexivity. In abundant song quotation and collage, contemporary poetry echoes the technologically enabled ubiquity of music, but it also vigorously presses back, especially in response to popular song.

Rae Armantrout commented in an interview with Lyn Hejinian, "I tend to focus on the interventions of capitalism into consciousness," and "I keep asking what happens to the subject—the 'cogito'—in a society where perceptions are commodities, already shrink-wrapped."[84] One such form of intervention that her poetry considers, along with television sitcoms and cartoons, tabloids, movies, advertising, television guides, and political speeches, is recorded popular song—commercial music as what Theodor Adorno calls "predigested" sentiment and sound.[85] Armantrout deserves special attention as the author of books of poetry that exemplify poetry's resistant if obsessive relation to popular song. In "New," a poem in *Versed* (2009), she quotes what was, according to *Billboard* magazine, the most popular single of 2006, Daniel Powter's "Bad Day," a song heard in an ad campaign for Coke and on the TV show *American Idol*:[86]

> The new pop song
> is about getting real:
>
> "You had a bad day.
> The camera don't lie."
>
> But they're lying
> to you
> about the camera.[87]

The song lyrics are isolated graphically in quotation marks and in the poem's only sequentially capitalized lines. "The camera don't lie" recycles a truism, supposedly authenticated by folksily non-grammatical idiom ("camera don't"), but the poem questions the veracity of the camera and the song, syntactically flipping "camera" and "lies" in a chiasmus with "lying" and "camera." The song lies, just as the camera lies, just as the prettifying war news lies ("Fallujah / is the new Antigua"), just as an apologetic car salesman lies ("around bumptious 3-D / Hondas") (45). Set against these deceptions, the poem concludes with a hard-etched imagist image:

> sunlight nibbles
> on pre-
> charred

terrain
in the electric fireplace. (45)

In contrast to the ads, news, and *Billboard* hit, the sunlight functions like the bare existential thereness in an imagist or objectivist poem, such as the feeding deer in George Oppen's "Psalm." But the supposed fireplace, as in Plato's allegory of the cave, is a mere copy of a copy, a technological reproduction of a fireplace that is in turn a reproduction of natural light, and its fake coals are "pre- / charred," like the prefabrications of pop songs, advertising, and the news media. Reversing the Platonic secondariness of writing to orality, Armantrout paradoxically represents song as shrink-wrapped, while poetry, accepting its fallenness as interdiscourse, is in a better position to interrupt and interrogate commercial language games, as demonstrated by Armantrout's clinical quotations, razor-sharp enjambments, and imagist precision. Drawn to but wary of music's distance-collapsing capacities, a poem seeks to "establish," in Armantrout's words, "a 'critical distance'" from such language, "to isolate and decontextualize examples of it so we can do a double-take, as in 'Did you hear *that*?' On the other hand, such language pervades our consciousness and partially composes it, so how can we really be separate from this material?"[88] In an age of ubiquitous popular songs and ads, our minds are partly made up of commodified musical verses; instead of trying to spring free from such predigested words and thoughts, Armantrout's poetry shuttles critically in the interstices between them.

"Did you hear *that*?" is also the question raised in Armantrout's "Soft Money," in *Money Shot* (2011). First published a year earlier in *Poetry* alongside an interview, the poem quotes a phrase from what Armantrout called the "objectionable" chorus and "male gaze" of the Duran Duran song "Rio," near the top of the pop charts in 1983 and selling over two million copies:

> her name is Rio she don't need to understand
> and I might find her if I'm looking like I can
> oh Rio, Rio hear them shout across the land
> from mountains in the north down to the Rio Grande[89]

Armantrout's poem questions the fantasized and eroticized self-sufficiency of the song's narcissistic dancer ("They're sexy / because"), exposing its contradictions ("because they're needy," "because / they don't need you," "because they pretend / not to need you").[90] She juxtaposes her unmarked quotation from the song ("don't need / to understand") with Archibald MacLeish's famous claim in "Ars Poetica," "A poem should not mean / But be,"[91] later a watchword for the New Criticism and for formalist poetry:

> They're across the border,
> rhymes with dancer—
>
> they don't need
> to understand.
>
> They're content to be
> (not *mean*),
>
> which degrades them
> and is sweet.[92]

Unlike the cloying rhymes in the Duran Duran song, this poem conspicuously doesn't rhyme "border" or "dancer," except conceptually. Dovetailing Duran Duran's pop lyrics with a definition of high-art lyricism, Armantrout compares the independence of the unreflective dancer with the New Critical ideal of wholeness, art unriven by anything outside itself. To this jagged conjunction she adds philosophical discourse about the unknowability of the "thing-in-itself" (or *Ding an sich*) and what she calls in the *Poetry* interview the "narcissistic abjection" of "Miss Thing," "slamming those two contexts together to see what sparks fly,"[93] not to mention the discourses of pop song and high-art aesthetics, all forced into her tight and narrow strophes. As she says elsewhere, "I quite often juxtapose discourses from different realms in order to see what happens when they come into contact, what kinds of friction can result."[94] Armantrout's juxtapositions put under scrutiny MacLeish's dictum and the idea of "poems as pretty but effete": "So is a poem a bit like the 'Rio Dancer' in the song? I'm hoping it isn't."[95] By engaging song, among other intertexts, the poem's dialogism is positioned against the contradictory ideal of self-sufficient beauty lauded in pop ("which degrades them / and is sweet") and against the pretty-but-effete autotelism pursued in New Critical and Kantian aesthetics. "Soft Money" is an anti–ars poetica ars poetica, intended not only to be but to mean. A poem, Armantrout suggests, depends on its musical, literary, and philosophical others, even as it contravenes them; it immerses itself in them, in this case echoing song's emphatic recursiveness in the anaphora "They're sexy," even as it skeptically reflects on them.

Armantrout describes her dialogic practice as "a poetics of collisions and overlaps":[96] "Various voices speak in my poems," in recognition that "[w]e all hear voices, on the radio, in the newspaper, in memory" (58). But insofar as Armantrout can be said to "speak-in-tongues" (105), to combine various kinds of "found language" (90), to write in "a number of unidentified voices" that create an "ambiguous identity position" (107), she is not merely replicating a pervasive condition in the age of the media. Collage, anti-autotelism, and heteroglossia need not dissolve a poem into its others. Instead, a work's vigorous grappling with song and other discourses, including its clinching of unexpected points of overlap among them, evinces the tensile dialogism perhaps more readily achieved in poetry than in some other discursive forms. In response to a question of Hejinian's about her "composite" and "collaging techniques," Armantrout affirms: "The compression of poetry can create these contested, conflicted spaces" (105). Building on a conception of identity as irreducibly heteroglot, she torques—tonally, ideologically, sonically—various discourses within the especially compressed, intricate, and self-reflexive language game that is poetry. Though resembling popular song in sometimes almost being "built entirely of spare parts of other songs,"[97] her poetry also differs from its often passive recycling of tropes, lines, and forms. For Armantrout, as for such precursors as

Oppen and Lorine Niedecker, poetry is a tool of precision and rigorous circumspection, not the "slavish devotion" often announced in, and demanded by, popular song.[98] Even so, it is difficult, she concedes in "Locality," to purge the mind of sung verses, even when vapid ("Is it nummy? Yeah, huh?")—verses that compel us to listen to them "again and again."[99] In an age of hypersaturation by song, poetry's more strenuous and difficult music must exist in an uneasy counterpoint with the catchy tunes in our heads.

From the vantage point of Armantrout's poetry, overly insistent repetition is the condition of popular song—clichés, recursive sound structures, songs revolving in the mind. Add to these the repetition of songs heard constantly on sound systems in public spaces, the subject of two poems in *Versed*. In "Remaining," the Eagles' number-one *Billboard* hit "'Hotel California' is on every sound system," and the poem offers imaginative release from this aural imprisonment by figuratively leaping to comparable scenes of entrapment in sitcoms and cartoons (108). In "Left Behind," which has "a singer intoning 'Venice Boulevard' / on a store sound system / late last night" (27), Armantrout metaphorically bridges this street song with an image of eucalyptus trees in the median strip as ballerinas: "Twisted and white, limbs / strike poses" (26). Although song has long been associated with liberation and spontaneity, for Armantrout popular song is often instead on the side of capital and coercion, and it is in this context that poetry's meta-metaphoric leaps, self-reflective spaces, and muted music offer an alternative, albeit thoroughly contaminated by its other. Through convergence with and self-differentiation from song, among other intergenres, her poetry teases out its specificities as poetry—attention to the constructedness of its metaphors and other literary devices, critical inspection of the various discourses it twists together and acknowledges its dependence on, precision of both lineal and conceptual enjambments, and imaginative openings through the restrictions and repetitions of mass culture.

Another poet affiliated with Language writing, Michael Palmer also takes up, and pushes back against, the song insistently stuck in the mind. "Autobiography 6," a poem in *The Promises of Glass*

(2000), begins by playing on a popular Irish folk song about a strong alcoholic drink:

> *My name is Johnny Jump-Up*
> *And I live in a shiny car*
> *And when I'm really happy*
> *It takes me very far*[100]

"Often this most post-modern of songs," the poem continues, "runs through my head" (20). Insofar as Palmer's poem is in quatrains, it visually extends the drinking song, but it sonically refuses its example: it limits end rhyme and regular iambic trimeter. Like Armantrout, Palmer mimics but breaks the tyranny of obsessive song in part by turning from the melodic to the visual, forging a likeness between the image in the song and another: like a driver buoyed up by happiness, or a person by drink, a boat "is buoyed upward to some extent" by "the weight / of the water it displaces—" (21). The next time Palmer returns to the ballad, he displaces the speaker's name and head (*"that is not my name / My head rolled down the marble stairs"*) (22), and the final rendition doesn't even rhyme. Postmodernizing a proto-postmodern song, the poem plays with but untunes and critically disassembles it.

This affiliative but adversarial approach to song may seem out of keeping with Palmer's partiality to music, his postsymbolist aspiration to pull poetry in the direction of music. More than once Palmer has quoted Zukofsky's famous "equation of 'Lower-limit speech / Upper-limit music'" as a framework for understanding poetry's internal spectrum; Zukofsky's poetry, perhaps like his own, sometimes evidences an "urgency to arrive at a musicality."[101] Glossing his objectivist predecessor, Palmer comments: "Song then is where harmony gathers, 'the upper limit,' turning the linear flow of living-dying back to its sources."[102] If so, then the friction between the musical and semantic poles that Lawrence Kramer and others discern in song has its corollary within poetry. It is what Agamben calls "the tension and difference . . . between sound and sense, between the semiotic sphere and the semantic sphere."[103] As semimusical, semisemantic genres, both song and poetry, in comparison with everyday speech, tend to privilege the signifier over the signified, words as sounds (and in poetry, often also as shapes) over words as meanings; yet Palmer and other contemporary poets acknowledge that poetry's bending of language in the direction of the signifier is less strong than the musical pull in song, and this divergence from song's still greater investment in the signifier over the signified often affords poetry a more critical edge.

Aware that traditional songs have long captivated the mind, Palmer alludes to the recent technological intensification of the friction between poetry and song. In a 2007 lecture, he describes riding in a subway car in New York City and noticing that many other passengers "are listening to MP3 players and iPods, plugs in their ears, wires dangling down . . . , carrying their isolation booths around with them." But wondering what they might be listening to, he then calculates that "it is not impossible, it is not mathematically inconceivable, that one or another has down-loaded poetry readings from various sites and is listening to them as we travel."[104] Calculating the statistical nonimpossibility that one passenger just might have been listening to poetry, Palmer concedes that although digital music players, websites, and podcasts have made poetry more readily available as sonic experience, literary verse nevertheless remains a tiny fraction of a digital soundscape dominated by popular song.

A fond but competitive relation to song animates "The Merle Asleep," a poem in *Company of Moths* (2005). Palmer invokes an age-old trope in figuring the poet as songbird:

Asked the Merle, of Sleep,
Are you the kingdom of sand or the blessèd moon?

Asked the Merle, asleep,
Who are these blindered travelers

choiring Amazing Grace, Haunted Heart,
All the Things You Are . . . ?

But Palmer reverses the usual scene of human envy for birdsong, since in this case, the merle cannot sing. It asks who these singers are

> while I can only speak
> of thimbleberry, limestone and wheat,
>
> of power lines and poles and shattered oaks
> though I'd prefer by far to sing,
>
> I who can only speak?[105]

Most merles and other European blackbirds sing in spring and summer, but Palmer's ironically can't—hence the merle's puzzled self-differentiation from the poem's singing travelers. Claiming in an interview that the merle "can't sing" but instead "squawks," Palmer spells out the stakes of this difference, which is ultimately a contrastive likening between poet and singer: "I often think that those of us who come to this impossible task of poetry come out of a disability with language, a lack of fluency rather than dazzling fluency. I think dazzling fluency leads to other media and other uses of language, rather than the impaired fluency of our squawkings."[106] If song makes the most fluent use of language, Palmer disavows the mellifluous, full-throated renditions of spirituals and popular songs, such as "Amazing Grace, Haunted Heart, / All the Things You Are"; a poem's verbal music is impeded or distorted, squelched or muted, unlike the smoothly rounded melodies of crooners and soaring flights of gospel singers. Although Palmer's poetry is more richly patterned with verbal "music" than that of many contemporary poets, thick with assonance and alliteration, repeated cadences and words, syntactic parallelism and inversion, it uses end rhyme sparingly—here in repeated words such as "of Sleep" and "asleep," "speak" and "speak?"—favoring instead end-of-line assonances such as "Heart" and "Are," or "asleep," "speak," and "wheat" that stop short of fully binding euphonies. Rhythmically, this poem plays with frequently anapestic cadences, but they are sandwiched with irregular rhythms. In contrast to Sleep's songlike and dreamy "kingdom of sand or the blessèd moon," the poet/bird, though aspiring to song, "can only speak" of the less beauteous and more starkly imagistic places where it forages and perches, delivered in series of three that subtly repeat cadences, vowels, and consonants in lines of iambic pentameter: "of thimble-berry, limestone and wheat, // of power lines and poles and shat-tered oaks." A world so violent, fractured, and degraded, including a gruesome "pit / of twined and mounded limbs,"[107] seems less suited to melodious song than the poem's interruptive hints at a partly strangulated music. "What of the singer robed in red // and frozen at mid-song / and the stone, its brokenness"? asks "Stone," another poem in the collection,[108] summoning auditory and visual tropes for the *cantus interruptus* that is poetry for Palmer.

Sound poems, as works that perform words primarily for their sonic value rather than semantic content, would seem to be a strong counterexample to the argument I've been making for affectionate contention between poetry and its "sister art." But interruption keeps even these most songlike contemporary poems from being completely assimilable to song. Admittedly, Tracie Morris's sound poems are, in a sense, songs, as works that live in vocal, occasionally melodic, performance. They come out of a rich tradition of African American musical and vocal improvi-sation, ranging from rap, slam poetry, and jazz scat to Black Arts poems by Amiri Baraka and Sonia Sanchez, as well as post-Dada avant-garde sound art.[109] Unlike most literary verse, the verbal content of Morris's sound poems—often a single sentence or a few lines—consists of simple texts that have scant existence on the page; they function more like the melodic head of a jazz tune, merely a point of departure that the improviser at first replays but over time deranges, scatters, and turns against itself, in what Mor-ris characterizes as "the deconstruction of standards in jazz that I had heard growing up."[110]

A sound poem such as "The Mrs. Gets Her Ass Kicked" is based on a song, the first verse of Irving Berlin's "Cheek to Cheek," as sung by Doris Day and others: "Heaven, I'm in heaven, / And my heart beats so that I can hardly speak. / And I seem to find the hap-piness I seek, / When we're out together dancing cheek to cheek."[111]

As Christine Hume notes, Morris's sound poetry, in repeating and riffing on such song lyrics, "provides a vocal bridge between musical improvisation and poetry."[112] Morris begins her performance of the piece by singing these lines straightforwardly, merely slowing them down.[113] But over time, in this as in other of her sound poems, she breaks up melody and rhythm, fragments words into other words and syllables, repeats lines and phrases with sudden ellipses and elisions. Having sung the head, she gets hung up on the phrase "when we're out," repeating it several times, then leaps up the tonal scale on the word "heart" before becoming locked in a stutter on the word "I," a dramatization of the subject's fear and immobility behind the veneer of domestic happiness. Separating out part-lines such as "I can hardly speak," or breaking out the first syllable of the word "heaven" until it becomes a frightened "hey, hey, hey," or devolving the word "heart" into a terrified "hard, hard, hard, hard," she splits up words to turn them into signifiers of the domestic abuse screened out by the popular standard but implicitly lurking behind the facade of homely bliss. At the same time that words are distended, repeated, and torn apart, sudden sprints up atonal intervals also jarringly fracture the melody. Song has morphed into antisong. Or in her words, "it's the deconstruction of the version as sung."[114] Similar procedures can be tracked through sound poems that are closer to recitative, such as Morris's "Africa(n)," which both speaks and shreds the line "It all started when we were brought here as slaves from Africa."[115] The poem enacts sudden operatic leaps on the second word of the phrase "when we" and shakes out from the sentence other statements, such as "It's all Africa" and "We all start in Africa." For all their indebtedness to song, these sound poems, in which interruptions derange and rearrange words and lines and melodies, turn song on its head. And despite their emphasis on sound, it is the twisting of the semantic values of words into other words, rather than the subordination of the semantic to the melodic, harmonic, and rhythmic, that ultimately bends these songlike works in the direction of poetry.

Insofar as contemporary poetry may be songlike, its self-understanding is more as the interrupted song, the stuttered song, the broken song than as "song" per se. From Charles Olson to

Susan Howe, Michael Palmer, and Charles Bernstein, the concept of the stutter has been useful to experimental poetry's self-conception.[116] But perhaps less expected is the importance of the stuttered song, the song of impeded fluency, in postconfessional poetry. And whereas the primacy of collage in experimental poetry makes song and other quotations virtually axiomatic, dialogized song may be less anticipated in lyric. Frank Bidart made his reputation as the author of emotionally volcanic dramatic monologues, but his more recent books, including *Watching the Spring Festival* (2008), have included tightly clenched lyrics, some of which make room, even in their cramped spaces, for sung verse, among other popular forms. "Poem Ending with Three Lines from 'Home on the Range'" ends as forecast by the title, except that the poem breaks the lines differently from the song:

The red man was pressed from this part of the West—

'tis unlikely he'll ever return to the banks of Red River,
    where
seldom, if ever, their flickering campfires burn.[117]

Bidart reproduces the words from an early twentieth-century version of the western song, but by visually interrupting its flow, he plays on and plays up the differences between poem and song: his lines do not coincide with the rhymes *pressed/West, return/River/ ever/burn*, and they enjamb a stanza ("West— // 'tis") and a phrase ("where / seldom"). Rewrapping the aural lines in his contrastive visual lines, he critically reframes a song in which "seldom is heard a discouraging word"—a nostalgic song that, glossing over mass historical violence, has been treated in different versions as an anthem endorsing white America's manifest destiny.[118]

Still, even with the song's obtuseness about historical atrocity, Bidart credits it with some awareness of abject loss, albeit partial and distorted. Opening with the memory of having dived into an ill-fated love relationship twenty-three years earlier, the speaker finds a musical setting for that painful loss not only in the cowboy song but also in verses from Ray Charles's 1962 R&B cover of a country song by Don Gibson:

Whenever Ray Charles sings "I Can't Stop Loving You"

I can't stop loving you. Whenever the unstained-by-guilt
cheerful chorus belts out the title, as his voice, sweet

and haggard reminder of what can never be remedied,

answers, correcting the children with "It's useless to say,"
the irreparable enters me again, again me it twists. (12)

Repeating the tune's title in a stanza-straddling echo, the poem highlights song's recursiveness, both structurally and as recorded sound, except that what might be pleasurable repetition in soul or country music looks, laid bare on the page, like pain that can't be alleviated. "It's useless to say" is devastating, decontextualized from the playful call and response between Ray Charles and the chorus, becoming instead an opening onto silence, which lingers visually in the white-space enjambments between lines and stanzas. The word "reminder" shares most of its letters with "remedied," but this orthographic repetition intimates not healing but ever-recurring agony. Song's voice- and music-embodied memory, which absorbs personal injury into communal interplay, becomes instead in a poetic text the melancholia of irremediable wounds, whether in lost love or collective trauma. The turning back on itself in the chiastic line "the irreparable enters me again, again me it twists" is a syntactic emblem of ever-revolving pain.

At times Bidart's poetry pays homage to popular song; the title of his collection *Star Dust* (2005), for example, recalls the famous 1920s song about song and its consolations. His verse bears out, in its depictions of cruelly thwarted homosexual love, what popular music seems to say about love more generally: "Love craved and despised and necessary / the Great American Songbook said explained our fate."[119] The poems also implicitly admire song for being able to survive across time, encapsulate an era, and musically embody powerful feelings. In the concluding sequence of *Watching the Spring Festival*, "Collector," Bidart writes,

> Lee Wiley, singing in your bathroom
> about "ghosts in a lonely parade,"
>
> is herself now one—(56)

Wiley's 1956 rendition of "Who Can I Turn To?" unwittingly anticipates both her own demise and her ghostly survival as a disembodied voice. Enclosed in the small space of the bathroom, her song is also emblematic, however, of an era of repressions and oversimplifications, as the poet indicates in his self-address:

> erased era you loved, whose maturity
> was your youth, whose blindnesses
>
> you became you by loathing. (56)

Glossing her career as singer and actor in a note, Bidart explains that Wiley's era "remains the period that, for solace and pleasure, I most often return to. But it was also a suffocating box," partly alleviated by his discovering Robert Lowell and Allen Ginsberg (n.p.). Along with film, pre-1960s popular song was the soundtrack of the era that formed him, beloved for allowing escapist refuge and hated for shutting out nonnormative sexuality and untidy affect. Once again the Latinate twisting of syntax, placing "blindnesses," the object of "loathing," a line before it, suggests the contortions of pain: at first the sentence seems to say "whose blindnesses // you became," thus conceding the era's influence, only to turn this meaning on its head by line's end with the word "loathing" ("you became you by loathing" the era's "blindnesses").

Though less caustic in his response to commercial song, Bidart resembles Armantrout in conceding his poetry's dialogic dependence on popular lyrics, even as he, like Palmer and Morris, differentiates the reflectiveness poetry affords by interrupting and twisting song. Also like Bidart, Jorie Graham represents song as an emotional time capsule of a historical moment, as suggested by the syntactic mirrorings and hectic repetitions in a poem in *Sea Change* (2008): "the tune of the latest song, the recording of what was at some moment the song / of the moment, the *it* song, the thing / you couldn't / miss—it was everywhere—everyone was singing it."[120] And like Bidart, Palmer, and Morris, Graham fashions an image for poetry as interruptive song, though in her case it is still more violent: "It is all you have / left, but its neck is open, the throat is / cut, you have not forgotten how to sing, or to want / to sing."[121] Poetry is the song of the wounded throat.

African American music in genres including the blues, jazz, and spirituals has long been an inspiring muse and rival other for American poets and continues to be so for Kevin Young, Patricia Smith, Harryette Mullen, and Terrance Hayes. Though entwined with and energized by song, their poetry should not be reduced, however, to would-be song, wannabe music, attentive as it is to its peculiar capacities and riches as writerly text. Kevin Young's work is perhaps an obvious example of recent poetry that is built around song forms. Young's *Jelly Roll* (2003) is subtitled *A Blues*; its title page parenthetically fictionalizes the poetry as being "composed & arranged by" Young; and its epigraph quotes most of Robert Johnson's 1936 song "Kind Hearted Woman Blues."[122] But even as they honor and draw on the form's stock tropes and techniques, these poems seldom follow the strict verse patterns of blues songs. "Aubade," a love poem, like most of the book's verse, has the terse wit and sexual longing of many blues songs and even ends with a blueslike full rhyme. But its first lines mark out its difference from the blues:

There is little else
I love: the small

of yr back, your thick
bottom

lip stuck out.[123]

As the poet enumerates, blazon-style, the beloved's parts, the cross-stanza enjambment of "bottom" momentarily and humorously introduces an extra body part, jutting out in a line all its own, before the seeming noun swivels into an adjective. Dependent on the visual arrangement on the page, this double entendre pays homage to the blues but registers the pun in distinctly literary form. The poem ends with a nod in the direction of the parting-lovers' dawn "song" of its title:

> Will you stay?
>
> Or rise, as sun
> does, & make us day?[124]

Comparing the beloved to the day-making sun, the poem plays on a central image in the aubade tradition, yoking the blues to a high-art literary form rooted in song.

Just as Young hybridizes the blues with aubade, in "African Elegy (Much Things to Say)," a sequence in *For the Confederate Dead* (2007), written in memory of a friend killed in a car crash, many of the individual poem titles are from Bob Marley songs once beloved by the dead man, and snatches of these and other songs thread through the poems. But despite this interweaving of poetry and song, Young implicitly differentiates song as a more communal art, the connective tissue among the mourners:

> The night of the day
> we buried you
> we sang every
> Bob Marley song we knew
>
> by heart or whatever
> it was that kept
> us up, and together—
> call it *gut*—[125]

Oral, performative, affective, and broadly familiar, Marley's reggae songs enable sociability, enwebbing the mourners in a collectivity that lives in and through song, by contrast to the poet's literary pseudosong: in lines that have nothing like the steady four-four time and broad social critique of reggae, Young's literary farewell recalls a series of solitary memories of the dead man, recounts in detail the mourning poet's process of grieving, and documents the mourner's travels to and from the funeral in Tanzania. Written in short-lined free verse, drawing affective power from bits and pieces of song, the long poem parades idiosyncrasies of a work that, if enriched by song, could hardly be sung or otherwise performed by an assembly of mourners.

Just as Young fuses the blues and the aubade, elegy and reggae, Patricia Smith, a slam as well as print poet, merges two forms that come out of vastly discrepant traditions in her "Hip-Hop Ghazal," which begins:

> Gotta love us brown girls, munching on fat, swinging blue
>   hips,
> decked out in shells and splashes, Lawdie, bringing them
>   woo hips.
>
> As the jukebox teases, watch my sistas throat the
>   heartbreak,
> inhaling bassline, cracking backbone and singing thru hips.[126]

Having set up a *qafieh*, or monorhyme (*swinging, bringing, singing*) and a *radif*, or refrain (*blue hips, woo hips, thru hips*), the poem finishes off its string of nonenjambed couplets, or *beyt*, with the required signature, or pen name (*takhallos*):

> Crying 'bout getting old—Patricia, you need to get up off
> what God gave you. Say a prayer and start slinging. Cue
>   hips.[127]

But while it rings the changes on the ghazal, the poem also resounds with rap's vernacular ("Gotta love"), boasting ("decked

out in shells and splashes"), carnality ("woo hips"), musical motifs ("the jukebox," "bassline"), feminine rhyme ("blue hips," "woo
hips"), and references to the deejay's spinning of discs ("Cue
hips"). Hip-hop itself is already, as seen above, a hybrid form, fusing sources that range from African Caribbean toasting to African
American funk and spoken-word poetry, while the anglophone
literary ghazal makes use of a Persian and South Asian variation (sometimes sung) on the Arabic ghazal. Smith's cross-genre
fusion works in part because rap and ghazal are both subgenres
often centered on desire, deploying end rhymes and internal
rhymes that persist and insist. Like Young's aubade blues and reggae elegy, and like Agbabi's hip-hop ghazal, Smith's transnational
oral-scribal hybrid makes amicable use of, and self-consciously
departs from, song.

In inventive amalgamations that open up possibilities for poetry, twenty-first-century poems playfully enmesh literary traditions with other oral, musical, and song forms. In *Sleeping with the
Dictionary* (2002), Harryette Mullen's "Jinglejangle" is inspired by
rhyming games, such as the banana or name game popularized
through recorded music in Shirley Ellis's 1964 "The Name Game"
and other hit songs: witness the key phrase "Anna banana" in
the line "Asian contagion analysis paralysis Anna banana ants in
your pants."[128] A later line embeds Jakobson's famous example of
"the poetic function of language," an assonantal and alliterative
presidential slogan:[129] "Icky Ricky I Like Ike ill pill ill will Increase
the Peace inky-dinky" (38). In song as in poetry, the sonic features
of language are privileged over the referential, but the humor in
Mullen's uproarious romp depends in part on juxtaposing words
and phrases that sonically and alphabetically replicate but semantically diverge, such as "date rape deadhead deep sleep dikes on
bikes" or "fungus among us fun in the sun funny money fur burger
fuzzy wuzzy" (35, 36). The lines force together rhyming, jingling,
alliterative, assonantal, and onomatopoetic words and phrases
taken from incongruous spheres—political slogans, TV commer-
cials, brand names, kids' cereals, jazz riffs, and so forth—but even
poetry as "musical" as this, strongly foregrounding the sonic di-

mension of language and cleverly hybridizing oral genres, doesn't dissolve into sound the heterogeneous worlds it evokes. The influence of blues, jazz, rap, and other musical forms is evident throughout Terrance Hayes's poetry in its rapid turns of thought, slippery language, and distorted forms. Hayes credits music and painting for inspiring his writing yet also distinguishes poetry from these other arts as a genre that is also a metagenre:

Though I studied painting growing up, I also studied, in a less academic sense, music: Coltrane, RUN DMC, James Brown, Roberta Flack, Bob Marley, chorus tunes (I was on chorus all through school—even in college, but don't let that get out). I suppose painting taught me as much about the ways to look, to see, as music did about the ways to hear and listen. . . . I know one reason I chose poetry over painting or music has to do with poetry's capacity to reflect, if not embody, all other art forms. This is probably why there are more poems about paintings and music and movies than there are paintings, music, and movies about poems. . . . I can do more as a poet, express more.[130]

Though an avid singer and painter, Hayes sees poetry as a uniquely encompassing genre, able to "reflect" and reflect on musical, painterly, and other forms ("about paintings and music . . .") even as it absorbs them. His poem "emcee," in *Hip Logic* (2002), embodies many rap ingredients but at the same time evinces, to recur to Bakhtin, "the ability of a language to represent another language," "to talk about it and at the same time to talk in and with it."[131] In keeping with rap, "emcee" samples two unattributed hip-hop songs, OutKast's "ATLiens" ("throw their hands in the air— // . . . *And wave 'em like they just don't care*") and Run-DMC's "King of Rock" ("*Sucka emcees can call me Sire*").[132] As in "King of Rock" and many other rap lyrics, its subject is the emcee. As if a rap boast, the poem calls attention to the emcee's low-riding "triple X / Jeans," his rhyming "about death," his composing "Explicit lyrics," his sending young dancers "into jerk patterns and grunts," his inspiring women to write his "phone number on their tongues," even his sporting a "grin of gold-plated windows" (5–6). But even as Hayes's poem likens itself to hip-hop in all these ways, it also (in a bracketed reference to vocal percussion) names an aspect of its musical kin that is beyond poetry, since to "beatbox   beatbox beatbox"—making sounds inseparable from the performer's lips, mouth, tongue, breath, voice, and mike—is to evade linguistic transcription, as well as all but the barest musical notation (6). In less flattering ways, the poem signals that it may be raplike but is not a rap, dislocating braggadocio from first person to second, making limited use of rap's resounding internal and end rhymes in sonic recursions that are less predictable than they are in rap, foregrounding the poem's aspiration to suppler and freer sonic arrangements. The texture of the figurative language also marks a divergence, demonstrating still greater reach than that of the verbally inventive group OutKast (e.g., in "ATLiens," the imaginative line "Cause I'm cooler than a polar bear's toenails"):[133]

> Your mind twists,
> Gleams like lights on the bends of a night-coaster
> The riders throw their hands in the air—(5)

Hayes's adaptation of a line from "ATLiens" highlights his poem's outpacing of its musical double in its figures of speech. Finally, the pants-dropping, sex- and self-infatuated emcee in Hayes's poem is, however admired, also the object of irony, as in the wordplay that collapses the alphabet, divinity, and a swollen microphone: "You are the Alpha and the Omegaphone" (5). In "emcee" and his other rap poems, by quoting and critically inspecting rap, by fondly adapting yet exceeding the bounds of the musical form in figuration, reflexivity, and formal arrangements, by acknowledging beatboxing and other aspects of hip-hop as beyond poetry's ken, Hayes both intertwines literary verse with rap and implicitly differentiates them.

Hayes has spoken admiringly of Langston Hughes's "synthesis of blues and poetry,"[134] and "The Things-No-One-Knows Blues" in *Hip Logic*, like Hughes's "The Weary Blues" and Young's

"Aubade," synthesizes poetic and song forms, "blues and poetry"; it is both like a blues and about the blues, except that Hayes is less reverent toward the musical form. The poem plays at the edges of blues song convention, in both form and content, while aggressively pushing in new directions. Instead of following the *aab* blues-song structure, the poem skews or splits the occasional rhyme it incorporates into most stanzas (e.g., *luxury/poetry, hot/bit, Orleans/degrees, the latch/wristwatch, portable ex/wistfulness*), with only one full rhyme, on "knee" and "agree," appropriately in lines about B. B. King's erotic caress of his guitar Lucille (9–10). So too Hayes, like Young and Hughes, remakes blues wordplay for the page:

> My favorite turtleneck sweater, the green,
> 50% rayon, 5% cotton (rest unknown) one,
>
> shrank in a tub of hot
> bath water. (9)

Downhearted and bankrupt, the speaker knows neither the rest of the sweater's contents nor restfulness—a parenthetical pun that in oral, rather than written, form would likely vanish. Later in the poem, Hayes ventures another scribal pun, in lines about lines that make use of orthographic and visual cues unavailable to the blues singer: "The lines on my palms slope like portable ex / & why graphs" (10). The blues is hyperbolic, but Hayes's poem's description of the speaker's and his family's physical, financial, and emotional hardships and woes are all the more extreme, ending in the hilariously exaggerated fear of his masculinity's possible demise: "I suspect my penis will / be fed to a swimming Gila // monster" (10). If honoring the blues, Hayes also distorts and exceeds the song form through his extravagant imaginative stretch and writerly play.

As we have seen, many contemporary poems engage song as living and even rival other, but the idea of poetry's inheritances from song—implicit in Hayes, Young, and Smith—emerges more explicitly in some twenty-first-century poems that are vividly transnational as well as transgeneric. The tour-guide protagonist of Cathy Park Hong's *Dance Dance Revolution* (2007), for example, virtually allegorizes poetry's descent from song, including this very poem, which opens with a nod to Dante's guide in the *Inferno* ("den I's taka ova / as talky Virgil").[135] The futuristic tour-guide narrator, speaking in a kaleidoscopically hybrid language that combines English and Korean with "Han-guk y Finnish, good bit o Latin / y Spanish . . . sum toto Desert Creole en evachanging dipdong" (25), had a mother who was a singer "so famous . . . / . . . even now . . . ju can buy her CD / en de world muzak section" (42). At the time of the daughter's birth, she sings a song that, according to her daughter, is the "longest song eva" (42), or as it is headlined in a poem title, "Song That Breaks the World Record" (41), before she tragically dies. Her daughter also becomes a celebrated voice, but unlike her singing mother, she earns fame as disembodied, radio-transmitted speech, recalling Salman Rushdie's Saleem Sinai in *Midnight's Children*. "I's don want to / fes n'won" (105), she explains, embarrassed by her baldness, but she agrees to the demand that she "gib dim / ye voice" (105) during a Korean uprising, when she becomes known as the "voice o Kwangju" (104). Hong's poetic sequence traces its length, voicing, and verbal playfulness to song, but she does things with translingual amalgamation, spelling, and puns that would be impossible to reproduce orally, even in the "longest song eva."

Among song's vestigial presences in poetry, surviving like a musical tailbone, is the refrain, a device that takes on new functions in the body poetic. A poet and songwriter identified with both Irish and American poetry, Paul Muldoon provides a fitting final example of poetry's intergeneric engagement with song, since he writes both for the page and for musical performance. In the witty lyrics composed for his rock group, his songs' themes, narratives, and historical allusions, their alternating and couplet rhymes, may create a denser and knottier texture than that of most rock lyrics, but they are more straightforward than comparable features of his poetry, which notoriously skews and disassembles rhyme patterns, reaches for arcane allusions, and scrambles narrative.[136] It would be difficult to imagine one of his challenging long poems, such as *Madoc*, performed by his rock band, and many of his rock songs would seem relatively lightweight printed in a collection of his poems. Muldoon brings us full circle to the songlike orature in postcolonial poetry, since he notes in an interview that song and poetry have often been "closely related" and even "indivisible": in Ireland, poetry was still recited to music well into the eighteenth century. But he also acknowledges that typically "they're actually trying to do somewhat different things": a song lyric by Leonard Cohen printed in a book of poems remains "rather steadfastly a song lyric. It needs something else. It may be recited as a poem, but for one reason or another, it's missing something. The poem conventionally brings its own music."[137]

The refrain is a point of both convergence and divergence between Muldoon's poems and songs. In the songs "The Adult Thing" and "You Got the Rolex (I Got the Rolodex)," the variations on the refrain are scant,[138] while the refrains in some of his poems, such as "The Loaf," "One Last Draw of the Pipe," and "Homesickness" in *Moy Sand and Gravel* (2002), mutate wildly. The function of the refrain in Muldoon's poems is usually more complex and less immediately apparent than it is in his songs; in "The Loaf," it organizes the poem's five stanzas around the five senses:

> When I put my finger to the hole they've cut for a dimmer
>   switch
> in a wall of plaster stiffened with horsehair
> it seems I've scratched a two-hundred-year-old itch
>
> *with a pink and a pink and a pinkie-pick.*[139]

The poet retrofits the inherited song structure of the refrain, like the wall of his old house in New Jersey. What appears at first to be a typical instance of the refrain's songlike subordination of the semantic to the sonic, because of the seeming nonsense, lexical repetitions, alliterations, and wordplay, turns out otherwise, as the refrain lines turn sequentially to each of the human senses, from touch ("*a pinkie-pick*") and hearing ("*a clinky-click*") to smell ("*a stinky-stick*"), sight ("*a winkie-wick*"), and taste ("*a linky-lick*") (51–52). The hole cut in the wall provides a sensory opening to the traumatic past, in particular the harsh labor and mass death by Asiatic cholera of Irish immigrants building the Delaware and Raritan Canal. At the end, the poet tastes the imaginary loaf baked from dung-transmitted whole grain, "*with a link and a link and a linky-lick*"—a line that enacts the "link" between these words and earlier instances of the refrain, between Irish American poet and earlier Irish immigrants, and between the poem and the song device it remakes in the compact "loaf" on the page (52). This and other twenty-first-century poems acknowledge and engage their musical inheritances, but far from merely pining for the prelapsarian unity of poetry and song, play, often extravagantly, in the gap between them.

•

Experimental, lyrical, sound, and performance poems pay homage to song, quote it, hybridize themselves with it, and adapt its conventions. Whether American, postcolonial, or otherwise, poetry and song will never be fully disentangled from one another, in part because poets will likely continue to echo and compose songs, and songwriters to write and assimilate poems (Bob Dylan's absorption of Pound and Eliot is an obvious example). Fluid in boundaries, poetry and song are constituted as genres in part by the intersections and frictions between them, the give-and-take between writerly or performative act and audience presuppositions, and the shifting criteria for inclusion and exclusion on the part of magazines, publishers, and syllabi, as of recording companies, concert halls, and clubs.[140] In the context of today's period style of collage and heteroglossia, the dialogism of contemporary poetry makes it still harder to draw clear lines between poetry and song, among other genres.

But to stop there, as if contemporary poetry and song were one—the poem-song, exemplar of the dissolved boundaries among postmodern arts—would be to miss poetry's frequent insistence on its specificity as poetry, the formal grounds of its art, however provisional and contextual. For as we've seen in poetry's dialogue with other close generic kin, such as newswriting and prayer, the novel, theory, and the law, it's a misapprehension of the relation between poetry and its others, if not quite an insult, to confuse them. Despite contemporary poetry's affiliative openness to song, despite its quoting of song lyrics and adaptation of song forms to the page, some literary verse, perhaps especially in the age of the iPod, also pushes back. Contemporary poems sometimes represent popular songs—more commercially viable than tuneless lyrics—as ubiquitous and invasive, piped into public spaces and transported on personal music players, permeating subjectivities with prepackaged phrases and feelings. They question the clichés, forms, and formulas that enweb popular song in capitalist mass production, defamiliarizing them and at the same time making from them new art. Incorporating song texts and structures, yet breaking their enchantment as they strip words of musical accompaniment and vocal grain, twenty-first-century poems both indulge and interpose a reflective distance on the affective, sonic, and linguistic allure of the "1,000 songs in your pocket." The fluency of most song runs into interruptive stutters and stammers in contemporary poetry's less regularized sound structures and freer verbal, syntactic, and imaginative arrangements. Twenty-first-century poems squeeze song together with other discourses in compressed and tense amalgamations, and, partly by the light struck from this inner friction, they gain a critical perspective on the vocabularies and forms they torque together. With enjambments that can range in their effects from the humorous to the violent, with extravagant typography and silent white spaces, contemporary poems remind us that, unlike songs, they have graphic as well as sonic dimensions (albeit song can be joined to spectacle in live concerts and music videos). Contemporary poetry often envies song for being more musical, affective, communal, vocal, performative, and Dionysian than mere textuality allows. Fondly affiliating itself with its "sister art," it derives energy and sustenance from its interplay with song's peculiar capacities. But at the same time that it *"aspires to the condition of music,"* in Walter Pater's words,[141] and encrypts its lost musical origins and musical ambitions, contemporary poetry is often para-song, metasong, pseudo-song, postsong, and even antisong. As we've observed with other intergenres, it is paradoxically in contemporary poems that draw especially close to songs, that are on the hazy and shifting boundary line between the arts—adapting blues riffs or rap boasts or ballad refrains, intercalating scribal and oral forms, showing off verbal music or immersing themselves in song lyrics—that poetry can be seen most clearly to define itself and illuminate its conditions of possibility.

For all these intergeneric tensions, the self-troping of poetry as song, from Yeats and Toomer to Agbabi and Breeze, Palmer and Hass, shows no signs of fading. When W. S. Merwin opens "The Nomad Flute" in *The Shadow of Sirius* (2008) with the line "You that sang to me once sing to me now," he summons an illustrious tradition in which poetry has called itself into being as song, as poetic "air": he hopes it may "survive," unlike the extinct "lions in China."[142] Despite such anxieties about the fate of poetry, it seems likely that poems, even as they draw attention to their differences from song, will continue to name themselves "songs," in recognition of enduring connections with their closest double, their musical alter ego and antagonist, one among several of their most inspiring and vexing others. Poetry will never be conclusively defined, but if recent works are any indication, it will continue to re-create itself in its affiliative and contentious dialogue with song and other others in whose mirror image it endlessly renews and rediscovers itself.

NOTES

CHAPTER 1: A DIALOGIC POETICS

1. W. B. Yeats, "Easter, 1916," in *The Variorum Edition of the Poems of W. B. Yeats*, ed. Peter Allt and Russell K. Alspach (New York: Macmillan, 1968), 391 [variant title, as originally published], 392; Gertrude Stein, "Sacred Emily," in *Gertrude Stein: Writings 1903–1932*, ed. Catharine R. Stimpson and Harriet Chessman (New York: Library of America, 1998), 395; Louise Bennett, "Jamaica Oman," in *Selected Poems*, corrected ed., ed. Mervyn Morris (Kingston, Jamaica: Sangster's Book Stores, 1983), 21.

2. *Oxford English Dictionary Online*, s.v. "poetry," 2.a., accessed December 17, 2012, http://dictionary.oed.com/.

3. W. H. Auden, *The English Auden*, ed. Edward Mendelson (London: Faber, 1977), 327.

4. *The Oxford Book of Modern Verse: 1892–1935*, ed. W. B. Yeats (New York: Oxford University Press, 1936), 1; *Against Expression: An Anthology of Conceptual Writing*, ed. Craig Dworkin and Kenneth Goldsmith (Evanston: University of Illinois Press, 2011), 576–77.

5. Auden, *English Auden*, 329.

6. Roman Jakobson, "What Is Poetry?" (originally published in Russian in 1933–34 and in English in 1976), trans. Michael Heim, in *Language in Literature*, ed. Krystyna Pomorska and Stephen Rudy (Cambridge, MA: Belknap–Harvard University Press, 1987), 368, 369. J. S. Mill also asks this question; see chapter 3 below.

7. Jakobson, "Linguistics and Poetics" (originally published in 1960), in *Language in Literature*, ed. Pomorska and Rudy, 70.

8. Jakobson, "What Is Poetry?," 369.

9. As examples of recent historical disaggregations of "lyric" and "poetry," understood to be modern Western constructions, see Virginia Jackson, "Lyric," in *The Princeton Encyclopedia of Poetry and Poetics,* 4th ed., ed. Roland Greene, Stephen Cushman, et al. (Princeton, NJ: Princeton University Press, 2012), 826–34, and Stephen Owen, "Poetry," in *Princeton Encyclopedia*, 1065–68.

10. Tzvetan Todorov, *Genres in Discourse,* trans. Catherine Porter (Cambridge: Cambridge University Press, 1990), 14; Jacques Derrida, "The Law of Genre,"

trans. Avital Ronell, *Critical Inquiry* 7 (1980): 65. Among special journal issues on genre, see "Remapping Genre," coordinated by Wai Chee Dimock and Bruce Robbins, *PMLA* 122, no. 5 (2007), and "Theorizing Genres I" and "Theorizing Genres II," ed. Ralph Cohen and Hayden White, *New Literary History* 34, nos. 2–3 (2003).

11. Hans Robert Jauss, *Toward an Aesthetic of Reception*, trans. Timothy Bahti (Minneapolis: University of Minnesota Press, 1982), 88.

12. Alastair Fowler, *Kinds of Literature: An Introduction to the Theory of Genres and Modes* (Cambridge, MA: Harvard University Press, 1982), 41.

13. A. K. Ramanujan, "Where Mirrors Are Windows," in *The Collected Essays of A. K. Ramanujan*, ed. Vinay Dharwadker (New Delhi: Oxford University Press, 1999), 8, 9.

14. Ralph Cohen, "History and Genre," *New Literary History* 17, no. 2 (1986): 205, 210.

15. Marianne Moore, "Poetry," in *The Poems of Marianne Moore*, ed. Grace Schulman (New York: Viking, 2003), 135; Stéphane Mallarmé [Bestow a purer sense on the language of the horde], "Le tombeau d'Edgar Poe," in *Collected Poems*, trans. Henry Weinfield (Berkeley: University of California Press, 2011), 71.

16. M. M. Bakhtin, *The Dialogic Imagination: Four Essays*, ed. Michael Holquist, trans. Caryl Emerson and Holquist (Austin: University of Texas Press, 1981), 285, 298, 286.

17. M. M. Bakhtin, *Speech Genres and Other Late Essays*, trans. Vern W. Mc-Gee, ed. Caryl Emerson and Michael Holquist (Austin: University of Texas Press, 1986), 92.

18. M. H. Abrams, *The Fourth Dimension of a Poem and Other Essays* (New York: W. W. Norton, 2012), 42.

19. Mutlu Konuk Blasing, *Lyric Poetry: The Pain and the Pleasure of Words* (Princeton, NJ: Princeton University Press, 2007), 3, 29, 35.

20. Susan Stewart, *Poetry and the Fate of the Senses* (Chicago: University of Chicago Press, 2002), 2, 12.

21. Jakobson, "What Is Poetry?," 378. The idea is also central to Roland Greene's entry "Poem" in *Princeton Encyclopedia*, 1046–48.

22. Jakobson, "Linguistics and Poetics," 69.

23. See Gary Saul Morson, *The Boundaries of Genre: Dostoevsky's "Diary of a Writer" and the Traditions of Literary Utopia* (Austin: University of Texas Press, 1981), 79.

24. Cohen, "History and Genre," 207.

25. On Bakhtin's dialogism and poetry, see Mara Scanlan, "Ethics and Lyric: Form, Dialogue, Answerability," *College Literature* 34, no. 1 (2007): 1–22; Roger Simmonds, "The Poem as Novel: Lawrence's Pansies and Bakhtin's Theory of the Novel," *English Studies* 84, no. 2 (2003): 119–44; Donald Wesling, *Bakhtin and the Social Moorings of Poetry* (Lewisburg: Bucknell University Press, 2003); Michael Eskin, "Bakhtin on Poetry," *Poetics Today* 21, no. 2 (2000): 379–91; David H. Richter, "Dialogism and Poetry," *Studies in the Literary Imagination* 23, no. 1 (1990): 9–27;

and Jonathan Monroe, *A Poverty of Objects: The Prose Poem and the Politics of Genre* (Ithaca, NY: Cornell University Press, 1987).

26. Bakhtin, *Dialogic Imagination*, 358.

27. Ibid.

28. Andrew Welsh, *Roots of Lyric: Primitive Poetry and Modern Poetics* (Princeton, NJ: Princeton University Press, 1978).

29. On Marvell and Herbert's adaptation of the adage into poetry, see Rosalie L. Colie, *Resources of Kind: Genre-Theory in the Renaissance*, ed. Barbara K. Lewalski (Berkeley: University of California Press, 1973), chap. 2. On Donne's *Anniversaries* in relation to Ignatian meditation, see Louis Martz, *The Poetry of Meditation: A Study in Religious Literature of the Seventeenth Century*, 2nd ed. (New Haven, CT: Yale University Press, 1962). On generic hybridization in the Renaissance and later, see, in addition to Colie, Fowler, *Kinds of Literature*, 181–88.

30. For relevant criticism, see the section below on poetry and the novel.

31. Daniel Albright, *Untwisting the Serpent: Modernism in Music, Literature, and Other Arts* (Chicago: University of Chicago Press, 2000), 5–6.

32. See Marjorie Perloff, *Radical Artifice: Writing Poetry in the Age of the Media* (Chicago: University of Chicago Press, 1991).

33. Marjorie Perloff, *Unoriginal Genius: Poetry by Other Means in the New Century* (Chicago: University of Chicago Press, 2010), 11.

34. Vanessa Place, "Miss Scarlett," *Poetry* 194, no. 4 (2009): 339–40. The poem was part of a cluster of flarf and conceptual writing. For a discussion of this poem and other examples, see Brian Reed, "In Other Words: Postmillennial Poetry and Redirected Language," *Contemporary Literature* 52, no. 4 (2011): 756–90. See also Kenneth Goldsmith, *Uncreative Writing: Managing Language in the Digital Age* (New York: Columbia University Press, 2011), and Perloff, *Unoriginal Genius*.

35. Perloff, *Unoriginal Genius*, and Goldsmith, *Uncreative Writing*.

36. Cathy Park Hong, "Decorated Wall," *Parnassus: Poetry in Review* 30, nos. 1/2 (2008): 607, and *Dance Dance Revolution* (New York: W. W. Norton, 2007).

37. Anne Carson, *Nox* (New York: New Directions, 2010).

38. Juliana Spahr, *Well Then There Now* (Boston: Black Sparrow, 2011).

39. Srikanth Reddy, *Voyager* (Berkeley: University of California Press, 2011).

40. Paul Guest, *My Index of Slightly Horrifying Knowledge* (New York: Ecco-HarperCollins, 2008).

41. Morson, *Boundaries of Genre*, 52.

42. Herbert Tucker, *Epic: Britain's Heroic Muse, 1790–1910* (New York: Oxford University Press, 2008), 269.

43. John Ashbery, "Self-Portrait in a Convex Mirror," in *Selected Poems* (New York: Penguin, 1986), 190.

44. Ashbery, "Soonest Mended," in *Selected Poems*, 87, 88, 89.

45. For critiques of this assumption, see Fowler, *Kinds of Literature*, 32; Adena Rosmarin, *The Power of Genre* (Minneapolis: University of Minnesota Press, 1985), 7–8; and Jahan Ramazani, *Poetry of Mourning: The Modern Elegy from Hardy to Heaney* (Chicago: University of Chicago Press, 1994), 23–28.

46. T. S. Eliot, "The Music of Poetry," in *On Poetry and Poets* (New York: Farrar, Straus and Giroux, 1957), 17.

47. Bakhtin, *Dialogic Imagination*, 4, 5.

48. Claiming that "[s]peech genres organize our speech in almost the same way as grammatical (syntactical) forms do," Bakhtin mentions, for example, military orders, business documents, scientific statements, proverbs, chronicles, contracts, legal texts, clerical documents, commentary, and official and personal letters; see his *Speech Genres*, 61, 78–79, 60–62.

49. In addition to Albright's *Untwisting the Serpent* and Perloff's *Unoriginal Genius* and *Radical Artifice*, see, for example, T. Austin Graham, *The Great American Songbooks: Modernism, Musical Texts, and the Value of Popular Culture* (New York: Oxford University Press, 2013); Frances Dickey, *The Modern Portrait Poem: From D. G. Rossetti to Ezra Pound* (Charlottesville: University of Virginia Press, 2012); Daniel Kane, *We Saw the Light: Conversations between the New American Cinema and Poetry* (Iowa City: University of Iowa Press, 2009); Elizabeth Bergmann Loizeaux, *Twentieth-Century Poetry and the Visual Arts* (Cambridge: Cambridge University Press, 2008); Bonnie Costello, *Planets on Tables: Poetry, Still-Life, and the Turning World* (Ithaca, NY: Cornell University Press, 2008); David Trotter, *Cinema and Modernism* (Oxford: Blackwell, 2007); Robert Crawford, ed., *Contemporary Poetry and Contemporary Science* (New York: Oxford University Press, 2006); and Susan McCabe, *Cinematic Modernism: Modernist Poetry and Film* (Cambridge: Cambridge University Press, 2005).

50. Cohen, "History and Genre," 204.

51. David Perkins, *A History of Modern Poetry: From the 1890s to the High Modernist Mode* (Cambridge, MA: Harvard University Press, 1976), 12, 14.

52. R. G. Cox, ed., *Thomas Hardy: The Critical Heritage* (New York: Barnes and Noble, 1970), xxii, xxiii; James Gibson, *Thomas Hardy: A Literary Life* (New York: Palgrave, 1996), 141; and Michael Millgate, *Thomas Hardy: A Biography Revisited* (Oxford: Oxford University Press, 2004), 384.

53. T. S. Eliot, *The Letters of T. S. Eliot* (New York: Harcourt Brace Jovanovich, 1988), 1:179n4; Herbert Leibowitz, *"Something Urgent I Have to Say to You": The Life and Works of William Carlos Williams* (New York: Farrar, Straus and Giroux, 2011), 183; Marianne Moore, *Becoming Marianne Moore: The Early Poems, 1907–1924*, ed. Robin G. Schulze (Berkeley: University of California Press, 2002), 36 (Schulze notes that the second edition sold 488 copies between January 5 and June 30, 1925); and A. David Moody, *The Young Genius, 1885–1920*, vol. 1 of *Ezra Pound: Poet* (Oxford: Oxford University Press, 2007), 378n2.

54. Wallace Stevens, *Collected Poetry and Prose*, ed. Frank Kermode and Joan Richardson (New York: Library of America, 1997), 970–74; Yeats to Olivia Shakespear, April 25, 1928, in *The Letters of W. B. Yeats*, ed. Allan Wade (New York: Macmillan, 1955), 742; and George Bornstein, *Material Modernism: The Politics of the Page* (Cambridge: Cambridge University Press, 2001), 77.

55. Kotti Sree Ramesh and Kandula Nirupa Rani, *Claude McKay: The Literary Identity from Jamaica to Harlem and Beyond* (Jefferson, NC: McFarland, 2006), 189.

56. See Lawrence Rainey, *Institutions of Modernism: Literary Elites and Public Culture* (New Haven, CT: Yale University Press, 1998), 154.

57. In the 2007 survey of books read in the previous year, 54 percent of respondents reported having read a book of popular fiction and 3 percent a book of poetry; see "Book Study," Associated Press–Ipsos Public Affairs, http://surveys.ap.org/data/Ipsos/national/2007-08-09%20AP%20Book%20Topline.pdf. In the 2004 NEH report "Reading at Risk," 45 percent of adults read fiction, 12 percent read poetry, and 5.9 percent listened to poetry readings, and the aggregate 14 percent of poetry readers or listeners in the 2002 survey had declined from 20 percent in 1992 and 1982; see http://www.nea.gov/pub/ReadingAtRisk.pdf. Had the surveys included advertising jingles and other nonliterary forms of poetry, the figures would, of course, look quite different: see Mike Chasar, *Everyday Reading: Poetry and Popular Culture in Modern America* (New York: Columbia University Press, 2012).

58. Bakhtin, *Dialogic Imagination*, 7.

59. On eighteenth-century poetry's adaptation of novelistic character, forms, and themes, see G. Gabrielle Starr, *Lyric Generations: Poetry and the Novel in the Long Eighteenth Century* (Baltimore: Johns Hopkins University Press, 2004); on the genres' interrelations in the Romantic period, see Marshall Brown, "Poetry and the Novel," in *The Cambridge Companion to Fiction in the Romantic Period*, ed. Richard Maxwell and Katie Trumpener (Cambridge: Cambridge University Press, 2008), 107–28.

60. Perkins, *History of Modern Poetry*, 234.

61. Ibid., 231–32.

62. E. A. Robinson to Arthur R. Gledhill, October 28, 1896, in *Selected Letters*, ed. Ridgely Torrence (New York: Macmillan, 1940), 13, and Robinson, "Richard Cory," in *Selected Poems*, ed. Robert Faggen (New York: Penguin, 1997), 9.

63. Pound to Harriet Monroe, January [?], 1915, in *The Selected Letters of Ezra Pound, 1907–1941*, ed. D. D. Paige (New York: New Directions, 1950), 48 (emphasis in original).

64. Stephen Fredman, *Poet's Prose: The Crisis in American Verse*, 2nd ed. (Cambridge: Cambridge University Press, 1990), 1. See also Marjorie Perloff, "Lucent and Inescapable Rhythms: Metrical 'Choice' and Historical Formation," in *Poetry On & Off the Page: Essays for Emergent Occasions* (Evanston, IL: Northwestern University Press, 1998), 116–40, and Monroe, *Poverty of Objects*.

65. Ezra Pound, "A Retrospect," in *Literary Essays of Ezra Pound*, ed. T. S. Eliot (New York: New Directions, 1935), 3.

66. Yeats, in *Oxford Book of Modern Verse*, ix, xi.

67. Eliot, "Music of Poetry," 23.

68. Michael André Bernstein, *The Tale of the Tribe: Ezra Pound and the Modern Verse Epic* (Princeton, NJ: Princeton University Press, 1980), 230. Building on this remark and Bakhtin, Patrick D. Murphy argues for the novelization of verse in the modern American long poem; see his "The Verse Novel: A Modern American Poetic Genre," *College English* 51, no. 1 (1989): 57–72.

69. Frank Bidart, "Ellen West," in *In the Western Night: Collected Poems* (New York: Farrar, Straus and Giroux, 1990), 109–21. On dramatic monologue as a novelistic model for lyric poetry, see Jonathan Culler, "Why Lyric?," *PMLA* 123, no. 1 (2008): 201–6.

70. See T. S. Eliot, "*Ulysses*, Order, and Myth," in *Selected Prose of T. S. Eliot*, ed. Frank Kermode (New York: Harcourt, 1975), 175–78; Ronald Bush, *The Genesis of Ezra Pound's Cantos* (Princeton, NJ: Princeton University Press, 1976), 193–97; William Carlos Williams, *I Wanted to Write a Poem: The Autobiography of the Works of a Poet*, ed. Edith Heal (Boston: Beacon, 1958), 72; Seamus Heaney, "Station Island" XII, in *Station Island* (New York: Farrar, Straus and Giroux, 1985), 92–94; and Charles W. Pollard, "Traveling with Joyce: Derek Walcott's Discrepant Cosmopolitan Modernism," *Twentieth Century Literature* 47, no. 2 (2001): 197–216.

71. Pound to Felix E. Schelling, July 9, 1922, in *Selected Letters*, 180. See John Espey, *Ezra Pound's "Mauberley"* (Berkeley: University of California Press, 1955), 49–62, and Russell J. Reising, "Condensing the James Novel: *The American* in *Hugh Selwyn Mauberley*," *Journal of Modern Literature* 15, no. 1 (1988): 17–34.

72. T. S. Eliot, "Henry James," in *Selected Prose*, 152, 151.

73. W. H. Auden, "At the Grave of Henry James," in *Selected Poems*, new ed., ed. Edward Mendelson (New York: Vintage, 1979), 119, 123.

74. D. H. Lawrence, *The Rainbow* (orig. 1915; Harmondsworth, UK: Penguin, 1981), 42.

75. Perkins, *History of Modern Poetry*, 96, 233, 12. For an even earlier instance of poetry's adaptation of novelistic character, forms, and themes, see Starr, *Lyric Generations*.

76. James Joyce, "Chamber Music," II, rpt. in *The Essential James Joyce*, ed. Harry Levin (London: Jonathan Cape, 1948), 442.

77. Joyce, *Essential James Joyce*, 465, 467.

78. See Marc C. Conner, ed., *The Poetry of James Joyce Reconsidered* (Gainesville: University Press of Florida, 2012).

79. See Robert Adams Day, "The Villanelle Perplex: Reading Joyce," *James Joyce Quarterly* 25, no. 1 (1987): 69–85.

80. Obi Nwakanma, *Christopher Okigbo, 1930–67: Thirsting for Sunlight* (Woodbridge, Suffolk, UK: James Currey, 2010), 109.

81. Christopher Okigbo, "Fragments out of the Deluge," in *Collected Poems* (London: Heinemann, 1986), 49. Subsequent page references appear in text. In earlier published forms, the numbering and ordering of the sequence were different.

82. Chinua Achebe, *Things Fall Apart* (New York: Fawcett Crest, 1969), 150.

83. Ibid., 94.

84. Helen Vendler, *Soul Says: On Recent Poetry* (Cambridge, MA: Belknap–Harvard University Press, 1995), 5.

85. Jonathan Culler, "Apostrophe," in *The Pursuit of Signs: Semiotics, Literature, Deconstruction*, 2nd ed. (Ithaca, NY: Cornell University Press, 2002), 152.

86. James George Frazer, *The Golden Bough: A Study in Magic and Religion*, abridged ed. (London: Macmillan, 1957), 703.

87. Christopher Okigbo, "The Limits," V–X, *Transition*, nos. 6–7 (1962): 39.

88. See Jonathan Culler, "What Is Theory?," in *Literary Theory: A Very Short Introduction* (New York: Oxford University Press, 1997), chap. 1.

89. See "Poetry and Theory: A Roundtable," convened by Bruce R. Smith, *PMLA* 120, no. 1 (2005): 97–107; Robert Baker, *The Extravagant: Crossings of Modern Poetry and Modern Philosophy* (Notre Dame, IN: University of Notre Dame Press, 2005); Michael Davidson, "Philosophy and Theory in US Modern Poetry," in *A Concise Companion to Twentieth-Century American Poetry*, ed. Stephen Fredman (Oxford: Blackwell, 2005), 231–51; Joanne Feit Diehl, "Poetry and Literary Theory," in *A Companion to Twentieth-Century Poetry*, ed. Neil Roberts (Oxford: Blackwell, 2001), 89–100; Marjorie Perloff, *Wittgenstein's Ladder: Poetic Language and the Strangeness of the Ordinary* (Chicago: University of Chicago Press, 1996); Mark Edmundson, *Literature against Philosophy, Plato to Derrida: A Defence of Poetry* (Cambridge: Cambridge University Press, 1995); Donald G. Marshall, ed., *Literature as Philosophy/Philosophy as Literature* (Iowa City: University of Iowa Press, 1987); and Hank Lazer, "Critical Theory and Contemporary American Poetry," *Missouri Review* 7, no. 3 (1984): 246–65.

90. Aristotle, *Poetics*, trans. S. H. Butcher, rpt. in *Criticism: The Major Texts*, rev. ed., ed. Walter Jackson Bate (New York; Harcourt Brace Jovanovich, 1970), 25. For Plato's critique of poetry, see the *Ion* and the *Republic*, especially bk. 10.

91. John Crowe Ransom, "The Concrete Universal: Observations on the Understanding of Poetry," pt. 1, *Kenyon Review* 16, no. 4 (1954): 554–64, and pt. 2, 17, no. 3 (1955): 383–407.

92. See, e.g., Jacques Derrida, "White Mythology," in *Margins of Philosophy*, trans. Alan Bass (Chicago: University of Chicago Press, 1982), 207–71. On Derrida and the philosophy-literature distinction, see Richard Rorty, "Deconstruction and Circumvention," in *Essays on Heidegger and Others* (Cambridge: Cambridge University Press, 1991), 85–106.

93. T. S. Eliot, *The Waste Land* (New York: Boni and Liveright, 1922), line 414 and note to line 411. At least in this moment Eliot contemplates solipsism, although he disavowed it in his dissertation. See Eliot, "Solipsism," in *Knowledge and Experience in the Philosophy of F. H. Bradley* (London: Faber, 1964), chap. 6.

94. Eliot to Sydney Schiff, August 4, 1920, in vol. 1 of *The Letters of T. S. Eliot*, ed. Valerie Eliot and Hugh Haughton, gen. ed. John Haffenden (New Haven, CT: Yale University Press, 2011), 483.

95. Wallace Stevens, "To an Old Philosopher in Rome," in *The Collected Poems of Wallace Stevens* (New York: Alfred A. Knopf, 1954), 508.

96. Eliot, "The Metaphysical Poets," in *Selected Prose*, 64.

97. Charles Simic, "Notes on Poetry and Philosophy," *New Literary History* 21, no. 1 (1989): 216.

98. See, e.g., James Longenbach, *Wallace Stevens: The Plain Sense of Things* (New York: Oxford University Press, 1991), 18–21, 299–302; George Whiteside, "T. S. Eliot's Dissertation," *ELH* 34, no. 3 (1967): 400–424; and Richard Shusterman, "Eliot as Philosopher," in *The Cambridge Companion to T. S. Eliot*, ed. Anthony David Moody (Cambridge: Cambridge University Press, 1994), 31–47.

99. Eliot to Norbert Wiener, January 6, 1915, in *Letters of T. S. Eliot*, 1:87, 88, 87.

100. Moore, "An Octopus," in *Poems of Marianne Moore*, 170.

101. Rorty, "Deconstruction and Circumvention," 86.

102. Kenneth Goldsmith, "Conceptual Poetics," *Dispatches: Journals*, Poetry-Foundation.org, January 22, 2007, 3, available at http://epc.buffalo.edu/authors/goldsmith/Goldsmith_ConceptualWriting.pdf (ellipsis in original). Goldsmith repeats and elaborates this claim in *Uncreative Writing*, 4. Goldsmith denies that conceptual writing is "theoretical," calling it "intuitive" instead; see his "Paragraphs on Conceptual Writing," http://epc.buffalo.edu/authors/goldsmith/conceptual_paragraphs.html.

103. Goldsmith, "Conceptual Poetics," 3.

104. See the overviews by Davidson, "Philosophy and Theory in US Modern Poetry," and Diehl, "Poetry and Literary Theory."

105. W. B. Yeats, "The Symbolism of Poetry," in *Essays and Introductions* (London: Macmillan, 1961), 154.

106. Ibid., 154.

107. Ibid., 161.

108. Yeats, "Nineteen Hundred and Nineteen," in *Variorum Edition*, 429. For a book-length reflection on this poem, see Michael Wood, *Yeats and Violence* (New York: Oxford University Press, 2010).

109. Yeats, "Nineteen Hundred and Nineteen," in *Variorum Edition*, 429.

110. Yeats, "Among School Children," in *Variorum Edition*, 445.

111. Yeats, "Meru," in *Variorum Edition*, 563. Ensuing quotations of the poem are from this page. Wood also connects "rule" and "thought" in the two poems; see *Yeats and Violence*, 106–7.

112. Martin Heidegger, *What Is Called Thinking*, trans. J. Glenn Gray (New York: Harper and Row, 1968), 89, 90, and "The Origin of the Work of Art," in *Poetry, Language, Thought*, trans. Albert Hofstadter (New York: Harper and Row, 1971), 74.

113. *Oxford English Dictionary Online*, s.v. "raven," etym., accessed December 7, 2012, http://dictionary.oed.com/.

114. "Blow, winds, and crack your cheeks! rage! blow! / You cataracts and hurricanoes, spout" (*King Lear* 3.2).

115. On the poem's enjambments, Irishness, and combination of Shakespearean and Petrarchan form, see Helen Vendler, *Our Secret Discipline: Yeats and Lyric Form* (Cambridge, MA: Belknap–Harvard University Press, 2007), 177–80, 341–45.

116. Yeats to Lady Elizabeth Pelham, January 4, 1939, in *Letters*, 922.

117. Stephen Fredman, "Intersections of the Lyrical and the Philosophical," *Sagetrieb* 12, no. 3 (1993): 8.

118. Edward [Kamau] Brathwaite, *The Development of Creole Society in Jamaica, 1770–1820* (Oxford: Clarendon, 1978), 237. On Philip's poem, see Rajeev S. Patke, *Postcolonial Poetry in English* (Oxford: Oxford University Press, 2006), 29–37; Lee M. Jenkins, *The Language of Caribbean Poetry: Boundaries of Expression* (Gainesville: University Press of Florida, 2004), 160–68; and Cristanne Miller, "Mixing It Up in M. Nourbese Philip's Poetic Recipes," in *Women Poets of the Americas*, ed. Jacqueline

Vaught Brogan and Cordelia Chávez Candelaria (Notre Dame, IN: University of Notre Dame Press, 1999), 233–53.

119. See Ngũgĩ wa Thiong'o, *Decolonising the Mind* (London: Heinemann, 1986), and Bill Ashcroft, Gareth Griffiths, and Helen Tiffin, *The Empire Writes Back: Theory and Practice in Post-colonial Literatures*, 2nd ed. (New York: Routledge, 2002), 37–76.

120. Marlene Nourbese Philip, "Discourse on the Logic of Language," in *She Tries Her Tongue: Her Silence Softly Breaks* (Charlottetown, PEI: Ragweed, 1989), 56. More recently Philip has published as M. NourbeSe Philip. Subsequent page references appear in text.

121. Marlene Nourbese Philip, "Managing the Unmanageable," in *Caribbean Women Writers: Essays from the First International Conference*, ed. Selwyn R. Cudjoe (Wellesley, MA: Calaloux, 1990), 297.

122. The recording can be accessed at Philip's website, http://www.nourbese .com/SoundClips/Discourse-She%20Tries-01.mp3.

123. Archibald MacLeish, "Apologia," *Harvard Law Review* 85, no. 8 (1972): 1508.

124. See Thomas C. Grey, *The Wallace Stevens Case: Law and the Practice of Poetry* (Cambridge, MA: Harvard University Press, 1991). Grey concedes the obliquity of the connection, devoting half the book to the separation between the two spheres, while suggestively arguing that Stevens's binary-dissolving pragmatism has important lessons for legal reasoning. For another work that examines an oblique relationship between law and poetry in the twentieth century, in particular the relation between confessional poetry and Supreme Court decisions on the right to privacy, see Deborah Nelson, *Pursuing Privacy in Cold War America* (New York: Columbia University Press, 2002).

125. On Reznikoff's use of legal documents in *Testimony*, see Michael Davidson, *Ghostlier Demarcations: Modern Poetry and the Material World* (Berkeley: University of California Press, 1997), 150–67.

126. Vanessa Place, "Global Conceptualisms: I Am an American," UbuWeb, June 6, 2012, http://www.ubu.com/papers/place_global.html.

127. M. NourbeSe Philip, *Zong!* (Middletown, CT: Wesleyan University Press, 2008), 211. Subsequent page references appear in text.

128. Paul D. Gewirtz, "Narrative and Rhetoric in the Law," in *Law's Stories: Narrative and Rhetoric in the Law*, ed. Peter Brooks and Paul D. Gewirtz (New Haven, CT: Yale University Press, 1996), 5.

129. Lorna Goodison, "Annie Pengelly," in *To Us, All Flowers Are Roses* (Urbana: University of Illinois Press, 1995), 27. Subsequent page references appear in text.

130. Conversation with poet, December 23, 2008.

131. Yon Maley, "The Language of the Law," in *Language and the Law,* ed. John Gibbons (London: Longman, 1994), 40.

132. Colin Dayan, *The Law Is a White Dog: How Legal Rituals Make and Unmake Persons* (Princeton, NJ: Princeton University Press, 2011), 53–57, 124–35.

133. *Compact Edition of the Oxford English Dictionary*, s.v. "one" 7.

134. Ibid., s.v. "one" 20: "Defined by a sb. in apposition" (b).

135. Lorna Goodison, *From Harvey River* (New York: Amistad-HarperCollins, 2007).

136. Lady Maria Nugent, *Lady Nugent's Journal of Her Residence in Jamaica from 1801 to 1805*, ed. Frank Cundall (London: Adam and Charles Black–Institute of Jamaica, 1907), 55. Ensuing page references appear in text.

137. Gewirtz, "Narrative and Rhetoric in the Law," 5.

138. A. K. Ramanujan, "On the Death of a Poem," in *The Collected Poems of A. K. Ramanujan* (Delhi: Oxford University Press, 1995), 142.

139. Percy Bysshe Shelley, "A Defence of Poetry," in *Shelley's Poetry and Prose*, ed. Donald H. Reiman and Sharon B. Powers (New York: W. W. Norton, 1977), 508, 487.

140. David Kader and Michael Stanford, eds., *Poetry of the Law: From Chaucer to the Present* (Iowa City: University of Iowa Press, 2010).

141. Pound, *Literary Essays*, 25–26; Northrop Frye, *Anatomy of Criticism* (Princeton, NJ: Princeton University Press, 1957), 244, 275.

CHAPTER 2: POETRY AND THE NEWS

1. William Carlos Williams, "Asphodel, That Greeny Flower," in *The Collected Poems of William Carlos Williams*, ed. Christopher MacGowan (New York: New Directions, 1986), 2:318.

2. John Hartley, *Popular Reality: Journalism, Modernity, Popular Culture* (London: Arnold, 1996), 3.

3. Wallace Stevens, "Williams," in *Opus Posthumous*, rev. ed., ed. Milton J. Bates (New York: Alfred A. Knopf, 1989), 213.

4. Wallace Stevens, "The Noble Rider and the Sound of Words," in *The Necessary Angel: Essays on Reality and the Imagination* (New York: Alfred A. Knopf, 1951), 20, 21, 23, 26, 36.

5. Walter Benjamin, "The Storyteller," in *Illuminations: Essays and Reflections*, trans. Harry Zohn, ed. Hannah Arendt (New York: Schocken Books, 1969), 89.

6. W. H. Auden, *The English Auden*, ed. Edward Mendelson (London: Faber, 1977), 327.

7. Benjamin, "Storyteller," 90–91.

8. Ibid., 89.

9. Walter Benjamin, "The Newspaper," in *Selected Writings*, trans. Rodney Livingstone et al., ed. M. W. Jennings et al. (Cambridge, MA: Belknap–Harvard University Press, 1996) 2:741.

10. Ibid., 2:742.

11. See Marjorie Perloff, *Radical Artifice: Writing Poetry in the Age of Media* (Chicago: University of Chicago Press, 1991).

12. Benjamin, "Storyteller," 91–92.

13. T. S. Eliot, "Tradition and the Individual Talent," in *Selected Essays*, 3rd ed. (London: Faber, 1951), 18.

14. Ludwig Wittgenstein, *Zettel*, ed. G. E. M. Anscombe and G. H. von Wright (Oxford: Blackwell, 1967), sec. 160, line 1. Jonathan Culler quotes the statement in English in *Structuralist Poetics: Structuralism, Language and the Study of Literature*

(Ithaca, NY: Cornell University Press, 1975), 162, and Marjorie Perloff cites it as an epigraph to *Wittgenstein's Ladder: Poetic Language and the Strangeness of the Ordinary* (Chicago: University of Chicago Press, 1996).

15. On the erosion of the "distinction between poetry and the most ephemeral of commodities, the daily newspaper," see Lawrence Rainey, *Institutions of Modernism: Literary Elites and Public Culture* (New Haven, CT: Yale University Press, 1998), 32.

16. Adelaide Morris, "Documentary Poetics," in *The Princeton Encyclopedia of Poetry and Poetics*, 4th ed., ed. Roland Greene, Stephen Cushman, et al. (Princeton, NJ: Princeton University Press, 2012), 373; Joseph Harrington, "Docupoetry and Archive Desire," *Jacket 2*, October 2011, jacket2.0rg/article/docupoetry-and-archive-desire; and Joseph Lease, "Poetry as Information," in *Princeton Encyclopedia*, 705–7.

17. Tristan Tzara, "Pour faire un poème dadaïste," in *Œuvres completes*, ed. Henri Béhar (Paris: Flammarion, 1975), 1:382; Kenneth Goldsmith, *Day* (Great Barrington, MA: The Figures, 2003).

18. Mark Nowak, *Coal Mountain Elementary* (Minneapolis: Coffee House, 2009).

19. Benedict Anderson, *Imagined Communities: Reflections on the Origin and Spread of Nationalism*, rev. ed. (London: Verso, 1991), 227.

20. Seamus Heaney, *"Anything Can Happen," Essay and Poem* (Dublin: Town-House, 2004), 11. All further quotations of the poem are to this page. For poems about 9/11 and subsequent public events, as well as statements by poets, see *The New American Poetry of Engagement: A 21st Century Anthology*, ed. Ann Keniston and Jeffrey Gray (Jefferson, NC: McFarland, 2012). For more 9/11 poems, see *Poetry after 9/11: An Anthology of New York Poets*, 2nd ed., ed. Dennis Loy Johnson and Valerie Merians (Brooklyn, NY: Melville House, 2011), and *September 11, 2001: American Writers Respond*, ed. William Heyen (Silver Spring, MD: Etruscan, 2002).

21. Anderson, *Imagined Communities,* 35.

22. John Guillory, "The Memo and Modernity," *Critical Inquiry* 31, no. 1 (2004): 110.

23. Heaney, *"Anything Can Happen,"* 13.

24. Ibid., 14.

25. W. H. Auden, "In Memory of W. B. Yeats," in *Selected Poems*, new ed., ed. Edward Mendelson (New York: Vintage, 1979), 80, 81. Making other minor revisions, Heaney later changes the last line: "Telluric ash and fire-spores boil away." See his "Anything Can Happen," in *District and Circle* (London: Faber, 2006), 13.

26. Auden, "September 1, 1939," in *Selected Poems*, 86. Ensuing page references appear in text.

27. John Fuller, *W. H. Auden: A Commentary* (Princeton, NJ: Princeton University Press, 1988), 492.

28. Auden, "Spain," in *Selected Poems*, 54.

29. Ibid., 52.

30. Auden, *The Orators*, in *English Auden*, 86. Ensuing page references appear in text.

31. Benjamin, "Karl Kraus," in *Selected Writings*, 2:440.

32. Benjamin, "The Author as Producer," in *Selected Writings*, 2:772.

33. Auden, "Psychology and Criticism," in *English Auden*, 357.

34. Keith Williams, *British Writers and the Media, 1930–45* (New York: St. Martin's, 1996), 23. For another detailed historical accounting of British newspaper circulation and the modernist response, see Patrick Collier, *Modernism on Fleet Street* (Aldershot, UK: Ashgate, 2006). Collier emphasizes the modernists' participation in journalism despite their aversions.

35. Louise Bennett, *Selected Poems*, corrected ed., ed. Mervyn Morris (Kingston, Jamaica: Sangster's Book Stores, 1983), 106. Because most of the ensuing poems appear not in Morris's authoritative edition (which leaves out many topical poems) but in an earlier collection, *Jamaica Labrish* (Kingston, Jamaica: Sangster's Book Stores, 1966), subsequent citations are of that edition and appear in text.

36. I explore Bennett's trickster irony, including toward the newspapers, in *The Hybrid Muse: Postcolonial Poetry in English* (Chicago: University of Chicago Press, 2001), chap. 5.

37. F. G. Cassidy and R. B. Le Page, eds., *The Dictionary of Jamaican English*, q.v. "pupa-lick," 2nd ed. (Kingston, Jamaica: University of West Indies Press, 2002), 367.

38. Benjamin, "On Proverbs," in *Selected Writings*, 2:582.

39. Barbie Zelizer, *Taking Journalism Seriously: News and the Academy* (Thousand Oaks, CA: Sage, 2004), 38.

40. Paul Durcan, "Newsdesk," in *The Laughter of Mothers* (London: Harvill Secker, 2007), 58.

41. Paul Durcan, "Tribute to a Reporter in Belfast, 1974," in *The Selected Paul Durcan*, ed. Edna Longley (Belfast: Blackstaff, 1982), 25.

42. Durcan, "Irish Hierarchy Bans Coloured Photography," in *Selected Paul Durcan*, 89.

43. James Joyce, *Ulysses*, ed. Hans Walter Gabler (New York: Vintage, 1986), 57. The paper was *Tit-Bits*, which provided a digest of stories and worldwide news.

44. Declan Kiberd, "*Ulysses*, Newspapers and Modernism," in *Irish Classics* (Cambridge, MA: Harvard University Press, 2001), 463. For another view of Joyce and the press, see Collier, *Modernism on Fleet Street*, chap. 4.

45. Kiberd, *Irish Classics*, 464.

46. Caroline Walsh as cited in Victor Luftig, "Poetry, Causality, and an Irish Ceasefire," *Peace Review* 113, no. 2 (2001): 163.

47. Marie-Louise Legg, *Newspapers and Nationalism: The Irish Provincial Press, 1850–1892* (Dublin: Four Courts, 1999), 175.

48. Christopher Morash, *A History of the Media in Ireland* (Cambridge: Cambridge University Press, 2010), 96, 130.

49. W. B. Yeats, *The Autobiography of William Butler Yeats* (New York: Macmillan, 1965), 313.

50. Ibid., 313.

51. Richard Ellmann, *Yeats: The Man and the Masks* (London: Faber, 1961), 80.

52. R. F. Foster, *The Apprentice Mage, 1865–1914*, vol. 1 of *W. B. Yeats: A Life* (New York: Oxford University Press, 1997), 482, 500.

53. Benjamin, *Selected Writings,* 2:369, 772.

54. W. B. Yeats, *The Variorum Edition of the Poems of W. B. Yeats*, ed. Peter Allt and Russell K. Alspach (New York: Macmillan, 1968), 818.

55. For a textual reading of the newspaper publication of "September 1913," see George Bornstein, *Material Modernism: The Politics of the Page* (Cambridge: Cambridge University Press, 2001), 55–64.

56. Hugh Oram, *The Newspaper Book: A History of Newspapers in Ireland, 1649–1983* (Dublin: MO Books, 1983), 105. See, however, the less flattering portrait in Padraic Yeates, "The Life and Career of William Martin Murphy," in *Independent Newspapers: A History*, ed. Mark O'Brien and Kevin Rafter (Dublin: Four Courts, 2012), 14–25.

57. Yeats, "To a Shade," in *Variorum,* 292. Ensuing quotations are also from this page.

58. Yeats, "To a Friend Whose Work Has Come to Nothing," in *Variorum,* 291.

59. Yeats, "Easter, 1916," in *Variorum,* 391–94. I include the comma in the title, as printed originally and in Yeats's lifetime (391).

60. "Criminal Madness," *Irish Independent*, May 4, 1916, 2. By May 13, however, the leading article's tone was more cautious, warning against further executions and the indiscriminate "rounding up" of all "sympathisers" (2). Although Murphy was assumed to have written the editorials, their author was Timothy R. Harrington; see Yeates, "Murphy," 24.

61. Louis MacNeice, *Modern Poetry: A Personal Essay* (Oxford: Oxford University Press, 1938), 198.

62. Louis MacNeice, *Autumn Journal* (New York: Random House, 1939), 22. Subsequent page references appear in text.

63. Ezra Pound, *ABC of Reading* (New York: New Directions, 1934, 1960), 29, 44.

64. Maol Muire Tynan, "Adams Says IRA Will Not React to Attacks," *Irish Times*, September 3, 1994, 5.

65. Dick Grogan, "Paisley to Organise Pan Unionist Forum," *Irish Times*, September 3, 1994, 5.

66. Michael Longley, "Ceasefire," *Irish Times*, September 3, 1994, 8. Ensuing quotations are from this page. A slightly revised version appears in Michael Longley, *Collected Poems* (London: Jonathan Cape, 2006), 225. See also readings of the poem by Fran Brearton, *Reading Michael Longley* (Tarset, UK: Bloodaxe Books, 2006), 210–13, and Peter McDonald, "Lapsed Classics: Homer, Ovid, and Michael Longley's Poetry," in *The Poetry of Michael Longley*, ed. Alan J. Peacock and Kathleen Devine (Gerrards Cross, UK: Colin Smythe, 2001), 45–46.

67. Andrew Welsh, *Roots of Lyric: Primitive Poetry and Modern Poetics* (Princeton, NJ: Princeton University Press, 1978), 93.

68. *The Iliad*, bk. 24.

69. Olivia O'Leary as cited by Darragh Doyle, "Olivia O'Leary Pays Tribute to Seamus Heaney," *Culch*, June 3, 2009, www.culch.ie/2009/06/03/olivia-o-leary -pays-tribute-to-seamus-heaney. See also Dennis O'Driscoll, "Heaney in Public," in *The Cambridge Companion to Seamus Heaney*, ed. Bernard O'Donoghue (Cambridge: Cambridge University Press, 2009), 56–72.

70. Seamus Heaney, *Stepping Stones: Interviews with Seamus Heaney*, interviewed by Dennis O'Driscoll (New York: Farrar, Straus and Giroux, 2008), 123–24.

71. Blake Morrison, *Seamus Heaney* (New York: Methuen, 1982), 55.

72. Seamus Heaney, *North* (London: Faber, 1975), 57. Ensuing page references appear in text.

73. Obit. for Gerard McLaverty, "The Last Victim of the Shankill Butchers," *Irish Times*, March 22, 2008, 12.

74. Paul Muldoon, "Lunch with Pancho Villa," in *Poems 1968–1998* (New York: Farrar, Straus and Giroux, 2001), 41. Ensuing citations appear in text.

75. Medbh McGuckian, "The Dream-Language of Fergus," in *Selected Poems, 1978–1994* (Winston-Salem, NC: Wake Forest University Press, 1997), 48.

76. Medbh McGuckian, *The Soldiers of Year II* (Winston-Salem, NC: Wake Forest University Press, 2002), 95.

77. Medbh McGuckian, *Captain Lavender* (Winston-Salem, NC: Wake Forest University Press, 1995), 9. See Edna Longley, *Poetry and Posterity* (Tarset, UK: Bloodaxe Books, 2000), 309.

78. McGuckian, "Life as a Literary Convict," in *Soldiers*, 18. Ensuing quotations are from the same page.

79. William Carlos Williams, *The Autobiography of William Carlos Williams* (New York: New Directions, 1967), 360, 361.

80. William Carlos Williams, *Selected Essays of William Carlos Williams* (New York: New Directions, 1969), 269.

81. William Carlos Williams, "The Present Relationship of Prose to Verse," unpublished essay at Yale University Library, as cited by Margaret Lloyd Bollard, "The 'Newspaper Landscape' of Williams' *Paterson*," *Contemporary Literature* 16, no. 3 (1975): 322.

82. Alan Trachtenberg, *The Incorporation of America: Culture and Society in the Gilded Age* (New York: Hill and Wang, 1982), 125.

83. Ezra Pound, "A Retrospect," in *Literary Essays of Ezra Pound*, ed. T. S. Eliot (New York: New Directions, 1935), 3.

84. On T. S. Eliot's view of the newspaper's verbal imprecision and emotionalism, despite his own journalistic involvements, see Collier, *Modernism on Fleet Street*, chap. 2.

85. Stevens, "Noble Rider," 35.

86. Andreas Huyssen, *After the Great Divide: Modernism, Mass Culture, Postmodernism* (Bloomington: Indiana University Press, 1986).

87. Williams, *Selected Essays*, 295.

88. Williams, *Autobiography*, 241.

89. John J. Pauly and Melissa Eckert, "The Myth of 'the Local' in American Journalism," *Journalism and Mass Communication Quarterly* 79, no. 2 (2002): 313, 316.

90. Williams, *Autobiography*, 391.

91. Ibid., 391, 392. Dewey actually wrote "the locality is the only universal"; see "Americanism and Localism," *Dial* 68, no. 6 (1920): 687.

92. Dewey, "Americanism and Localism," 685, 686.

93. William Carlos Williams, prologue to *Kora in Hell* (1919), rpt. in *Imaginations*, ed. Webster Schott (New York: New Directions, 1970), 24–25. On Williams and other American modernists' nativism, see Walter Benn Michaels, *Our America: Nativism, Modernism, and Pluralism* (Durham, NC: Duke University Press, 1995).

94. On nineteenth-century US poems printed in newspapers, see Paula Bernat Bennett, *Poets in the Public Sphere: The Emancipatory Project of American Women's Poetry, 1800–1900* (Princeton, NJ: Princeton University Press, 2003), 1–10, 69–85.

95. William Carlos Williams, *Paterson*, rev. ed., ed. Christopher MacGowen (New York: New Directions, 1992), 280n98. Ensuing page references appear in text.

96. *Oxford English Dictionary Online*, s.v. "so be it," 3.a., accessed December 15, 2012, http://dictionary.oed.com/.

97. Louis L. Martz, "'Paterson': A Plan for Action," *Journal of Modern Literature* 1, no. 4 (1971): 516.

98. Williams, *Paterson*, 280n97.

99. On Williams's enjambments, including their relation to Milton's, see Stephen Cushman, *William Carlos Williams and the Meanings of Measure* (New Haven, CT: Yale University Press, 1985), chap. 1.

100. Unpublished manuscript, cited in Mike Weaver, *William Carlos Williams: The American Background* (Cambridge: Cambridge University Press, 1971), 120.

101. Williams, *Paterson*, 256n9.

102. Édouard Glissant, *Caribbean Discourse: Selected Essays*, trans. J. Michael Dash (Charlottesville: University Press of Virginia, 1989), xii, 134–44.

103. Weaver, *William Carlos Williams*, 152.

104. William Carlos Williams, *I Wanted to Write a Poem: The Autobiography of the Works of a Poet*, ed. Edith Heal (Boston: Beacon, 1958), 72.

105. Williams, *Autobiography*, 52; Weaver, *William Carlos Williams*, 7, 15.

106. Pauly and Eckert, "Myth of 'the Local,'" 310.

107. Harrington, "Docupoetry," and Morris, "Documentary Poetics," 372–73.

108. *New York Post*, July 17, 1959, 3.

109. Edward Brunner, *Cold War Poetry* (Urbana: University of Illinois Press, 2001), and Deborah Nelson, *Pursuing Privacy in Cold War America* (New York: Columbia University Press, 2002).

110. Frank O'Hara, "The Day Lady Died," in *The Collected Poems of Frank O'Hara*, ed. Donald Allen (New York: Alfred A. Knopf, 1971), 325. Ensuing quotations are from this page. On the poem's French and cold war contexts, see Marjorie Perloff, *Poetry On & Off the Page: Essays for Emergent Occasions* (Evanston, IL: Northwestern University Press, 1998), chap. 4. On its engagements with mass culture, including the "pulp press," see Robert von Hallberg, *American Poetry and Culture, 1945–1980* (Cambridge, MA: Harvard University Press, 1985), 177–79.

111. O'Hara, "Poem (Lana Turner Has Collapsed)," in *Collected Poems*, 449. Ensuing quotations are from this page.

112. Zelizer, *Taking Journalism Seriously*, 38–39.

113. Frank O'Hara, "Personism: A Manifesto," in *Collected Poems*, 499.

114. Nelson, *Pursuing Privacy*, 5

115. Roman Jakobson, "Linguistics and Poetics," in *Language in Literature*, ed. Krystyna Pomorska and Stephen Rudy (Cambridge, MA: Belknap–Harvard University Press, 1987), 67, 68.

116. Hartley, *Popular Reality*, 35.

117. Jakobson, "Linguistics and Poetics," 66.

118. M. M. Bakhtin, *The Dialogic Imagination: Four Essays*, ed. Michael Holquist, trans. Caryl Emerson and Holquist (Austin: University of Texas Press, 1981), 324.

119. Hartley, *Popular Reality*, 124.

120. Ibid., 3.

121. Robert Duncan, "Up Rising, Passages 25," in *Selected Poems*, ed. Robert J. Bertholf (New York: New Directions, 1993), 117. Ensuing page references appear in text. On the poem's contexts, see Eric Keenaghan, "Life, War, and Love: The Queer Anarchism of Robert Duncan's Poetic Action during the Vietnam War," *Contemporary Literature* 49, no. 4 (2008): 634–59.

122. D. H. Lawrence, "The American Eagle," in *The Complete Poems*, ed. Vivian de Sola Pinto and F. Warren Roberts (New York: Viking, 1971), 414.

123. See Cary Nelson's introduction to his anthology of American Spanish Civil War poetry, *The Wound and the Dream* (Urbana: University of Illinois Press, 2002), 1–61.

124. Carolyn Forché, *The Country between Us* (New York: Harper and Row, 1981), 16. Ensuing quotations are from this page.

125. On "Fission" and adolescence, see Stephen Burt, "'Tell Them No': Jorie Graham's Poems of Adolescence," in *Jorie Graham: Essays on the Poetry*, ed. Thomas Gardner (Madison: University of Wisconsin Press, 2005), 260–68.

126. Jorie Graham, "Fission," in *The Dream of the Unified Field: Selected Poems, 1974–1994* (Hopewell, NJ: Ecco, 1995), 101.

127. Ibid., 102.

128. J. L. Austin, *How to Do Things with Words* (Cambridge, MA: Harvard University Press, 1962).

CHAPTER 3: POETRY AND PRAYER

1. Immanuel Kant, *Religion within the Boundaries of Mere Reason*, trans. Allen W. Wood, in *Religion and Rational Theology*, trans. Wood and George Di Giovanni (Cambridge: Cambridge University Press, 1996), 210; Jean-Louis Chrétien, "Wounded Speech," in *The Ark of Speech*, trans. Andrew Brown (New York: Routledge, 2004), 21.

2. Sylvia Plath, "Years," in *The Collected Poems*, ed. Ted Hughes (New York: Harper and Row, 1981), 255.

3. Charles Simic, "To the One Upstairs," in *Jackstraws* (New York: Harcourt Brace, 1999), 63.

4. Simic, "Mystic Life," in *Jackstraws*, 82, 85.

5. Paul de Man, "Lyrical Voice in Contemporary Theory," in *Lyric Poetry: Be-*

yond New Criticism, ed. Chaviva Hošek and Patricia Parker (Ithaca, NY: Cornell University Press, 1985), 61; Jonathan Culler, "Apostrophe," in *The Pursuit of Signs: Semiotics, Literature, Deconstruction*, 2nd ed. (Ithaca, NY: Cornell University Press, 2002), 137. See also William Waters, *Poetry's Touch: On Lyric Address* (Ithaca, NY: Cornell University Press, 2003). For a critique of apostrophe as often abstracting and idealizing poetry from historically situated acts of address, see Virginia Jackson, *Dickinson's Misery: A Theory of Lyric Reading* (Princeton, NJ: Princeton University Press, 2005), 118–65.

6. Kant, *Religion*, 210n.

7. Ibid., 212, 210n. See also Chrétien, "Wounded Speech," 20.

8. Culler, "Apostrophe," 142. Culler comments on the "embarrassment" (135) of apostrophe as "the pure embodiment of poetic pretension" (143).

9. John Stuart Mill, "Thoughts on Poetry and Its Varieties," *Crayon* 7, no. 4 (1860): 93, 95.

10. W. B. Yeats, *Per Amica Silentia Lunae*, in *Later Essays*, ed. William H. O'Donnell, vol. 5 of *The Collected Works of W. B. Yeats* (New York: Charles Scribner's Sons, 1994), 8.

11. Aristotle states that among different kinds of speech, "a prayer . . . is neither true nor false" in *On Interpretation*, trans. Jean T. Oesterle (Milwaukee, WI: Marquette University Press, 1962), 60; I. A. Richards, *Science and Poetry*, 2nd ed. (London: K. Paul, Trench, Trubner, 1935).

12. Wallace Stevens, "The Emperor of Ice-Cream," in *The Collected Poems* (New York: Alfred A. Knopf, 1954), 64.

13. Roman Jakobson, "Linguistics and Poetics," in *Language in Literature,* ed. Krystyna Pomorska and Stephen Rudy (Cambridge, MA: Belknap–Harvard University Press, 1987), 67, 68.

14. Simone Weil, *Gravity and Grace*, trans. Arthur Wills (New York: Putnam, 1952), 170.

15. W. H. Auden, "Work, Carnival and Prayer," unpublished essay (Berg Collection), quoted in Arthur Kirsch, *Auden and Christianity* (New Haven, CT: Yale University Press, 2005), 159.

16. Helen Gardner, *Religion and Literature* (London: Faber, 1971), 157.

17. A. R. Ammons, "Hymn," in *Collected Poems, 1951–1971* (New York: W. W. Norton, 1972), 39.

18. See Joseph A. Junmann, *Christian Prayer through the Centuries*, trans. John Coyne, ed. Christopher Irvine (New York: Paulist, 2007).

19. A. D. Nuttall, *Overheard by God: Fiction and Prayer in Herbert, Milton, Dante and St John* (New York: Methuen, 1980), 9.

20. M. M. Bakhtin, *The Dialogic Imagination: Four Essays*, ed. Michael Holquist, trans. Caryl Emerson and Holquist (Austin: University of Texas Press, 1981), 358.

21. Leslie Marmon Silko, "Prayer to the Pacific," in *Storyteller* (New York: Seaver, 1981), 179.

22. Culler, "Apostrophe," 146.

23. J. L. Austin, *How to Do Things with Words* (Cambridge, MA: Harvard University Press, 1962).

24. Geoffrey Hill, "A Prayer to the Sun," in *Collected Poems* (New York: Oxford University Press, 1986), 79. The poem memorializes Miguel Hernández, a Catholic Communist poet who died in Fascist Spain.

25. Kinereth Meyer and Rachel Salmon Deshen, *Reading the Underthought: Jewish Hermeneutics and the Christian Poetry of Hopkins and Eliot* (Washington, DC: Catholic University of America Press, 2010), 14.

26. William T. Noon, S.J., *Poetry and Prayer* (New Brunswick, NJ: Rutgers University Press, 1967), 29. See also the discussion of "self-forgetfulness" and the quotations from various saints who suggest the self-extinguishing quality of prayer (24).

27. T. S. Eliot, "Little Gidding," in *The Complete Poems and Plays* (London: Faber, 1969), 192.

28. Gardner, *Religion and Literature*, 123.

29. Samuel Johnson, "Waller," in *The Lives of the Most Eminent English Poets; with Critical Observations of Their Works*, ed. Roger Lonsdale, 4 vols. (Oxford: Clarendon-Oxford University Press, 2006), 2:53.

30. Kevin Hart, "Poetry and Revelation: Hopkins, Counter-Experience and *Reductio*," *Pacifica* 18 (2005): 263, and "Transcendence in Tears," in *Gazing through a Prism Darkly*, ed. B. Keith Putt (New York: Fordham University Press, 2009), 128.

31. See Kevin Hart, "Religion and Poetry," in *The Princeton Encyclopedia of Poetry and Poetics*, 4th ed., ed. Roland Greene, Stephen Cushman, et al. (Princeton, NJ: Princeton University Press, 2012), 1153–57.

32. T. S. Eliot, "Religion and Literature," in *Selected Prose of T. S. Eliot*, ed. Frank Kermode (New York: Farrar, Straus and Giroux, 1975), 99.

33. Other prominent figures include William Carlos Williams, Edith Sitwell, Claude McKay, Jean Toomer, Theodore Roethke, James Wright, Charles Olson, John Berryman, Dylan Thomas, Robert Lowell, Amy Clampitt, Anne Sexton, Galway Kinnell, W. S. Merwin, Wole Soyinka, Mary Oliver, Lucille Clifton, Susan Howe, Lyn Hejinian, Michael Palmer, Jorie Graham, Les Murray, Carol Ann Duffy, Li-Young Lee, and Jacqueline Osherow.

34. Gerard Manley Hopkins, "O Deus, ego amo te," in *The Poetical Works of Gerard Manley Hopkins*, ed. Norman H. MacKenzie (Oxford: Clarendon-Oxford University Press, 1990), 106–7. Ensuing quotations appear in text, but to avoid distraction, most of the metrical marks have not been reproduced.

35. K. J. Healy, "Prayer (Theology of)," in *New Catholic Encyclopedia* (Detroit: Gale, 2002), 11:593.

36. Ibid., 594.

37. Ibid., 595.

38. James Finn Cotter, *Inscape: The Christology and Poetry of Gerard Manley Hopkins* (Pittsburgh: University of Pittsburgh Press, 1972), 236.

39. Gerard Manley Hopkins, *The Sermons and Devotional Writings of Gerard Manley Hopkins* (London: Oxford University Press, 1959), 240. See also the definition of enemy specifically as "the devil," along with examples, in the *Oxford English Dictionary Online*, s.v. "enemy," 1b, accessed December 15, 2010, http://dictionary.oed.com/.

40. William Empson, *Seven Types of Ambiguity*, rev. ed. (New York: New Directions, 1947), 225.

41. *Oxford English Dictionary Online*, s.v. "chervil," accessed November 10, 2010, http://dictionary.oed.com/.

42. William Blake, "The Marriage of Heaven and Hell," in *The Complete Poetry and Prose of William Blake*, rev. ed., ed. David V. Erdman (New York: Anchor/Doubleday, 1982), plate 5, p. 35.

43. Harold Bloom, *Ruin the Sacred Truths: Poetry and Belief from the Bible to the Present* (Cambridge, MA: Harvard University Press, 1989), 125.

44. Nuttall, *Overheard by God*, 15.

45. Hopkins, *Poetical Works*, 443n.

46. Healy, "Prayer," 595.

47. Jill Muller, *Gerard Manley Hopkins and Victorian Catholicism* (New York: Routledge, 2003), 96.

48. *Oxford English Dictionary Online*, s.v. "pied," 1a, 1b, accessed November 10, 2010, http://dictionary.oed.com/.

49. *Oxford English Dictionary Online*, s.v. "dappled," etym., accessed November 10, 2010, http://dictionary.oed.com/.

50. *Oxford English Dictionary Online*, s.v. "fickle," 1, etym., 2 quot., accessed November 10, 2010, http://dictionary.oed.com/.

51. Helen Vendler, *The Breaking of Style: Hopkins, Heaney, Graham* (Cambridge, MA: Harvard University Press, 1995), 16–21.

52. T. S. Eliot, *After Strange Gods: A Primer of Modern Heresy* (New York: Harcourt, Brace, 1934), 52.

53. T. S. Eliot, "Leçon de Valéry," *Listener* 37, no. 939 (1947): 72. See also Peter Ackroyd, *T. S. Eliot: A Life* (New York: Simon and Schuster, 1984), 160.

54. T. S. Eliot, "A Note on Poetry and Belief," *Enemy* 1 (1927): 16. On Eliot's skepticism, see Jeffrey M. Perl, *Skepticism and Modern Enmity* (Baltimore: Johns Hopkins University Press, 1989).

55. T. S. Eliot, review of Marianne Moore's *Poems* and *Marriage*, *Dial* 75 (1923): 597; Walter Pater, *The Renaissance: Studies in Art and Poetry*, rpt. in *Selected Writings of Walter Pater*, ed. Harold Bloom (New York: Columbia University Press, 1974), 55.

56. T. S. Eliot, "The Interpretation of Primitive Ritual" (1913), in vol. 1 of *Online Complete Prose of T. S. Eliot*, ed. Ronald Schuchard and Jewel Spears Brooker (Baltimore: Johns Hopkins University Press, forthcoming).

57. T. S. Eliot, *Ara Vus Prec* (London: Ovid, 1920).

58. Augustine, *The Confessions of Saint Augustine*, trans. Edward B. Pusey (New York: E. P. Dutton, 1900), 271.

59. T. S. Eliot, *The Waste Land* (New York: Boni and Liveright, 1922), lines 309–10. Ensuing references appear in text.

60. On Eliot's use of the *shantih* mantra and the importance of the blank line, see Cleo McNelly Kearns, *T. S. Eliot and Indic Traditions: A Study in Poetry and Belief* (Cambridge: Cambridge University Press, 1987), 226–29.

61. Eliot, "The Hollow Men," in *Complete Poems and Plays*, 85. Ensuing page references appear in text.

62. The Book of Common Prayer (London: Collins, 1921), 36. The doxology appears in later versions of Matthew but not in the oldest manuscripts.

63. Robert Crawford, *The Savage and the City in the Work of T. S. Eliot* (Oxford: Clarendon-Oxford University Press, 1987), 154, 157.

64. Barry Spurr, *"Anglo-Catholic in Religion": T. S. Eliot and Christianity* (Cambridge: Lutterworth, 2010), 98.

65. T. S. Eliot, "Lancelot Andrewes," in *Selected Essays*, 3rd ed. (London: Faber, 1951), 346.

66. Ronald Schuchard, *Eliot's Dark Angel: Intersections of Life and Art* (New York: Oxford University Press, 1999), chaps. 9 and 10.

67. Eliot, "Ash-Wednesday," in *Complete Poems and Plays*, 90.

68. Helen Gardner, *The Art of T. S. Eliot* (London: Faber, 1949), 114.

69. Eliot, "Choruses from *The Rock*," in *Complete Poems and Plays*, 158, 162, 166.

70. Gardner, *Art of T. S. Eliot*, 67; John Booty, *Meditating on Four Quartets* (Cambridge, MA: Cowley, 1983), 40; and A. David Moody, *"Four Quartets*: Music, Word, Meaning and Value," in *The Cambridge Companion to T. S. Eliot* (Cambridge: Cambridge University Press, 1994), 148.

71. Eliot, "The Dry Salvages," in *Complete Poems and Plays*, 189. Ensuing page references appear in text.

72. Spurr, *"Anglo-Catholic,"* 20; Kenneth Paul Kramer, *Redeeming Time: T. S. Eliot's "Four Quartets"* (Lanham, MA: Cowley–Rowman and Littlefield, 2007), 127.

73. Eliot, "Dante," in *Selected Essays*, 258.

74. Unpublished manuscript at Yale University Library, as quoted in Schuchard, *Eliot's Dark Angel*, 150.

75. Eliot, "Dante," 269.

76. For Eliot's criticism of Yeats, among other modern heretical writers, see *After Strange Gods*, 47–51.

77. W. B. Yeats, "A Dialogue of Self and Soul," in *The Variorium Edition of the Poems of W. B. Yeats*, ed. Peter Allt and Russell K. Alspach (New York: Macmillan, 1957), 478. Ensuing page references appear in text.

78. Aristotle, *Poetics* 9.1, trans. S. H. Butcher, rpt. in *Criticism: The Major Texts*, ed. Walter Jackson Bate (New York: Harcourt Brace Jovanovich, 1970), 25.

79. The classic study of the influence of this tripartite Ignatian meditative structure on poetry is Louis Martz, *The Poetry of Meditation: A Study in Religious Literature of the Seventeenth Century*, 2nd ed. (New Haven, CT: Yale University Press, 1962).

80. Noon, *Poetry and Prayer*, 153–54.

81. Seamus Heaney, *Station Island* (New York: Farrar, Straus and Giroux, 1985), 122n, 92–93.

82. Patrick Kavanagh, "Canal Bank Walk," in *Collected Poems*, ed. Antoinette Quinn (London: Allen Lane–Penguin, 2004), 224.

83. James Weldon Johnson, preface to *The Book of American Negro Poetry*, rev. ed., ed. Johnson (New York: Harcourt Brace Jovanovich, 1931), 41.

84. On his agnosticism, see James Weldon Johnson, *Along This Way: The Autobiography of James Weldon Johnson* (New York: Viking, 1933), 30.

85. Kant, *Religion*, 211n.

86. James Weldon Johnson, "Listen Lord: A Prayer," in *God's Trombones: Seven Negro Sermons in Verse* (New York: Viking, 1927), 13. Ensuing page references appear in text.

87. Johnson, *Along This Way*, 31.

88. Johnson, preface to *American Negro Poetry*, 18.

89. Philip Larkin, "Aubade," in *The Complete Poems of Philip Larkin*, ed. Archie Burnett (London: Faber, 2012), 115. Ensuing references appear in text. On Larkin as "agnostic" or "Anglican agnostic," see Andrew Motion, *Philip Larkin: A Writer's Life* (London: Faber, 1993), 485. For an overview of Larkin on religion, see Kateryna A. Rudnytzky Schray, "'To Seek This Place for What It Was': Church Going in Larkin's Poetry," *South Atlantic Review* 67, no. 2 (2002): 52–64.

90. Christopher Hitchens, ed., *The Portable Atheist* (Philadelphia: Da Capo, 2007).

91. Compare William Blake's question "When the Sun rises do you not see a round Disk of fire somewhat like a Guinea?" The respondent instead sees a host of angels. See "A Vision of the Last Judgment," in *Complete Poetry*, ed. Erdman, 565–66.

92. Larkin, *Complete Poems*, 467n1. See also "an angel standing in the sun" in Revelation 19. Seamus Heaney reads "Solar" as a prayer or hymn in "The Main of Light," in *The Government of the Tongue: Selected Prose, 1978–1987* (London: Faber, 1988), 16–20.

93. Louis Zukofsky, *Prepositions: The Collected Critical Essays of Louis Zukofsky*, expanded ed. (Berkeley: University of California Press, 1981), 12.

94. Maeera Y. Shreiber, *Singing in a Strange Land: A Jewish American Poetics* (Stanford, CA: Stanford University Press, 2007), 180.

95. Ibid., 181. See also Shreiber's reading of Oppen's "Psalm," ibid., 188–92.

96. George Oppen, "Psalm," in *New Collected Poems*, ed. Michael Davidson (New York: New Directions, 2002), 99. Ensuing quotations are from this page.

97. On Heidegger's influence on Oppen, see Peter Nicholls, *George Oppen and the Fate of Modernism* (Oxford: Oxford University Press, 2007), 62–72.

98. Dennis Young, "Anthologies, Canonicity, and the Objectivist Imagination: The Case of George Oppen," in *No Small World: Visions and Revisions of World Literature*, ed. Michael Thomas Carroll (Urbana, IL: National Council of Teachers of English, 1996), 150.

99. Percy Bysshe Shelley, "Ode to the West Wind," in *Shelley's Poetry and Prose*, ed. Donald H. Reiman and Sharon B. Powers (New York: W. W. Norton, 1977), 223.

100. Wallace Stevens, "Of Mere Being," in *Opus Posthumous*, ed. Samuel French Morse (New York: Alfred A. Knopf, 1957), 117. In later published editions of the poem, Holly Stevens revised "bronze distance" to "bronze decor"; see *Opus Posthumous*, rev. ed., ed. Milton J. Bates (New York: Alfred A. Knopf, 1989), 141.

101. Stevens, "Of Mere Being," 118.

102. Oppen to William Bronk, December 21, 1962, in *The Selected Letters of George Oppen*, ed. Rachel Blau DuPlessis (Durham, NC: Duke University Press, 1990), 73.

103. Louise Glück, "Disruption, Hesitation, Silence," *American Poetry Review* 22, no. 5 (1993): 31.

104. See, however, Roger Gilbert's discussion of the "religious turn" in 1990s poetry in "Awash with Angels: The Religious Turn in Nineties Poetry," *Contemporary Literature* 42, no. 2 (2001): 238–69. See also Jeanne Foster, *A Music of Grace: The Sacred in Contemporary American Poetry* (New York: Peter Lang, 1995).

105. Shreiber, *Singing*, 195, 197.

106. Louise Glück, "Matins," in *The Wild Iris* (Hopewell, NJ: Ecco, 1992), 12. Ensuing quotations from this poem are from this page.

107. Glück, "Matins," in *Wild Iris*, 13. Ensuing quotations from this poem are from this page.

108. Charles Wright, "Jesuit Graves," in *Black Zodiac* (New York: Farrar, Straus and Giroux, 1997), 57.

109. Charles Wright, "Confessions of a Song and Dance Man," in *Scar Tissue* (New York: Farrar, Straus and Giroux, 2006), 16.

110. Charles Wright, *Halflife: Improvisations and Interviews, 1977–87* (Ann Arbor: University of Michigan Press, 1988), 129–30.

111. David Lehman, foreword to *The Best American Poetry 2008*, ed. Charles Wright (New York: Scribner–Simon and Schuster, 2008), xiv; Wright, *Halflife*, 1988), 5.

112. Edward Hirsch, "The Visionary Poetics of Philip Levine and Charles Wright," in *The Columbia History of American Poetry*, ed. Jay Parini (New York: Columbia University Press, 1993), 778, 795.

113. Wright, "Confessions," 16.

114. Bonnie Costello, "Charles Wright's *Via Negativa:* Language, Landscape, and the Idea of God," *Contemporary Literature* 42, no. 2 (2001): 329.

115. Charles Wright, "Stone Canyon Nocturne," in *China Trace* (Middletown, CT: Wesleyan University Press, 1975), 47.

116. William Croswell Doane, "Ancient of Days," in *The Hymnal, 1940* (New York: Church Publishing, 2001), 274.

117. Charles Wright, "Apologia Pro Vita Sua," in *Black Zodiac*, 3–4.

118. Charles Wright, "The Gospel According to Yours Truly," in *Sestets* (New York: Farrar, Straus and Giroux, 2009), 24.

119. Wright, "Little Prayer," *Virginia Quarterly Review* 83, no. 3 (2007): 113.

120. Wright, "Clear Night," in *China Trace*, 61.

121. Okigbo, "Heavensgate," in *Collected Poems* (London: Heinemann, 1986), 19.

122. Kamau Brathwaite, "Irae," in *Middle Passages* (Newcastle upon Tyne, UK: Bloodaxe Books, 1992), 90.

123. Kamau Brathwaite, "Irae," in *Middle Passages* (New York: New Directions, 1993), 119–20.

124. Okot p'Bitek, *"Song of Lawino" and "Song of Ocol"* (London: Heinemann, 1984), 74. Ensuing page references appear in text.

125. Okot p'Bitek, *African Religions in Western Scholarship* (Kampala: East African Literature Bureau, 1971), 62.

126. Agha Shahid Ali, "About Me," in *Call Me Ishmael Tonight: A Book of Ghazals* (New York: W. W. Norton, 2003), 61. Ensuing references appear in text. *Ar-Rahim* is also transliterated as *al-raheem*.

127. Agha Shahid Ali, "Rooms Are Never Finished," in *Rooms Are Never Finished* (New York: W. W. Norton, 2002), 56. Ensuing references appear in text.

128. On the sequence and related poems, see Khaled Mattawa, "Writing Islam in Contemporary American Poetry: On Mohja Kahf, Daniel Moore, and Agha Shahid Ali," *PMLA* 123, no. 5 (2008): 1590–95.

129. A. K. Ramanujan, "Classics Lost and Found," in *The Collected Essays of A. K. Ramanujan*, ed. Vinay Dharwadker (Delhi: Oxford University Press, 1999), 190. Ensuing page references appear in text.

130. See Fred W. Clothey, *The Many Faces of Murukan* (The Hague: Mouton, 1978), which as a dissertation helped inspire Ramanujan's sequence.

131. Ezra Pound, *Make It New* (London: Faber, 1934); T. S. Eliot, "Tradition and the Individual Talent," in *Selected Prose*, 39.

132. Ramanujan, "Prayers to Lord Murugan," in *The Collected Poems of A. K. Ramanujan* (Delhi: Oxford University Press, 1995), 117. Ensuing page references to the sequence appear in text.

133. R. Parthasarathy, "How It Strikes a Contemporary: The Poetry of A. K. Ramanujan," *Literary Criterion* 12, nos. 2–3 (1976): 196.

134. Bruce King, *Three Indian Poets: Nissim Ezekiel, A. K. Ramanujan, Dom Moraes* (Madras: Oxford University Press, 1991), 78.

135. Stevens, *Opus Posthumous*, rev. ed., 186.

CHAPTER 4: POETRY AND SONG

1. Giorgio Agamben, *The End of the Poem: Studies in Poetics,* trans. Daniel Heller-Roazen (Stanford, CA: Stanford University Press, 1999), 32, 33.

2. James William Johnson, "Lyric," in *The New Princeton Encyclopedia of Poetry and Poetics*, 3rd ed., ed. Alex Preminger and T. V. F. Brogan (Princeton, NJ: Princeton University Press, 1993), 714.

3. Jacques Derrida, *Of Grammatology*, trans. Gayatri Chakravorty Spivak (Baltimore: Johns Hopkins University Press, 1976), 199.

4. W. B. Yeats, "Speaking to the Psaltery," in *Essays and Introductions* (London: Macmillan, 1961), 13. Subsequent page references appear in text. See Ronald Schuchard, *The Last Minstrels: Yeats and the Revival of the Bardic Arts* (New York: Oxford University Press, 2008).

5. Ezra Pound, *Literary Essays of Ezra Pound*, ed. T. S. Eliot (New York: New Directions, 1968), 91, and *Selected Prose, 1909–1965* (New York: New Directions, 1973), 37.

6. Pound, *Selected Prose*, 37.

7. See John F. Waterhouse, "Gerard Manley Hopkins and Music," *Music and Letters* 18, no. 3 (1937): 227–35.

8. Langston Hughes, "The Negro Artist and the Racial Mountain," *The Nation* 122, no. 3181 (1926): 693, 694.

9. Langston Hughes, "The Weary Blues," in *The Collected Poems of Langston Hughes*, ed. Arnold Rampersad and David Roessel (New York: Random House, 1994), 50. I discuss at greater length this poem's straddling the line between blues song and blues poem in *Poetry of Mourning: The Modern Elegy from Hardy to Heaney* (Chicago: University of Chicago Press, 1994), 144–47.

10. Langston Hughes, "Note on Blues," in *Fine Clothes to the Jew* (New York: Alfred A. Knopf, 1927), xiii.

11. Jean Toomer, "Song of the Son," in *Cane*, ed. Darwin T. Turner (New York: W. W. Norton, 1988), 14.

12. Ibid.

13. Other "American" examples include Robert Frost, Ezra Pound, Wallace Stevens, Edna St. Vincent Millay, Countee Cullen, Langston Hughes, Hart Crane, Theodore Roethke, Louis Zukofsky, Louise Bogan, W. H. Auden, Charles Olson, George Oppen, John Berryman, Gwendolyn Brooks, Robert Duncan, Robert Creeley, A. R. Ammons, Denise Levertov, Mark Strand, Kathleen Fraser, and Michael Palmer; other "postcolonial" examples include Adil Jussawalla, Kamau Brathwaite, Lenrie Peters, Kofi Awoonor, Dennis Brutus, Steve Chimombo, David Dabydeen, Grace Nichols, Lorna Goodison, Niyi Osundare, and Odia Ofeimun.

14. Robert Lowell, "Skunk Hour," in *Collected Poems*, ed. Frank Bidart and David Gewanter (New York: Farrar, Straus and Giroux, 2003), 192; Kenneth Goldsmith, *Head Citations* (Great Barrington, MA: Figures, 2002), 7.

15. Jacques Roubaud, "Prelude: Poetry and Orality," trans. Jean-Jacques Poucel, in *The Sound of Poetry / The Poetry of Sound*, ed. Marjorie Perloff and Craig Dworkin (Chicago: University of Chicago Press, 2009), 18.

16. Lawrence Kramer, *Music and Poetry: The Nineteenth Century and After* (Berkeley: University of California Press, 1984), 129.

17. Ibid., 127.

18. Kramer, *Musical Meaning: Toward a Critical History* (Berkeley: University of California Press, 2002), 53.

19. Ibid., 52.

20. Martin Boykan, "Reflections on Words and Music," *Musical Quarterly* 84, no. 1 (2000): 127.

21. Boykan, "Reflections," 135.

22. James Anderson Winn, *Unsuspected Eloquence: A History of the Relations between Poetry and Music* (New Haven, CT: Yale University Press, 1981), x.

23. John Hollander, *Vision and Resonance: Two Senses of Poetic Form*, 2nd ed. (New Haven, CT: Yale University Press, 1985), 289 (on Valéry), 291 (quotations).

24. Mark W. Booth, *The Experience of Songs* (New Haven, CT: Yale University Press, 1981), 7, 8.

25. Ibid., 13.

26. Charles O. Hartman, "The Criticism of Song," *Centennial Review* 19, no. 2 (1975): 104, 102.

27. Booth, *Experience of Songs*, 187.

28. Amy Clampitt, "Syrinx," in *The Collected Poems of Amy Clampitt* (New York: Alfred A. Knopf, 1997), 363.

29. Christophe Den Tandt, "Staccato, Swivel and Glide: A Poetics of Early Rock 'n' Roll Lyrics," in *Sound as Sense: Contemporary US Poetry &/in Music*, ed. Michel Delville and Christine Pagnoulle (Brussels: Peter Lang, 2003), 79.

30. Christopher Ricks, *Dylan's Visions of Sin* (New York: Ecco-HarperCollins, 2004), 13.

31. Roland Barthes, "The Grain of the Voice," in *Image, Music, Text*, trans. Stephen Heath (New York: Farrar, Straus and Giroux, 1977), 182, 183, 188. Among recent books on poetry in performance, see Lesley Wheeler, *Voicing American Poetry: Sound and Performance from the 1920s to the Present* (Ithaca, NY: Cornell University Press, 2008).

32. Robert Pinsky, "The Uncreation," in *The Figured Wheel: New and Collected Poems, 1966–1996* (New York: Farrar, Straus and Giroux, 1996), 53.

33. Lucille Clifton, "last words," in *Mercy* (Rochester, NY: BOA Editions. 2004), 15.

34. Tim Nolan, "At the Choral Concert," *Ploughshares* 33, no. 4 (2007/2008): 146.

35. Sebastian Matthews, "Barbershop Quartet, East Village Grille," *Chattahoochee Review* 28, nos. 2/3 (2008): 42.

36. Friedrich Nietzsche, *The Birth of Tragedy and The Genealogy of Morals*, trans. Francis Golffing (Garden City, NY: Doubleday–Anchor Books, 1956), 37–42.

37. C. K. Williams, *The Singing* (New York: Farrar, Straus and Giroux, 2003), 4.

38. Ibid., 5.

39. Alberto Ríos, "The Boleros," in *The Dangerous Shirt* (Port Townsend, WA: Copper Canyon, 2009), 95.

40. Ibid., 96.

41. D. A. Powell, "callas lover," *Poetry* 191, no. 4 (2008): 302.

42. Ibid., 302.

43. Kamau Brathwaite, *History of the Voice*, rpt. and rev. in *Roots* (Ann Arbor: University of Michigan Press, 1993), 279, 281.

44. My transcription from Lord Kitchener, "If You're Not White You're Black," *London Is the Place for Me: Trinidadian Calypso in London, 1950–56*, CD (Honest Jons Records, 2002).

45. Frantz Fanon, *Black Skin, White Masks*, trans. Charles Lam Markmann (New York: Grove, 1967), 192.

46. Ibid., 60, 148.

47. Ibid., 38, 18.

48. Stuart Hall, "Cultural Identity and Diaspora," in *Identity: Community, Culture, Difference*, ed. Jonathan Rutherford (London: Lawrence and Wishart, 1990), 231.

49. Kofi Awoonor, "Songs of Sorrow," rpt. in *The Penguin Book of Modern African Poetry*, ed. Gerald Moore and Ulli Beier, 4th ed. (London: Penguin, 1998), 103–4.

50. Robert Fraser, *West African Poetry: A Critical History* (Cambridge: Cambridge University Press, 1986), 17–18.

51. Okot p'Bitek, *"Song of Lawino" and "Song of Ocol"* (London: Heinemann, 1984), 42.

52. Ibid., 34, 35.

53. "Okot p'Bitek (1978)," in *Conversations with African Writers*, ed. Lee Nichols (Washington, DC: Voice of America, 1981), 250.

54. Okot p'Bitek, interview by Bernth Lindfors, *World Literature Written in English* 16, no. 2 (1977): 283. Okot also tells the story in *Conversations*, 244.

55. Here and in the preceding chapter I draw on my lengthier discussion of Okot p'Bitek in *The Hybrid Muse: Postcolonial Poetry in English* (Chicago: University of Chicago Press, 2001), chap. 6.

56. Wole Soyinka, "Procession," in *A Shuttle in the Crypt* (London: Rex Collings–Eyre Methuen, 1972), 41.

57. Jean Binta Breeze, *"Riddym Ravings" and Other Poems*, ed. Mervyn Morris (London: Race Today, 1988), 58. Subsequent references appear in text. "'Ribbit' (rivet)," writes Jenny Sharpe, "is a DJ term for describing the state of being caught in a heavy dub beat"; see her "Cartographies of Globalization, Technologies of Gendered Subjectivities: The Dub Poetry of Jean 'Binta' Breeze," in *Minor Transnationalism*, ed. Françoise Lionnet and Shu-mei Shih (Durham, NC: Duke University Press, 2005), 274.

58. Claude McKay, "The Tropics of New York," in *Complete Poems*, ed. William J. Maxwell (Urbana: University of Illinois Press, 2004), 154.

59. Jean Binta Breeze, *"The Arrival of Brighteye" and Other Poems* (Newcastle upon Tyne: Bloodaxe Books, 2000), 53. Subsequent page references appear in text.

60. Patience Agbabi, "R.A.W.," in *R.A.W.* (London: Izon Amazon-Gecko, 1995), 49.

61. Tim Brennan, "Off the Gangsta Tip: A Rap Appreciation, or Forgetting about Los Angeles," *Critical Inquiry* 20, no. 4 (1994): 677.

62. Ezra Pound, "A Retrospect," in *Literary Essays*, 3.

63. Brennan, "Off the Gangsta Tip," 681.

64. Patience Agbabi, "Prologue," in *Transformatrix* (Edinburgh: Payback Press–Canongate, 2000), 9. Subsequent page references appear in text.

65. Roman Jakobson, "Linguistics and Poetics," in *Language in Literature*, ed. Krystyna Pomorska and Stephen Rudy (Cambridge, MA: Belknap–Harvard University Press, 1987), 73, 69.

66. Lesego Rampolokeng, "Libéte," *Boundary 2*, 33, no. 2 (2006): 32.

67. Lesego Rampolokeng, "rap 31," in *Horns for Hondo* (Fordsburg, South Africa: Congress of South African Writers, 1990), 54–55.

68. For an overview of rap's poetic form, see Adam Bradley and Andrew DuBois, introduction to *The Anthology of Rap*, ed. Bradley and DuBois (New Haven, CT: Yale University Press, 2010), xxxi–xl.

69. See John Hollander, *The Untuning of the Sky: Ideas of Music in English Poetry, 1500–1700* (Princeton, NJ: Princeton University Press, 1961), 13–14; Marc Berley, *After the Heavenly Tune: English Poetry and the Aspiration to Song* (Pittsburgh, PA: Duquesne University Press, 2000), 1; and Terence Allan Hoagwood, *From Song to Print: Romantic Pseudo-songs* (New York: Palgrave-Macmillan, 2010).

70. Michael Palmer, "Period (Senses of Duration)," in *Code of Signals: Recent Writings in Poetics*, ed. Palmer (Berkeley, CA: North Atlantic Books, 1983), 243.

71. Robert Hass, "Three Dawn Songs in Summer," in *Time and Materials* (New York: Ecco-HarperCollins, 2007), 6.

72. Jim Elledge, introduction to *Sweet Nothings: An Anthology of Rock and Roll in American Poetry* (Bloomington: Indiana University Press, 1994), xviii, xix.

73. David Wojahn, contributor's comment in *Sweet Nothings*, ed. Elledge, 266.

74. Stephen Burt, "'O Secret Stars Stay Secret': Rock and Roll in Contemporary Poetry," in *This Is Pop: In Search of the Elusive at Experience Music Project*, ed. Eric Weisbard (Cambridge, MA: Harvard University Press, 2004), 201, 207.

75. James Merrill, *Collected Poems*, ed. J. D. McClatchy and Stephen Yenser (New York: Knopf–Random House, 2001), 669. Subsequent page references appear in text.

76. See Helen Vendler, *Last Looks, Last Books: Stevens, Plath, Lowell, Bishop, Merrill* (Princeton, NJ: Princeton University Press, 2010), 130–35.

77. Johanna Drucker, "Not Sound," in *Sound of Poetry*, ed. Perloff and Dworkin, 238.

78. Apple, "Apple Presents iPod," October 23, 2001, http://www.apple.com /pr/library/2001/oct/23ipod.html.

79. T. Austin Graham, "T. S. Eliot and Ubiquitous Music, 1909–1922," in *Music and Literary Modernism: Critical Essays and Comparative Studies*, ed. Robert P. McParland (Newcastle, UK: Cambridge Scholars, 2006), 217.

80. Walter Benjamin, "The Work of Art in the Age of Mechanical Reproduction," in *Illuminations: Essays and Reflections*, trans. Harry Zohn, ed. Hannah Arendt (New York: Schocken Books, 1969), 219.

81. T. Austin Graham, *The Great American Songbooks: Modernism, Musical Texts, and the Value of Popular Culture* (New York: Oxford University Press, 2013), chap. 1.

82. Kramer, *Musical Meaning*, 3.

83. Apple, "iPod + iTunes Timeline," 2011, http://www.apple.com/pr/products /ipodhistory/.

84. Rae Armantrout, *Collected Prose* (San Diego, CA: Singing Horse, 2007), 120.

85. Theodor W. Adorno, *Essays on Music*, ed. Richard Leppert, trans. Susan H. Gillespie (Berkeley: University of California Press, 2002), 445.

86. Gary Trust, "Best of the 2000s: Part 1," *Billboard*, December 22, 2009, http:// www.billboard.com/articles/columns/chart-beat/266342/best-of-the-2000s-part-1.

87. Rae Armantrout, *Versed* (Middletown, CT: Wesleyan University Press, 2009), 45. Subsequent page references appear in the text.

88. Armantrout, *Collected Prose*, 92.

89. Rae Armantrout, interview about "Soft Money," *Poetry* 196, no. 1 (2010): 20.

90. Rae Armantrout, "Soft Money," in *Money Shot* (Middletown, CT: Wesleyan University Press, 2011), 37.

91. Archibald MacLeish, "Ars Poetica," in *Collected Poems, 1917–1982* (Boston: Houghton Mifflin, 1985), 107.

92. Armantrout, "Soft Money," 37.

93. Armantrout, interview, 21.

94. Armantrout, *Collected Prose*, 89.

95. Armantrout, interview, 20.

96. Armantrout, *Collected Prose*, 57. Subsequent page references appear in text.

97. Booth, *Experience of Songs*, 9.

98. Armantrout, "Locality," in *Versed*, 22.

99. Ibid., 22.

100. Michael Palmer, "Autobiography 6," in *The Promises of Glass* (New York: New Directions, 2000), 20. Subsequent page references appear in the text.

101. Michael Palmer, *Active Boundaries: Selected Essays and Talks* (New York: New Directions, 2008), 240, 241.

102. Palmer, "Period (Senses of Duration)," 253.

103. Agamben, *End of the Poem*, 109.

104. Palmer, *Active Boundaries*, 5–6.

105. Michael Palmer, "The Merle Asleep," in *Company of Moths* (New York: New Directions, 2005), 45.

106. Michael Palmer, "The Recovery of Language," interview by Sarah Rosenthal, in *A Community Writing Itself: Conversations with Vanguard Writers of the Bay Area*, ed. Rosenthal (Champaign, IL: Dalkey Archive, 2010), 190.

107. Palmer, "The Merle Asleep," in *Company of Moths*, 46.

108. Palmer, "Stone," in *Company of Moths*, 8.

109. Tracie Morris, "Sound Making Notes," in *American Poets in the 21st Century: The New Poetics*, ed. Claudia Rankine and Lisa Sewell (Middletown, CT: Wesleyan University Press, 2007), 210–11.

110. Ibid., 210.

111. Doris Day, "Cheek to Cheek," in *Hooray for Hollywood*, LP (Columbia 1128–2, 1959).

112. Christine Hume, "Improvisational Insurrection: The Sound Poetry of Tracie Morris," *Contemporary Literature* 47, no. 3 (2006): 428.

113. Tracie Morris, "The Mrs. Gets Her Ass Kicked," rec. October 28, 2008, www.writing.upenn.edu/pennsound/x/Morris.html.

114. Morris, "Sound Making Notes," 212.

115. Tracie Morris, "Africa(n)," rec. October 28, 2008, www.writing.upenn.edu/pennsound/x/Morris.html.

116. See Gilles Deleuze, "He Stuttered," trans. Constantin V. Boundas, in *Gilles Deleuze and the Theatre of Philosophy*, ed. Constantin V. Boundas and Dorothea Olkowski (New York: Routledge, 1994), 23–29, and Craig Dworkin, "The Stutter of Form," in *Sound of Poetry*, ed. Perloff and Dworkin, 166–83.

117. Frank Bidart, *Watching the Spring Festival* (New York: Farrar, Straus and Giroux, 2008), 12. Subsequent page references appear in the text.

118. "Home on the Range" (1910 version), in *Cowboy Songs and Other Frontier Ballads*, collected by John A. Lomax and Alan Lomax, rev. ed. (New York: Macmillan, 1938), 425.

119. Bidart, "Valentine," in *Watching*, 21.

120. Jorie Graham, "Undated Lullaby," in *Sea Change* (New York: Ecco, 2008), 53.

121. Graham, "No Long Way Round," in *Sea Change*, 55.

122. Kevin Young, *Jelly Roll* (New York: Alfred A. Knopf, 2003), n.p.

123. Young, "Aubade," in ibid., 36.

124. Ibid.

125. Kevin Young, "One Love," in *For the Confederate Dead* (New York: Alfred A. Knopf, 2007), 142.

126. Patricia Smith, "Hip-Hop Ghazal," *Poetry* 190, no. 4 (2007): 254.

127. Ibid.

128. Harryette Mullen, "Jinglejangle," in *Sleeping with the Dictionary* (Berkeley: University of California Press, 2002), 34. Subsequent page references appear in text.

129. Jakobson, "Linguistics and Poetics," 70.

130. Terrance Hayes, "'The Poet in the Enchanted Shoe Factory': An Interview with Terrance Hayes," interview by Charles Henry Rowell, *Callaloo* 27, no. 4 (2004): 1070.

131. M. M. Bakhtin, *The Dialogic Imagination: Four Essays*, ed. Michael Holquist, trans. Caryl Emerson and Holquist (Austin: University of Texas Press, 1981), 358.

132. Terrance Hayes, "emcee," in *Hip Logic* (New York: Penguin, 2002), 5. Ensuing page references appear in text.

133. OutKast, "ATLiens," CD (Atlanta: LaFace Records, 1996).

134. Hayes, "Poet in the Enchanted Shoe Factory," 1077.

135. Cathy Park Hong, *Dance Dance Revolution* (New York: W. W. Norton, 2007), 25. Subsequent page references appear in the text. Hong's sequence also dialogizes the popular video game after which it is named, significant to Hong in part for its genesis out of "cultural zigzagging" between the West and Japan; see Cathy Park Hong, interview by Joshua Kryah, *Poets & Writers* (online only), July 11, 2007, http://www.pw.org/content/interview_poet_cathy_park_hong?cmnt_all=1.

136. See Paul Muldoon's song lyrics in *General Admission* (Oldcastle, County Meath, Ireland: Gallery, 2006) and *The Word on the Street: Rock Lyrics* (New York: Farrar, Straus and Giroux, 2013).

137. Paul Muldoon, "Paul Muldoon in Conversation," *Poets.org*, Academy of American Poets, June 2011, http://www.poets.org/viewmedia.php/prmMID/22380#.

138. Paul Muldoon, "The Adult Thing" and "You Got the Rolex (I Got the Rolodex)," *Little Star: A Journal of Poetry and Prose*, February 14, 2011, http://littlestarjournal.com/blog/2011/02/paul-muldoon-and-the-wayside-shrines/.

139. Paul Muldoon, "The Loaf," in *Moy Sand and Gravel* (New York: Farrar, Straus and Giroux, 2002), 51. Subsequent page references appear in text.

140. On a personal note, I have learned well the role played by two different kinds of lists, namely tables of contents of literary anthologies, having served as an editor, and music playlists for radio stations, having volunteered as a jazz (and at first classical) disc jockey at community radio stations through the 1980s and 1990s.

141. Walter Pater, *The Renaissance: Studies in Art and Poetry*, rpt. in *Selected Writings of Walter Pater*, ed. Harold Bloom (New York: Columbia University Press, 1974), 55.

142. W. S. Merwin, "The Nomad Flute," in *The Shadow of Sirius* (Port Townsend, WA: Copper Canyon, 2008), 5.

INDEX

Abercorn Café explosion, 101
Abrams, M. H.
  *The Fourth Dimension of a Poem and
    Other Essays,* 7
Achebe, Chinua
  Things Fall Apart, 25–31
Adams, Gerry, 92
Adams, John, 118
address
  and poetry, 128–29, 166, 168
  See also apostrophe
Adorno, Theodor, 214
Africa, 24, 64, 172, 194–95, 223
  African diaspora, 198
  African diasporic poetry, 208
  poetry, and song, influence on in,
    198–200
African Americans
  music of, and American poetry,
    inspiration for, 227
  prayer-sermons of, 157
  spirituals of, 159, 186–87
  verse of, 158
  as writers, 157
Agamben, Giorgio, 184, 219
Agbabi, Patience, 9, 203–7, 208–10,
  230, 238
  literary verse, use of, 206
  "Prologue," 204–7
  rap techniques of, 203
  "R.A.W.," 203–4

"Word," 204
  wordplay of, 206
Ai (poet), 20
Albright, Daniel, 9
alētheia, 40
Alexie, Sherman, 23
Ali, Agha Shahid, 182
  "From Amherst to Kashmir," 177–78
  "God," 176, 178
  "In," 176
  "Lenox Hill," 176–77
  and prayer, 8, 143, 175–78, 183
  Rooms Are Never Finished, 176
  "Srinagar Airport," 178
  "Summers of Translation," 178
America
  See United States
American Idol (television series), 214
American Indians, 117
Amistad incident, 48
Ammons, A. R., 262n13
  "Hymn," 131
Anaximander
  On Nature, 32
"Ancient of Days" (hymn), 169
Anderson, Benedict, 67, 69, 81, 104
Anderson, Marian, 75
Andrewes, Bishop Lancelot, 148
apostrophe, 54, 71, 154, 169, 187
  and lyric poetry, 29–30, 128–29, 132
  See also address